W
R
E
C
K
E
D

COLL THRUSH

University of Washington Press / Seattle

IN ASSOCIATION WITH

Center for the Study of the Pacific Northwest

Unsettling Histories from the Graveyard of the Pacific

W R E C K E D

Wrecked was made possible in part by a grant from the Emil and Kathleen Sick Fund of the University of Washington's Department of History.

Additional support was provided by generous gifts from Michael Burnap, William Donnelly, Suzanne Ragen in memory of Brooks Ragen, Cynthia Lovelace Sears, Allen Shimada in memory of Captain Albert E. Theberge (NOAA), Sheryl and Mark Stiefel, and Michael T. Wing.

Design by Mindy Basinger Hill / Composed in 11.8 × 16 pt Garamond Premier Pro

29   28   27   26   25   5   4   3   2   1

Printed and bound in Canada

CENTER FOR THE STUDY OF THE PACIFIC NORTHWEST *sites.uw.edu/cspn/*

UNIVERSITY OF WASHINGTON PRESS *uwapress.uw.edu*

LIBRARY OF CONGRESS CATALOGING-IN-PUBLICATION DATA
Names: Thrush, Coll-Peter, 1970– author. | Center for the Study of the Pacific Northwest, issuing body.
Title: Wrecked : unsettling histories from the graveyard of the Pacific / Coll Thrush.
Other titles: Unsettling histories from the graveyard of the Pacific
Description: Seattle : University of Washington Press, in association with Center for the Study of the Pacific Northwest, 2025. | Series: Emil and Kathleen Sick book series in Western history and biography | Includes bibliographical references and index.
Identifiers: LCCN 2024059310 (print) | LCCN 2024059311 (ebook) | ISBN 9780295753768 (hardcover) | ISBN 9780295753775 (ebook)
Subjects: LCSH: Shipwrecks—Northwest Coast of North America. | Shipwrecks—Washington (State)—History. | Shipwrecks—Oregon—History. | Navigation—Northwest Coast of North America—History. | Indians of North America—Northwest Coast of North America—History. | Northwest, Pacific—Colonization—History.
Classification: LCC G525 .T484 2025 (print) | LCC G525 (ebook) | DDC 910.9164/32—dc23/eng/20250208
LC record available at https://lccn.loc.gov/2024059310
LC ebook record available at https://lccn.loc.gov/2024059311

♾ This paper meets the requirements of ANSI/NISO Z39.48-1992 (Permanence of Paper).

*To the coast
and all its peoples,
human and otherwise.*

Shipwreck is always the most significant moment.
FERNAND BRAUDEL / "History and the Social Sciences"

A boat, even a wrecked and wretched boat,
still has all the possibilities of moving.
DIONNE BRAND / *Thirsty*

CONTENTS

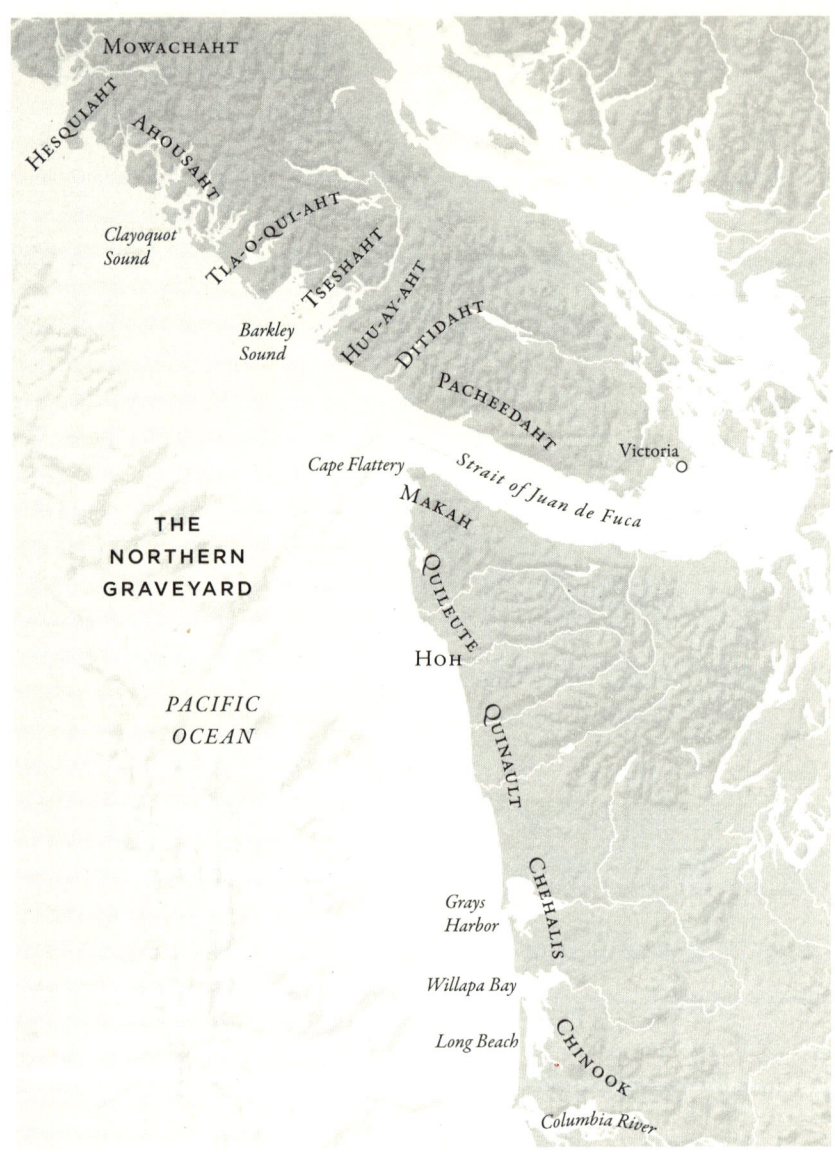

MOWACHAHT

HESQUIAHT

AHOUSAHT

TLA-O-QUI-AHT

*Clayoquot
Sound*

TSESHAHT

HUU-AY-AHT

DITIDAHT

*Barkley
Sound*

PACHEEDAHT

Victoria ○

Cape Flattery

Strait of Juan de Fuca

MAKAH

**THE
NORTHERN
GRAVEYARD**

QUILEUTE

HOH

*PACIFIC
OCEAN*

QUINAULT

CHEHALIS

*Grays
Harbor*

Willapa Bay

Long Beach

CHINOOK

Columbia River

The northern and southern Graveyard, with important geographical features, selected towns, and Indigenous peoples mentioned in the text. *Maps designed by Eric Leinberger*

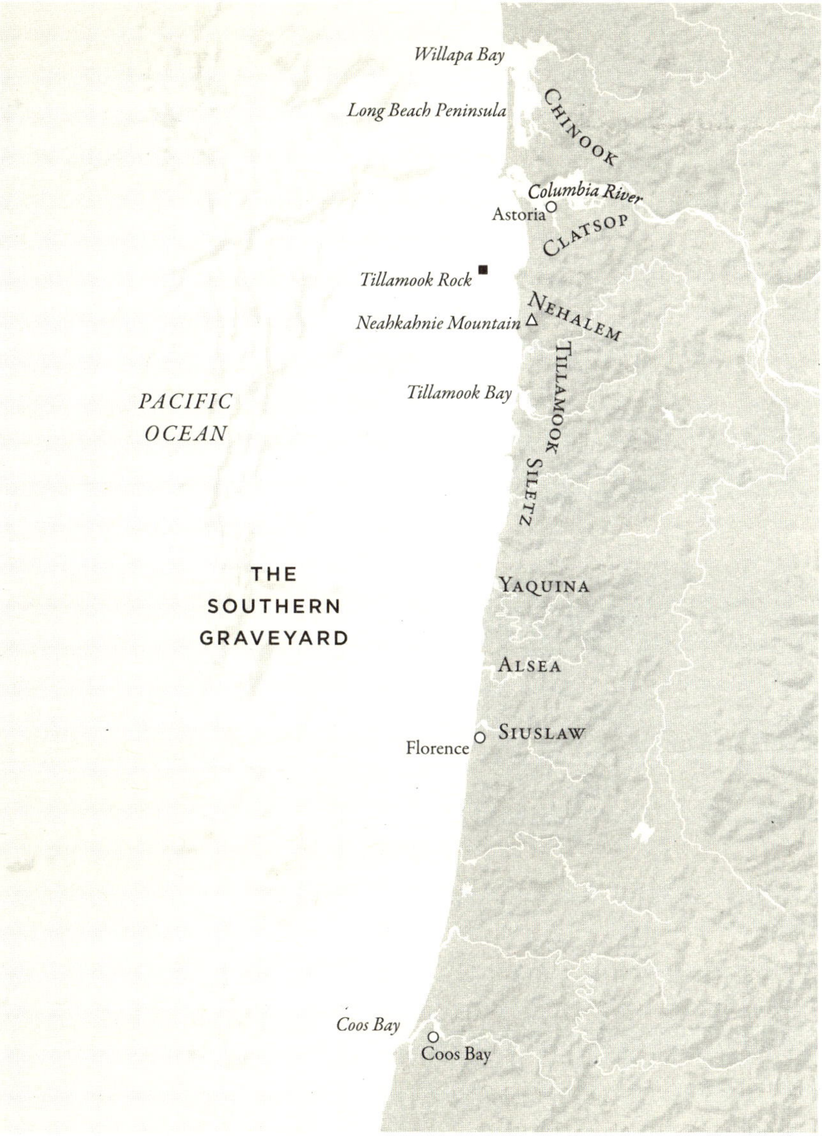

Willapa Bay

Long Beach Peninsula

CHINOOK

Columbia River

Astoria

CLATSOP

Tillamook Rock

NEHALEM

Neahkahnie Mountain

Tillamook Bay

Tillamook

PACIFIC
OCEAN

SILETZ

THE
SOUTHERN
GRAVEYARD

YAQUINA

ALSEA

SIUSLAW

Florence

Coos Bay

Coos Bay

A View from the Shore

THE LIGHT IS DIM, and the Pacific horizon seems to list. It's very early morning, with no dawning sun over the hills to the east, just the promise of a gradual brightening in the sky. For now, the clouds are leaden. In an hour, they will be the color of oyster shells. There is a light rain spitting, the sort of precipitation that few take seriously in this part of the world. The tide is far, far out, ebbing still but about to turn, and the dun sands are hard and cold. In the distance, the gray ocean roils as it withdraws. Figures are moving on the beach, my extended family among them. Folks are dressed in rain gear and rubber boots, fanning out across the places where the seawater has only just pulled away. The grown-ups stalk the beach, looking for small dimples in the sand known as clam shows, as the children follow sleepily behind or race the trailing edge of the water like sandpipers. Some adults carry shovels; others carry clam guns, cylinders of galvanized aluminum, capped at one end save for a small hole, and a long T-shaped handle. *Here's one*, someone stage-whispers, then waves to their compatriots. All along the beach, others are finding shows of their own. Those with shovels begin digging energetically, while those bearing the cylinders calmly plunge the metal into the ground with a *shhhhhhh*, place their thumb over the hole, then with another *shhhhhhh* bring up a perfect column of dark brown sand. And in it, with any luck, the treasure: a gold-green ovoid, fragile but with sharp edges, and the creature that lives inside of it. A Pacific razor clam.

It is sometime in the early 1970s, probably in the late fall. My mom's parents have parked their fifth-wheel camper, long and white behind a red Ford pickup, at a trailer park in the tiny coastal community of Grayland in southwestern Washington. They have gone there for years, since my mom and her two brothers were young, and will for a few more, until the annual harvest is largely shut down to protect the disappearing clams. The rest of the family—aunts and uncles, four cousins, my parents and me—visits on weekends, using the trailer on its concrete pad as a base for the harvest. No shovels for us; we have guns. Later, us kids explore the dunes, silvery brown and shot through with blue-gray grasses and beach strawberries, while the adult men gather around the firepit to stare at the flames and swap talk. Inside the trailer, my aunts and my mom remove the clam's pale gray-brown flesh, revealing the shell's purple and white interior. My grandmother pushes the meat through an antique grinder she has attached to the tiny kitchen counter. She fries some up for a celebratory dinner, and what's left is frozen for Thanksgiving and Christmas—it simply is not a holiday without clam patties on the table.[1]

And then there was the wreck. Our trips to tidewater Washington almost always included a side quest to Ocean Shores, at the north side of the entrance to Grays Harbor. There, SS *Catala* lay rusting and off-kilter at Damon Point. Ocean Shores, with its raucous go-karts, souvenir shops full of shells pilfered from around the world, and wide beach perfect for driving, was a respite from suburbia and a place of small wonders—*Catala*, at least to me, being the most wondrous thing of all. Older children and adults alike climbed on and into the ship, taking photos that played with its tilt. I mostly remember being too young to be allowed on board myself, but I can still practically smell the rust, and as in my memory of the clam beach at Grayland, the world seems to be an odd angle, all catawampus and unsettling. Others I've talked to remember the ship fondly, even if some acquired nasty scrapes or even broke arms or ankles

My childhood shipwreck: SS *Catala* at Damon Point in Ocean Shores, Washington, photographed here in 1968. *Ocean Shores Public Library*

messing around inside. Seemingly from a mysterious past, *Catala* punctuated the coast with a history that demanded our attention.

Catala's past wasn't all that mysterious, really. Built in Scotland in 1925 and capable of carrying close to three hundred passengers, it had once steamed weekly between Vancouver, British Columbia; Prince Rupert in northern BC; and Stewart, near Alaska. In later years, it served as a hotel ship during the 1962 Seattle World's Fair, then as a floating restaurant in California. It eventually found its way to Grays Harbor, where it was to be used as a home base for recreational salmon fishing. But on New Year's Day 1965, a massive Pacific storm blew into the bay, and the relentless winds and surging waves battered *Catala* until it came unmoored and ran ashore. No one died in the wreck; the only casualties were economic. There is little romance or drama in the story of *Catala*, and yet there it was, looking like *Titanic*'s smaller sibling and a bit like *Cotopaxi*, the ship abandoned by aliens in the Gobi Desert in 1977's *Close Encounters of the Third Kind*. And here it is still in my mind, half a century later. What few knew at the time is that *Catala* was leaking oil into the sand and was also filled with asbestos: in the flooring, in the wiring, in the bulkheads. And hovering over it all was the rotten, salty, and gorgeous scent of the sea.[2]

On those same trips to the Washington coast, there was one other place that hinted at a larger and perhaps more unsettling world: Marsh's Free Museum in the town of Long Beach. Just north of the Columbia on a long, narrow peninsula made mostly of dunes and bogs, Long Beach was yet another popular destination for folks from Puget Sound country and the Portland, Oregon, area. Fudge shops, arcades, and fish-and-chips places predominated, but Marsh's, a classic curiosity cabinet of a shop founded in 1921, was the premier tourist attraction, second only to the ocean itself. Along with everything from a taxidermied two-headed calf to a collection of antique revolvers, the real star of the show at Marsh's was Jake, an "alligator man" made from a crocodilian's desiccated body and a small mummified human torso.[3] Like a good clam beach and the site of *Catala*, the museum was a required stop on any trip to the coast, and it left an indelible mark on my imagination.

It was also here that a seed of this book was planted. On the wall at Marsh's, something that looked like a cross between a nautical chart and a treasure map hung, maybe between a case full of stuffed birds and one of those machines that stretches pennies—I don't remember exactly. The map included the Columbia River and the Washington and southern British Columbia coasts; the land was colored in a pale parchment-gold and the sea a bright blue. The water bristled with dozens of little black symbols, each a ship sinking by the stern and representing a wreck like *Catala* or something much worse. The same beaches where we clammed and flew kites, I remember realizing, looked out on places of danger and disaster. The poster was titled with a single phrase. For a bookish boy who had already been spending his childhood hopped up on ghost stories and who was simultaneously terrified and fascinated by the sea, it was a phrase that elicited chills and curiosity in equal parts and that has stayed with me until now: The Graveyard of the Pacific.

This so-called graveyard—an apt name, given its deadly history— lies just off the American states of Oregon and Washington and along the long western coastline of Vancouver Island in Canada's British Columbia. It is an exceptionally dangerous stretch of water, full of strong currents, battered by intense storms, hemmed with rocky coastlines and shifting sands, and studded with difficult bar crossings. In particular, the mouth of the Columbia and the entrance to the Strait of Juan de Fuca have claimed many ships and even more lives and livelihoods over the past two and a half centuries. All told, more than two thousand ships have gone down or come ashore in the Graveyard, making it one of the most lethal places among all the oceans of the world.[4] The density of marine misfortune in the region has inspired an extensive literature; beginning in the late nineteenth century, when the phrase was first coined, the Graveyard of the Pacific spawned not only disaster but a great deal of writing about the ships that sank or smithereened themselves here. Crafted by maritime and local historians with prodigious knowledge of the archive and intimate understanding of shipboard life, these works have kept alive the stories of the ships and their crews and passengers, serving almost as an elegy.[5]

As for me, I come to the waterline from a different direction. I've never been in the navy or the merchant marine, and I don't sail or dive. Indeed, big water makes me more than a little nervous. Even before I knew about the great earthquake and tsunami that devastated this entire coast in January of 1700, something I would eventually come to write about early in my career, I found wide expanses of beach unsettling, especially at a low night tide when the sea threatened distantly, flashing white in the darkness and hissing across a too-broad strand. As a child, it chilled me that the sea kept churning even when the lights of human life turned off; it seemed like it could move in on us at any moment. (The truth, of course, was that it could.) Lying awake and anxious inside my grandparents' trailer or my mother's tent, I could hear it, out there in the dark. All of this is to say that, in the words of poet W. S. Merwin, I am "dry-shod."[6]

Ultimately, then, mine is a view from the shore, and this book is only nominally a maritime or nautical history. It is less concerned with the technological, economic, or legal elements of marine vessels; rather, it is primarily engaged with questions about meaning-making along the coast, where shipwrecks remain, even in the relative safety of the twenty-first century, iconic and exceptionally evocative elements of regional popular history. In short, I am far more interested in the afterlives of the wrecks herein than I am in the mechanics of disaster itself, and in what the history and historiography of shipwreck in this place can tell us about the patterns and shapes of history along the coasts of Oregon, Washington, and British Columbia. The result is a story about relations between Indigenous peoples and newcomers, between sailors and salvagers, between people and place, and between the past and the present. The Graveyard—from SS *Catala* to the many wrecks included in this book—is one place where we have met each other and told stories, stories that help the tellers and listeners or readers make sense of our lives together. More often than not, those stories were told by gawkers on the shore, by newspaper editors or church ministers, or by Indigenous knowledge keepers or settler poets, as much as they were by actual survivors. These stories, and the ships around which they have flowed, are the subjects of what follows. At the core of this book is a set of related questions: What does it mean to call something a "graveyard"? What sorts of aspirations, desperation, and fates inhere in such a name? What sort of claim on place and territory does such a phrase suggest, and how might it reveal important themes in the region's history?

If mine is a view from the shore, it is also a white settler's view.[7] Raised in the treaty territory of the Muckleshoot Indian Tribe and now living and working in the traditional, ancestral, and unceded territories of the Musqueam, Squamish, and Tsleil-Waututh First Nations, my career has largely centered on one question in particular: What has it meant across time to "belong" to a place in the context of colonialism? With ancestors that arrived in North America in the seventeenth, eighteenth, and nineteenth centuries from various places in Europe, I do not view this as an abstract question; indeed, my very genealogy is bound up in centuries-long (and ongoing) processes of dispossession and genocide. In fact, according to Ancestry.com, my earliest ancestor to arrive in North America, John Proctor, was a shipwreck survivor. A passenger on the Virginia Company's *Sea Venture*, he experienced the wreck of that ship on Bermuda in 1609 when it was on its way to James Town, an English settlement founded in the many-peopled land of Tsenacomoco. Proctor would eventually make it to Virginia, and he and his family are among the much-venerated "Ancient Planters." *Sea Venture*, meanwhile, became an inspiration for Shakespeare's *Tempest*.

Each of us is entangled in the consequences of the past, even if those consequences have played out very differently depending on where we come from or where we stand. Each of us, and perhaps especially white settlers, thus has the right and responsibility to engage with this history if we are to understand our now. At its core, this book is an extended meditation on these questions of belonging and responsibility, written in the spirit of learning from, amplifying, and supporting Indigenous survivance and futurity.[8] At the same time, I recognize that it is only a book. "The sea is not a metaphor," Hester Blum has warned, and, as Eve Tuck and K. Wayne Yang remind us, neither is decolonization, the project of acknowledging, supporting, and helping to enact Indigenous sovereignties of place and personhood.[9] Which is to say, a book can't be enough: it doesn't return lands and waters to their traditional owners. Yet I do believe that better stories can help create conditions for better relations and realities, and it is with that intention that I offer this history.

This history is meant to unsettle, then, in two senses of the word. First, it is meant to offer histories that challenge the widespread and easy nostalgia associated with the Graveyard of the Pacific. Instead of romantic, picturesque, or titillating tales of marine disaster, I offer troubling histories that include significant amounts of violence, particularly directed toward Indigenous people. These histories are intended to unsettle and disorient the reader, particularly if they are already familiar with many of the stories of the Graveyard. Second, this history is meant to unsettle in that its goal is to disrupt histories that always place settlers at the center of the story and, with that in mind, to unsettle readers' sense of the shape of the region's history as a whole. The "unsettling" of *Wrecked*'s subtitle, then, is both adjective and verb, both a description and a doing. The central conceit of the book—the notion of colonialism wrecking itself on Indigenous shores—is meant to unsettle both reader and history itself.

Meanwhile, back in Ocean Shores, the local interpretive center holds fragments of long-gone *Catala*, many donated by area residents who had taken away pieces of the ship over the years it rested at Damon Point. The artifacts range from china plates to log books, from the ship's nameplate to its anchor. Together, they capture something of the gravity of the now-lost ship for those of us who encountered it from the late 1960s to the early 1980s. Like the objects retrieved from wrecks up and down the coast—or in some cases, like the remains of the ships themselves—the relics of *Catala* are anchor points and holdfasts for storytelling about the region, its past, and its present. They, just like Indigenous oral traditions, settler reminiscences, or federal marine incident reports, are now part of the archive of the Graveyard, serving as reminders of the overwhelming power of the Pacific, of the storms and waters that roll in across distances that beggar description. They are the detritus of the past, but they are far from wretched and dead; instead, they are just waiting to tell new stories. Here are a few.

W
R
E
C
K
E
D

A Fragile Machine

What We Talk about When
We Talk about Shipwreck

THE FETCH OF THE PACIFIC reaches for thousands of miles here, sending heavy weather across great distances: winds from south and west, waves against cobble and sand, rains combed by dense rainforests of spruce and cedar and salal. From at least November through to spring, storms alternately caress and pummel these shores, leaving their traces in tree-hung mosses and runnels down black sea cliffs. Even in the relatively dry summers, the sodden reality of the dark half of the year is remembered in deep and wide leaves of spiked devil's club and lush deer and sword ferns and in the fogs that embrace the shore but give way to sun just a half mile inland. But the winters, it's true, can seem endless, and it is in those gloaming months that the Graveyard of the Pacific has captured most of its casualties, as the darkness and weather confounded navigation and wrested control from captains and crew.

Faced with these challenges, all up and down the coast, the Canadians and the Americans built lighthouses to send the promise of safety back into the dim fetch. Some are today automated, others still managed by human hands, and even a few are now left dark. Built on the points and prominences of the British Columbia, Washington, and Oregon coasts, some take their names from older Indigenous words on the land—Umpqua, Yaquina, Tillamook, Tatoosh, Carmanah—while others have monikers inspired by colonial presences: Heceta, Meares,

Disappointment. Resisting the unending and punishing generosity of the great ocean, the lighthouses serve as markers of modernity on an ancient waterscape, holding out hope against seemingly eternal storms.

In January of 1906, the light at Cape Beale had been guarding the entrance to Vancouver Island's deep and islanded Barkley Sound for more than thirty years. Its keepers were the Pattersons, Thomas and Minnie,[1] and in the wee hours of Tuesday the twenty-third, the couple received a panicked message over the telegraph line that wound south through the forest: a ship had gone ashore nearby. Not long after, they heard pounding on their door, and when they opened it to the dark night, they found nine desperate and bedraggled men who had been through hell. From between chattering teeth, the men told their story: their ship, a passenger steamer called SS *Valencia*, had run onto a submerged reef some three miles south of Cape Beale. In the ensuing chaos, the men had seen full lifeboats launched over the side of *Valencia* only to overturn in the crashing surf or be smashed against the ship's metal hull. The nine men had been cast ashore, battered and bloodied, then somehow climbed the island's cliffs before making their way along the undergrowth-crowded telegraph line trail to the lighthouse. As they settled in to warm themselves, behind them in the dark and pounding surf, *Valencia* would take another day and a half to die.[2]

———————

Why does shipwreck catch in our mind? I think there are a few reasons. One is straightforward: with a powerful combination of dread and fascination, we fear death by drowning. The notion of green water pouring first into our ship and then into our lungs terrifies. That vicarious frisson is real. Shipwreck is also a destroyer of livelihood, of cargoes lost and investments failed; such catastrophes can thwart even the most wealthy or ambitious among us, whether passenger or crew. And survivors face their own travails, in the form of deprivation, precarity, and the loneliness of the wrecked. Whether in terms of life, livelihood, or the trauma of the castaway, maritime tragedy has a deep and profound pull on us—not just in terms of individual ship*wrecks*, but also through the concept and metaphor of ship*wreck*.

It is no surprise, then, that shipwrecks and shipwreck have been something like muses throughout Western history. From Egyptian papyri telling of men cast away on magical islands to illustrations of drowning shipmates on ancient Greek amphorae—let alone the epics of Homer—shipwrecks had a place in the imaginative seascapes of the ancient world. In medieval Ireland, mythical stories of sea voyages in search of new, otherworldly lands and new converts were always shadowed by the potential for both wreck and salvation. In early modern Portugal, France, and elsewhere, shipwreck narratives circulated widely and both thrilled their readers and offered new ways to talk about everything from the human body to the prospects of empire (more on that below).[3] In later centuries, romantic poets and painters in Britain both drew on shipwreck as a motif to produce massively popular maritime fantasies just as their nation's sea-flung empire was nearing its nineteenth-century apogee. And of course, the sinking of *Titanic* in 1912 has held the world enrapt for more than a century, its doom an arguably overdetermined metaphor for the hubris of modernity.[4] Author Michael Titlestad writes that "wrecks generate floods of texts, which are subsequently anthologised, fictionalised, adapted, and translated into other media. We have never stopped speaking and writing about wrecks."[5]

There is another potency to shipwreck, however, one that moves out in waves and ripples from the wreck site into existential realms. This is the fear of losing what the ship in question represents: the relationship with a benevolent nature, an ocean-spanning empire, or even the very future itself. Whether in the Mediterranean, on the Northwest Coast, or in the middle of the North Atlantic, shipwreck can capsize the idea that "progress" is inevitable, just as the sublime and uncaring deep renders us flotsam. As metaphor, shipwreck might be used to represent anything from the dissolution of a marriage to the collapse of an entire society—a shipwreck doesn't have to be literal to signify harm. In the case the Graveyard of the Pacific, for example, one man's kayak journey across the terrifying Columbia River Bar elicited commentary on his tempestuous relationship with his own father. "I had imagined our project as a salvage operation," he writes, "one involving the recovery of something lost in childhood and reconciliation with the ghosts of our fathers." Referencing the hundreds who have died attempting to cross the bar, Randall Sullivan continues by writing that the victims of the Columbia "were innumerable but not nameless, and those closest to us in the spectral gathering were the ghosts of our fathers, and of the boys Ray and I had once been. *All together now, brothers,* I sang silently, *all together now, those who are gone, and we who shall soon be.* All of us have lived through it. And even if we are dead, that is still true."[6]

But shipwreck is more than metaphor. It is also meto*nym*, the thing itself. As shipwreck scholar Sara Rich argues, marine vessels literalize metaphor.[7] A ship is a material microcosm of what it represents: that lost load of lumber will be used by coastal people to build things and transform their home-scapes; that naval vessel both represents and *is* the military-industrial complex; that man who has shackled his fellow humans in the hold also embodies the transhemispheric institution of slavery. Shipwreck invites us to attend to the relationship between the material and symbolic, between, say, sunken doubloons in a pirate's chest and the self-fashioning of a maritime imperial culture.

And always, shipwreck stories show the seemingly capricious agency of the nonhuman. As literary scholar Steve Mentz writes, "Shipwreck makes palpable the stark contradiction between human desires and mortal limits. These stories . . . balance out our hopes for an ordered universe against our knowledge of the costs the disorienting world extracts from its inhabitants."[8] In the case of *Valencia*, its destruction in January 1906 would focus public attention not just on the vagaries of the weather, on the actions of a single ship's captain, or on the mechanics of rescue, but on the very nature of modern life along the northwestern coast of North America.

————

Built in Philadelphia and launched in 1882, SS *Valencia* was over 250 feet long and weighed some 1,600 tons. Used as an army transport during the Spanish-American War, it was later purchased by the Pacific Coast Steamship Company, a firm that also owned railroads and coal mines up and down the West Coast. In this, the vessel was imbricated and implicated in the workings of American empire. Then, in early 1906, *Valencia* was assigned to the San Francisco–Seattle run. On its second voyage on this route, having left San Francisco on January 20, 173 people were aboard when the ship ran off course in a dense fog. Just before midnight on Monday, January 22, *Valencia* struck a rock reef near the shore of Vancouver Island, ripping open a hole in its bow. Captain Oscar M. Johnson was reported to have cried out, "My God, where are we?" before ordering the ship to pull away from the reef as water began pouring into its single-hulled, uncompartmentalized hold. As it turned, *Valencia* was pushed back into the reef by the high swells, stern-first this time. Within minutes, it was clear the steamer was going down, only fifty yards from the cliff-girded shore.

The crew began launching boats, two of which immediately overturned, pitching their occupants into the violent waters. The tule-reed life preservers worn by passengers and crew alike proved virtually useless, and the terror only intensified when *Valencia*'s lights suddenly went out. The captain and crew tried to calm the panicking passengers; one stewardess went from cabin to cabin, whistling happily and reassuring those huddled there that they would soon be rescued.[9] Meanwhile, waves had begun washing over the deck, sending even more people into the water. Lines were fired toward shore, but with no one there to secure them, they might as well have never been fired at all. Several men tried

The only known photograph of SS *Valencia* on the rocks of southern Vancouver Island in 1906. *British Columbia Archives*

to swim lines ashore but were either forced back or were dashed fatally against the rocks. Some twenty people climbed into the rigging of the foretop mast, but the structure soon collapsed, and all were thrown into the surf. *Valencia* was coming apart.

Soon, other ships arrived at the scene. The tugs *Salvor* and *Czar*, along with the Pacific Coast Steamship Company's *Queen City*, arrived by Tuesday evening, when they found the steamer's deck completely submerged and thirty to forty people in the rigging or gathered at the stern. But it was too dark and dangerous to approach, and the ships could get within only half a mile of *Valencia*. By Wednesday morning, the PCSC's *City of Topeka* had also appeared on the scene, while *Queen City* was ordered to return to Victoria and then resume its journey to San Francisco. Two life rafts, with a total of thirty people aboard, were rescued by *City of Topeka* crew members. Meanwhile, three linemen maintaining the telegraph line that ran along the shore of the island began working their way to the site as darkness fell, carbide headlamps lighting their way through the heavy underbrush. They finally reached the wreck location on Thursday morning. The entire spectacle lay before them: the broken ship, the passengers high in the riggings, the other ships standing by. And then, around noon, a giant wave came and turned the whole thing over. Some people grabbed pieces of wreckage but were drawn into the pounding surf, while others were carried seaward. All of them would die. "I could do nothing for the poor creatures," recalled one of the linemen, "and they were swept away before my eyes."[10] In the end, only thirty-seven of *Valencia*'s passengers and crew would survive. All were men; no women or children made it to safety.

The tragedy of *Valencia* was reported nearly in real time by Victoria and Seattle newspapers. Headlines like "Survivor Tells Story of Wreck," "Fated Craft's Last Moments," "Boy Missing," and "Irony of Fate"—all within a single issue of the *Seattle Star*—portrayed the disaster as it was happening, an agonizing accounting of terror and pathos.[11] They reported, for example, that rescued men had seen women aboard *Valencia* singing hymns as the ship fell apart around them. Among these was "Nearer, My God, to Thee," a song that would also be heard on the sinking *Titanic* six years later.[12] Then, once *Valencia* had settled on the bottom, came the reports of bodies and the recriminations. For weeks after the wreck, newspapers in Seattle and Victoria would report the grim search for the steamer's dead. Many were unidentifiable, having been worn almost to bones in the relentless surf. Some were buried in shallow graves onshore, to be exhumed later, while others were taken onto ships to be brought to the cities for proper burial. As more and more bodies were recovered, public discourse got hotter and hotter about the cause of the disaster and exactly who or what was to blame. The ensuing US federal investigation enrapt the public in the region and far beyond. The captains of *Salvor* and *Czar* charged each other with

Painter J. D. Gall created this piece, titled *Seventy-Five Search for Succor but in Vain*, to commemorate the tragedy of *Valencia*. Of note are the observers on the cliffs in the foreground and the ships standing by out at sea. *British Columbia Archives*

cowardice for not approaching, while public attention focused on the decision to send away *Queen City*, seemingly abandoning *Valencia* to its fate in an example of "unamerican conduct."[13] Meanwhile, the editors of the *Seattle Star* warned that the investigation would be "nothing else but a clean white-wash for the Pacific Coast Steamship company."[14] In the end, nature itself was found guilty, along with the lack of lifesaving infrastructure on that part of the Vancouver Island coast.

One ephemeral source from this moment of grief and acrimony brings together the emotional heft of the disaster with calls for practical ways to avoid another one like it. Written by Seattle composer Philip French and dedicated to both Theodore Roosevelt and Edward VII, the song begins:

> We were sailing o'er the ocean blue, our ship was homeward bound
> To friends and loved ones waiting on the shores of Puget Sound.
> Our dear ones think we're coming soon to greet them with our love,
>> But sadly they receive the news of wrecked upon the shore
>> But sadly they receive the news of wrecked upon the shore.

After taking on the voice of the victims, the sad tune describes the terror and heartbreak of the actual sinking:

> When sleeping in our Berths at night upon the raging sea
> We hear the cry we're on the rocks and sinking in the sea.
> There's A Ship in sight they all cried out, but help it gave us none,
>> Poor mothers cry for their dear ones upon the raging sea
>> Poor mothers cry for their dear ones upon the raging sea.

> A line was shot from ship to shore, from aching hearts for help;
> We pulled from shore by loving hands, poor souls on board to help.
> The line did break and proved itself so rotten in the sea.
>> The heart doth break for those loved ones who will return no more;
>> The heart doth break for those loved ones who will return no more.

The song then ends with a plea for modernization, combining the raw emotion of previous verses with a practical proposal that more lighthouses be built in the region posthaste:

> Ah, then let us with our cousins weep, across from shore to shore,
> And let us both improve our coasts in love and unity,
> And help poor Jack to face the storms, and cross the raging seas,
>> And give him light from shore to shore, to lead him safe on sea—
>> And give him light from shore to shore, to lead him safe on sea.
> Our coasts of rocks, from shore to shore, protection ought to have,

To guide us in our darkest hours in storms upon the sea;
Our flags are two; but we are one, in storm upon the sea.
　　Then let us do our best for those upon the raging sea,
　　Then let us do our best for those upon the raging sea.[15]

The piece does several things. First, it articulates perfectly the sentimentality of its era and its genre, capturing post-Victorian emotionality and the norms of early twentieth-century lyricism. Unspeakable tragedy has a language. Second, it highlights the transnational nature of the colonial Northwest Coast: shipwreck brought two settler nations together. Lastly, it is a vision of history as a narrative of progress in which the light of modernity shines into benighted places. Likely unheard since the first years of the twentieth century, "The Loss of the *Valencia*" was a way of talking about the relationship between past, present, and future; it both heralded and lamented the wonders and costs of modernity. Meanwhile, lighthouses have historically been linked closely to narratives of empire and modernity; European observers of lighthouse construction in colonized places such as Southeast Asia, for example, routinely made the connection between the building of a light and the light of European and white racial supremacy over others, paired with a beaming Christianity.[16] Taken together, these readings of the song suggest that Philip French, those who played his music and sang his lyrics, and likely their audiences all understood *Valencia* not just as a singular tragedy but as a rupture in the story of civilization. Meanwhile, the deaths of scores of people provoked further claims on place by layering settler grief, horror, and victimhood onto the coast of Vancouver Island.

Indeed, others at the time often found themselves talking about more than *Valencia* whenever the wreck was on their tongues. As Steven Biel has shown in his cultural history of the loss of *Titanic*, wrecks can "expose and come to represent anxieties about modernity . . . a kind of 'social drama' in which conflicts were played out and American culture in effect thought out loud about itself."[17] Six years earlier, *Valencia* had

DOES IT PAY?

Recriminations flew after the wreck of *Valencia*, including this *Seattle Star* editorial cartoon that questioned the entire project of industrial modernity.

already provoked the same responses, just as the same hymns drifted over both disasters. In one *Seattle Star* cartoon, for example, the illustrator portrays Hermes, the fleet-footed god of journeys, standing atop a coin and a pile of skulls, surrounded by wrecked ships, a crashed automobile, and a derailed train. In bold, shouty letters at the top, the visual editorial clamors, "DOES IT PAY?"—"it" being the speed and greed of the modern age. Behind Hermes, the dark clouds of the twentieth century gather.[18] If, as essayist and photographer Allan Sekula writes, the arrival of the steamship heralded the triumph of the straight line over the wind-blown wanderings of sail, then this cartoon showed that at times those modern trajectories could also point toward doom with much higher body counts than those of the past.[19] Anxieties triggered by the loss of *Valencia* were thus ways of thinking with and feeling through the entire project of creating a pair of settler societies on the Northwest Coast.

Valencia interrupted history by raising doubts about the material and even moral costs of progress.

Practically before *Valencia* had settled into the sands and cobbles near the reef that had torn it open, commentators on the tragedy demanded not just culpability but change. In Victoria, critics looked to the federal government. "Another wreck is added to the list of wrecks that have strewn the coast," went one editorial, "and one more appeal goes up to the authorities at Ottawa to hasten their hand."[20] On the American side, another editorial argued in all caps that the time for talk was long past: "THERE ARE FIFTY AND MAYBE A HUNDRED AMERICAN VESSELS TO EVERY ONE OF ANY OTHER COUNTRY PASSING THE SAME POINT. THEN WHY SHOULD ... CITIZENS OF THE UNITED STATES LAY BACK AND WAIT FOR OUR CANADIAN NEIGHBORS TO MAKE THE FIRST MOVE FOR PROTECTION OF LIFE AND SHIPPING."[21] Such editorials were far from impotent; indeed, change would happen quickly. Within a year of *Valencia*'s destruction, lifesaving stations had been established nearby at the tiny island communities of Ucluelet and Tofino, an additional lightship was installed at the mouth of the Strait of Juan de Fuca, and an entirely new lighthouse would be completed in 1908 at Pachena Point, close to the site of *Valencia*'s grave. Meanwhile, the barely visible path that the survivors had used to get to the Pattersons' front door at Cape Beale was turned into a permanent rescue trail, with implications for the future.

———————

The imaginary of settler colonialism is based on ambition and, ultimately, a certain kind of hope. In the case of the United States, for example, settler colonialism was grounded in the widespread and persistent belief that inherent European superiority, when it encountered supposed wilderness or savagery as in the arid West of the nineteenth century, created a new, even more robust figure called the American.[22]

This formulation is still popular as a historical framework, along with its relatives the outlaw-frontiersman-as-real-American, the white savior, the noble savage, the pretendian, and the Indian mascot. Similar kinds of stories are part of the Canadian tradition as well, although on the imagined Canadian frontier, the hero is no outlaw but the law itself, in the figure of the Mountie. Meanwhile, the presence of Indigenous peoples in these stories is either one of exaggerated stereotypes or near-complete invisibility; rarely do they include Indigenous people and peoples as complex, dynamic, or in some cases even extant. These mythologies, which have been challenged for decades, if not longer, by individuals and collectives both inside and outside settler society, continue to shape national and regional cultures despite recent turns toward a more nuanced and accurate accounting of the past and its relevance for the present.

These mythologies can also be called prophecies. There are three settlerist prophecies in particular that relate to shipwreck.[23] The first is that the story of humanity will be one of increasing control over our species' environment, which in turn will make an endlessly abundant nature flourish. This story—an example of what literary scholar Mark Rifkin calls "settler common sense"—was particularly convincing among white American and Canadian citizens and subjects in the last half of the nineteenth century and the first decades of the twentieth century.[24] *Valencia* wrecked right in the middle of that range of time; indeed, the steamship more generally was born out of that exact story of progress. While by *Valencia*'s time, many people on the Northwest Coast had begun to realize the limitations of natural resources, the best solution remained further intervention, in this case through the increasingly influential ideology of modern conservation. This hopeful certainty was at the heart of the settler project, and it continues to influence both policy and popular culture throughout the region.

The second prophecy of settler colonialism is that Indigenous peoples would disappear through a process that we now call genocide. Genocide can take the form of mass murder and introduced diseases or legal systems such as blood quantum, Indian status, or tribal termination that made sure that there were as few legal "Indians" around as possible. Genocide can also come as a story. This particular prophecy cleaves Indigenous people from history itself, casting them as unchanging relics who, sadly or not, are doomed to vanish either physically or legally or both. This is a deep and enduring narrative that Indigenous studies scholar Jean M. O'Brien has called "lasting," in which Indigenous people are declared locally extinct, and which is invariably paired with the "firsting" of settler origin stories.[25] In some ways, the era of *Valencia* was the height of this sort of thinking, in which federal, provincial, and state policies in both nations targeted Indigenous land (and sea) tenures, languages, and family structures through theft, containment, criminalization, or forced assimilation. The height of the age of steam, for example, was also the era of the criminalization of the potlatch under Canada's Indian Act. Meanwhile, the conditions of life in Indigenous North America were understood by settlers as inevitable; never mind that they, their diseases, and their policies had created the conditions for that diminished life.

The current colonial jurisdictions that include the Graveyard of the Pacific—Oregon, Washington, and British Columbia, along with the United States and Canada—have very different histories of Indigenous dispossession. In coastal Oregon, unratified treaties and massive reductions in a reservation that once stretched for about half of the state's coast meant that few Indigenous people still live in their traditional territories. At the mouth of the Columbia, the Chinook Nation, despite not being recognized by the federal government, is engaging in resurgence just like other communities and nations up and down the coast. On the coast of Washington, many Indigenous communities avoided full relocation (but not restrictions on movement) and now have reservations in their traditional homelands and homewaters. On Vancouver Island, where there have been only a handful of treaties—fourteen in the 1850s and one in 2006—much of the land remains technically unceded, while small reserves exist along the coast, often in places of traditional use. For all their differences, there is a common story here of attempted genocide but also one of persistence and resilience. Everywhere on these shores, Indigenous tribes and nations are resurging, perhaps best embodied in the long canoe journeys undertaken every summer by crews of Indigenous pullers, knitting together long-standing community relationships and contemporary solidarities all along the coast. The prophecy of Indigenous disappearance is a lie.[26]

A third prophecy of settler colonialism—that the past will stay in the past—emerges from the other two. If progress was inevitable, traumas such as the loss of *Valencia* would recede into the past, as society moved, technologically and otherwise, into an always-improving future in which Indigenous peoples would play no meaningful part. But not all shipwrecks stayed submerged; indeed, as we shall see, many ships resurfaced long after they were first lost, and *Valencia* was one of them. Twenty years after the steamer went down, a Victoria man was walking the shore of Vancouver Island when he came across a five-foot spar bearing the name of the doomed ship. Described in one newspaper as "long-remembered," *Valencia* had seemed to suddenly reappear in the form of debris.[27] Then, in 1935, *Valencia*'s fifth lifeboat was found drifting and empty in Barkley Sound, a bizarre and haunting reminder of the disaster nearly three decades on.[28] The disaster has also been ensconced in regional history through regular retrospective newspaper coverage and through the publication of histories of the Graveyard.[29] On the hundredth anniversary of the disaster, in 2006, local organizers held a commemoration at the University of British Columbia's Bamfield Marine Sciences Centre, not far from the wreck site, and the tragedy was classified as a National Historic Event by Parks Canada.[30] Perhaps the most famous tragedy in the history of the Graveyard of the Pacific, *Valencia* continues to inspire and edify. The past is not past. As Christina Sharpe has written, the wakes of ships—whether those of the Middle

Passage or the world of passenger liners—prove that "the past that is not past reappears, always, to rupture the present."[31]

———————

Every shipwreck in this book took place in Indigenous space. As an example, Cape Beale, where this introduction began, might have been named in 1787 for a British ship's purser, but it had already carried another moniker for a very long time. To the Huu-ay-aht Nuu-chah-nulth people, it is *chi·maqatsaɬ*, a name referring to an aquatic monster that sometimes swallowed canoes passing the cape. It was also a site that carried stories about drift whaling, in which maritime dangers could cost the lives of even the most skilled hunters. Meanwhile, a nearby site is known as *chi:t-sa:wpshi:ɬ*, a place with currents that people were careful to avoid lest their canoes be pulled into the rocks. These names are histories in and of themselves, attesting to the long presence of the Huu-ay-aht, the depth of their knowledge of the place and its waters, and, in a way, their own version of shipwreck.[32]

Then came the Cape Beale Lighthouse. First lit in 1874, the beacon had been hard-won. Again and again, the local land- and seascape had confounded colonial efforts to survey the site and begin construction, and Indigenous people, especially from the Huu-ay-aht, had paddled into the gap. Using skills and watercraft honed perfectly for the local environment, they provided transportation to and from the site during surveys, construction, and operation; they carried the mail; they piloted settler ships through the treacherous waters. While usually paid for this labor, Huu-ay-aht people also saw the lighthouse as merely a new presence in their well-established territory and its legal system. They continued using the site in traditional and accustomed ways—butchering a whale within smelling range of the keepers' house, for example—and helped themselves to lumber and food when they visited *chi·maqatsaɬ*. Meanwhile, new relations were built; the first keepers' offspring often played with Huu-ay-aht children and learned their language, and records kept at the lighthouse show a mix of both conflict and confluence taking place there in the last quarter of the nineteenth century. Thus, while the Cape Beale lighthouse was a clear example of settler colonial incursion into Huu-ay-aht territory, it also spurred complex relationships at the local level, and the truth of ongoing Indigenous territoriality there rarely seemed in question, at least in practical terms.[33]

Thirty-two years after the lighthouse was completed and just to its south, Indigenous people appear everywhere in the archives of *Valencia*. The linemen's ultimately pointless journey to the site of the wreck, for example, depended on a river crossing in a Ditidaht canoe, and while local Indigenous people were not recorded in the press coverage or investigation as being on the scene of the disaster as it happened, they would play a central role in its aftermath. Local people, mostly likely from both the Huu-ay-aht and Ditidaht Nations, were the primary collectors of the bodies that littered the shores around what would become known as Valencia Bluffs, their cedar canoes far superior to settlers' ships in the difficult littoral. They earned up to ten dollars per body.[34] As they did this harrowing work, they either buried the dead on-site for later exhumation or took them to a local settler outpost, where they were placed in rough wooden caskets to await departure for Victoria or Seattle.[35] Locals also contributed to what would become the "wrecklore" of *Valencia*, some reporting to officials that they had found a sea cave buzzing with flies and blocked by a large boulder, discovering inside a lifeboat cradling eight skeletons. It was surmised that the boat had been carried over the boulder by a high wave and then had become trapped inside the cavern. It was also surmised that the "Indians" might have made up the story. Certainly, the lifeboat in question has never been found.[36] Indigenous people, then, were often part of the story of shipwreck, even in a period when they were thought to be on the verge of extinction as distinct peoples.

More than a century after the destruction of *Valencia*, the lineman's path and later the rescue trail that replaced it have now become the world-famous West Coast Trail in Pacific Rim National Park. As anthropologist Lauren Harding has shown, those who walk the rugged trail often carry with them ideas of wilderness that erase Indigenous history and obscure ongoing Ditidaht and Huu-ay-aht presence in the area.[37] At the same time, a close look at the official Parks Canada map of the present-day trail offers Indigenous place-names alongside symbols representing the many shipwrecks that took place here, including *Valencia*. Near the bluffs that now bear the steamer's name, there is *tsakkawis* (Head Pointing Straight Down toward Beach, anglicized as Tsocowis Creek) and *tlaadiwa* (Pieces of Blubber on the Beach, the Klanawa River).[38] These Ditidaht words, which appear on the map alongside their Huu-ay-aht counterparts, are evidence that despite the intrusion of colonial infrastructure into Indigenous space in the wake of *Valencia*, that trail now alerts those who hike it to a deeper Indigenous past as well as to an undeniable Indigenous present.

———————

In his widely influential work on the slave ship, historian Marcus Rediker describes maritime vessels as "those strange and powerful European machines,"[39] and the history of the Northwest Coast was indelibly shaped by the power of these floating fragments of empire. They carried with them a particular kind of future; as Frances Steel writes, imperial tools such as steamships "possessed an enlightening power and a civilising agency; they heralded the collapse of distance and a progressive universalism."[40] *Valencia* was no different. But what the story of that doomed steamer tells us is something quite distinct from the inevitable march of empire: instead, it highlights the fragile nature of the machinery of the ship, as well as of the machine of colonialism itself.

To claim that colonialism might be fragile might seem counterintuitive, but it is very much in keeping with current thinking about the nature of empires. In her work on campaigns of resistance against the British Empire in places such as India and Kenya, historian Antoinette Burton argues for a vision of fraught colonial "progress": "There were always dangers lurking at the edges—dangers that could give settlement a semi-permanent feel, make occupation look precarious, and cast a dubious light on the promise of explorer David C. Livingstone's three Cs: commerce, civilization, and Christianity. Despite the abstract appeal of the upward arc of imperial progress and even the concrete reality of empire's global reach, imperialism on the spot was downright rocky, its realities grimmer and more alarming than the tuneful imperative of *Rule, Britannia!* allows. The turbulence of empire deserves more attention."[41] Similarly, anthropologist Gastón Gordillo writes that the history of wrecks and ruination emphasizes "interruption, debris, constellation, and catastrophe in opposition to . . . the ideology of progress."[42] Such approaches to the past are what historical sociologist Renisa Mawani has called a "critical porthole" on the workings of power, in the sense that they capsize the seemingly inevitable march of colonial modernity by highlighting the ways in which empire was fraught and never a given.[43]

Scholarly thinking about shipwrecks also makes reference to the possible conflicting meanings of maritime misfortune. In his work on Portuguese shipwreck narratives, historian Josiah Blackmore argues that such stories "collectively manifest a counterhistoriographical impulse to the official textual culture of imperialism."[44] That is to say, accounts of wrecking often challenge dominant stories of colonial success by highlighting the moments where colonialism simply did not work. At the same time, other scholars argue that shipwreck stories can actually shore up narratives of empire. For example, the historian of early America Amy Mitchell-Cook claims, in contrast to Blackmore, that shipwreck narratives "were always ones of stability, where traditional understandings of social order were reestablished."[45] I lean more toward Blackmore's argument, while also recognizing that powerful stories of colonial hierarchies and ambitions could gather around shipwrecks even as the actual material consequences of maritime disaster challenged those things. Shipwreck, I argue, interrupts the smooth functioning of both power and history.

Why might we want to tell stories of colonial fragility, when we can see the results of settler colonialism all around us, in the forms of environmental degradation and systemic racism? What is the point of a history in which the settler project is framed as a precarious thing, or even a failure? First, such a history offers an opportunity to challenge the inevitability of our present moment, which was not the result of inexorable and impersonal forces but the outcome of myriad individual decisions and countless seemingly random events. Second, the notion of colonialism as a failing project—failing in the sense that its founding prophecies are proving to be false—opens space for the recognition of Indigenous resurgence and sovereignty.[46] Lastly, it encourages us to think about the ways in which we have, all of us—Indigenous and settler alike—inherited the wreckage of the past and are in the process of finding ways to live in that debris.

Wrecked makes a case for the ways in which shipwreck can tell us about how people on the Northwest Coast made sense of colonialism and of their shared history in this place. The first two chapters place Indigenous histories at the center of the story. Chapter 1 shows how Indigenous legal orders, such as the notion that anything that came ashore belonged by definition to the local people, had significant implications for those who had survived shipwreck in the early nineteenth century. Chapter 2, meanwhile, limns the transition between the fur trade and full-on settler colonialism, arguing that early episodes of violence between Indigenous people and newcomers became iconic stories that fueled later state violence against Indigenous communities in the wake of shipwrecks, especially on Vancouver Island. Turning primarily to settlers, chapter 3 illustrates the effect that quotidian maritime misfortune had on settlers' ideas about themselves and about history in the late nineteenth and very early twentieth century, while chapter 4 looks at the ways that the physical remains of shipwrecks—flotsam, jetsam, and cargo alike—contributed to everyday coastal culture in the nineteenth and twentieth centuries for both settlers and Indigenous people. Chapter 5 brings us closer to the present by placing together stories about ghosts and oil to make the case that shipwrecks in the later twentieth century are emblematic of the haunting challenges of the Anthropocene. Running in reverse chronological order from 2022 to 1693—moving in a sort of tidal fashion—chapter 6 peels back the layers of wrecklore that have accreted around a single early shipwreck, arguing that Indigenous knowledge is the foundation of regional historical tradition. Lastly, a meditation on a remaining hulk (one that you will see decomposing slowly over time in the photos between chapters) asks us to consider what it means to live with and amid the wreckage of the past.

Which is to say that this is not a typical maritime history, if it is maritime history at all. The nautical histories of shipwreck in the Graveyard of the Pacific have already been told by authors more informed and experienced than me about the nature of shipboard life and the economic, technological, and legal details of each case. I can do no better. Instead, I offer an account that uses shipwreck to tell a larger story of historical change, with an emphasis on the nature of colonialism in this place. In this, *Wrecked* is in keeping with a tiny but growing literature that we might call "critical wreckography." It includes the scholarship of people such as Steve Mentz, who illustrates the ways in which early modern Atlantic shipwrecks such as the famed *Sea Venture*, wrecked at Bermuda in 1609, heralded the much larger story of the arrival of the Anthropocene. Meanwhile, in her analysis of shipwreck archaeology, multidisciplinary scholar Sara Rich suggests that such labor invokes Christian savior narratives while also shoring up long-standing ideas about empire and colonialism. Australian theorist Killian Quigley similarly uses shipwreck to discuss broader themes, including the multispecies nature of wrecks, encrusted with marine life, that blur the boundaries between artifact and ecology. With *Wrecked*, my goal is to bring critical wreckography to bear on the Northwest Coast, a region that until quite recently has not drawn the attention of scholars who work in cultural studies, and to contribute to both academic and broader public conversations about empire and colonialism, particularly in the North American West.[47]

———————

Four years after *Valencia* went down, the *Victoria Colonist* reported on the progress that had been made since the terrible events of January 1906. "The day of greatest danger at sea is over," the writer claimed. "Better navigating, better charts, better appliances make bad accidents rare, better equipment, double bottoms, bulkheads, air chambered lifeboats make escape comparatively easy in case of bad accident; wireless telegraphy assures speedy succor. It is very different now to what it was in years gone by. Little by little, it is becoming safer to go down to the sea in ships."[48] The tragedy of *Valencia* had spurred progress. In this way and others, settlerist (and Indigenous) stories of shipwreck can tell us a great deal about the contours of history on the Northwest Coast. In doing so, they unsettle the expected stories of settler triumph and Indigenous decline.

Whatever its broader cultural meaning, *Valencia*, like many other shipwrecks in the Graveyard of the Pacific, left wakes in lives. For a long time after the disaster, for example, some area residents refused to board ships because of what was known as the "*Valencia* horror."[49] In October 1907, meanwhile, thirty-four-year-old Josephine Lombardi of Seattle, whose husband, William, had died with *Valencia*, went missing. She had been inconsolable in her widowhood, and that October day, she left her two children with a nurse and took her own life by jumping into the waters of the city's Lake Union.[50] Seven years later, in 1914, "Old John" Anderson, who had been a crew member aboard *Valencia* on its final voyage, was picked up for vagrancy on the Seattle waterfront by a rookie police officer. The *Seattle Star* reported on Anderson's previous bravery and the bleakness of his later life:

The mass grave of *Valencia*'s unidentified dead in Seattle's Queen Anne cemetery.
Photo by Sarah Fox

When the vessel, pounding on the rocks, began settling, and drove the survivors to cold positions on the spars, John was there with his cheering words and strong arms. He kept a score of half-frozen victims clinging to those spars hours after they would have given up otherwise, and then finally he himself went down, but managed to grab a bit of wreckage. But he was exposed in that freezing water for 24 hours, and now "Old John" is a derelict himself, always wandering along the waterfront, always striking his hands together and muttering. All the old officers know him and let him alone. But the new officer didn't. So "Old John" was in police court this morning. After several officers pleaded his case he was dismissed.[51]

Such were the very human costs of maritime disaster. For all the larger critiques of settler colonialism, these are also stories of very real personal trauma. People like the Lombardis and John Anderson were more than functionaries of empire; they were also victims of the same currents of history that brought colonial modernity to the shores of the Graveyard of the Pacific.

Just as the black rocks of Vancouver Island opened a hole in its metal hull, *Valencia* opens a hole in history, through which we might step into a different story of the Northwest Coast, one in which colonialism was not always successful, in which maritime failure was in fact quite common, and in which the aims of settler society all too easily went onto the shoals. To reframe the history of the region through marine misfortune is to widen the cracks in the machinery of empire by attending to the moments in which those things ran aground on the realities of the British Columbia, Washington, and Oregon coasts. The Graveyard of the Pacific, as it was already known by the time *Valencia* descended into its watery tomb, is a space that cradles a shadow history of the Northwest Coast. Certainly, the ships that wrecked in this region were only a small fraction of those that traveled its coastlines, but at the same time, those that were lost offer a valuable perspective that sheds new light on the region's past. It is a history in which the outcome was not a foregone conclusion, in which the myriad vagaries of wind, tide, stone, sand, fog, night, and human error determined the outcome, not just of particular ships but of the entire colonial project, which in most tellings can seem so inevitable and inexorable. Instead, the story here is one of colonial fears, settler fragilities, and the limits of technology. At the same time, it is clear that many who lived on and with the coast were transformed, for worse and sometimes for better, by the experience and afterlives of maritime disasters, in both the stories they told and in more material ways. When we talk about shipwreck, then, we speak of the most basic truths of this part of the world: that it, like its peoples, did not give itself up to empire easily or willingly. And indeed, maybe never gave itself up at all.

This painting by an unknown artist,
painted sometime after 1906,
shows the British bark *Peter Iredale*
at sail in stormy seas.

*Image courtesy of Columbia River
Maritime Museum, Astoria, Oregon*

ONE

Everything That Comes Ashore Is Mine

A Pacific World Wrecks on an Indigenous Coast

THE SKY IS OFTEN LOW over Grays Harbor, a large embayment north of the Columbia River in what is now Washington State. Named for Robert Gray, who in 1792 captained the first foreign ship to enter it, the wide bay accepts the flow of rivers with names that attest to much older understandings of place than that of an American explorer and trader: rivers like the Wishkah ("stinking water"), its muddy banks and bridges to huddle under made famous by local boy and grunge icon Kurt Cobain.[1] The de facto capital of Grays Harbor is Aberdeen, once the world's busiest lumber port but now a town that struggles in the wake of that same industry's decline. Histories of Grays Harbor speak to the global flows of capital, the movement of workers and wood, and the sometimes-violent conflicts that emerged from the intersection of those things. It is, in other words, a quintessentially Pacific setting. A hard place today with a hard past, Grays Harbor's hunger for commerce saw brick and mortar, concrete and steel, iron, and of course local cedar and fir forever transform its rivers and shores.[2]

In February of 1855, a gathering took place on another river flowing into Grays Harbor. The Chehalis is a slow tributary, wending out of low hills, and was once hemmed in by deep forests on either side, the very trees that would kick-start Aberdeen and other nearby towns in the decades to come. In a clearing among those trees, leaders of local

At the 1855 Chehalis River treaty negotiations between the leaders of coastal nations and Washington Territory governor Isaac Ingalls Stevens, shipwrecks were a subject of conversation and conflict. *Franz R. and Kathryn M. Stenzel Collection of Western American Art. Yale Collection of Western Americana, Beinecke Rare Book and Manuscript Library*

Indigenous communities had come together to meet with a young American and his entourage. That man's name was Isaac Ingalls Stevens, and he was both governor of Washington Territory and territorial superintendent of Indian affairs. He had come to treat with the headmen of the peoples who lived around the bay and along the nearby outer coast, part of a hastily organized treaty campaign that would ultimately cede much of Washington Territory to the United States. On the table were the most important issues facing Indigenous peoples and newcomers alike: the future of the lands and waters, the rights to the wealth of those things, and the building of relationships between two radically different societies. At the Chehalis River, hunting and fishing were primary sub-jects of debate between Stevens and the local dignitaries, as was access to ancestral lands that would be taken over by the Americans. And, perhaps surprisingly, they also spoke of shipwrecks.

Kah-kow-en, an elderly chief from the Chehalis people, made it very clear that places where ships came ashore belonged to his tribe. In the summary of his comments, he is purported to have stated quite simply that "the sea beach was his country. He did not want to leave it." Another leader, Chah-lat from the northern shore of Grays Harbor, noted that while he wanted only a small place for his house, he also "wanted a scope on the beach where things floated up of which he got a good deal." Other participants in the negotiations agreed. Two Chinook headmen from the south, Nah-kotti and Moos-moos, stated firmly that "when anything came ashore on the weather beach, whales or anything, they wanted one half." This included wrecks: Nah-kotti is also reported to have said that he "wanted the same privileges as the white man as to travel and labor, to pick up wrecks &c on the beach. Would give up half he found." And another Chehalis chief, Tleyuk, said, "I want the beach. Everything that comes ashore is mine. (Whales and wrecks.)" Stevens, for his part, had a clear response: "As to whales they were theirs," he told those gathered, "but wrecks belonged to the owners and if the Indians found them, they were to tell the wreckmaster and they would be paid a share of what they saved. They must not hide things." Wrecked vessels, then, were indicative not just of capricious seas but of competing sovereignties.[3]

Similar conversations happened in other places that treaty season. On his visit to the Quileute people north along the coast, Stevens made maritime disaster central to his admonitions to the locals. According to a Quileute elder named Hallie George, who spoke to ethnographer Leo Frachtenberg in the early twentieth century, discussions between the governor and Quileute headmen focused to no small extent on the disposition of wrecks. Stevens gave the gathered Quileute tools—axes, saws, shovels, and more—out of gratitude for how they had treated previous castaway sailors. Then, according to George, Stevens gave a speech to the Quileute. "Every time you see a White man drifted ashore," he is recorded to have said, "take good care of him. The reason I have given you the White people's working tools, is that you have taken care of the White people when they have needed care."[4]

Stevens was almost certainly referring to the previous year's wreck of the steamer *Southerner*, which came ashore at Akalat, the large, cliff-encircled island just off the main Quileute community of La Push. The crew remained at La Push for a year, showing the Quileute how to use iron tools and bake bread, and distributing twenty-dollar gold pieces among the community in thanks for their hospitality.[5] In the early twentieth century, George told Frachtenberg about what had happened after *Southerner* hit the rocks:

> A long time ago, a big steamer ran ashore on a rock at James Island. There were many White people on the steamer that grounded on the rock. Many things were washed ashore from the steamer, and the Indians picked up everything. As they did not know what forks were, they used them in order to brush the dog blankets, and they used the "hard tacks" by rolling them about on the beach.
>
> But the Quileute took care of the Whites[,] feeding them and giving them a place to sleep. They even gave one White man a pretty woman for a wife while he was here. The White people stayed a long time in Quileute-land. Some of the White people learned to speak the Quileute language because none of them could speak the language of the White people.

In return for their treatment of the survivors, the Quileute were given sheets of canvas, and George's memories included an account of the castaways playing on swings in La Push, suggesting that the trauma of shipwreck could be leavened.[6]

Meanwhile, Quileute leader Arthur Howeattle confirmed much of Hallie George's account of the steamer's destruction, adding that his ancestor Chief Howeattle had brought dried and fresh salmon to the survivors and then invited them into his home, in part to protect them from more hostile elements in the community. The sailors remained for half a year, feasting often with the people, and when they were finally rescued, one of the steamer's crew even gave a speech of gratitude. Then, Arthur Howeattle noted, "about a year or two after the Chief received a good powerful paper from the U.S. Government to show up with when he saw white people, and during his old age the U.S. Government put up a good building for shelter and furnished clothes and food to live on in his old age."[7] Indeed, a quarter century after the wreck, in 1878, Indian agent Charles Willoughby offered a personal recommendation for Chief Howeattle, noting that "during the distress of those aboard the ill-fated *Southerner*, this man rendered both assistance and succor. I strongly recommend him to the respect of all whitemen who may come in contact with him."[8] This was what "everything that comes ashore is mine" could look like: Quileute responsibility for all those in their territory.

Back in 1855, as Governor Stevens visited the peoples of the coast, he kept hearing about shipwrecks. While among the Makah at the northwesternmost tip of Washington Territory, for example, shipwrecks were on the negotiating block as Stevens and his functionaries engaged in treaty conversations with the people of Neah Bay.[9] A relatively recent incident no doubt informed the discussion. In 1851, the Hudson's Bay Company brigantine *Una* was forced ashore at Neah Bay by a December gale. Soon after, the Makah relieved the ship of its cargo and burned it to the waterline.[10] The tensions over not just lands and waters but over the fate of ill-starred vessels highlighted what was at stake: the very future of Indigenous-settler relations as Washington Territory began to be flooded with land- and wealth-hungry newcomers. The negotiations also served to establish a basic truth of the region: that Indigenous societies had long-standing legal orders that had existed since time immemorial, and which would not easily be dislodged by Stevens and those who followed him. The peoples of what would come to be known as the Graveyard of the Pacific had complex ways of managing their relationships with each other, with nonhuman relatives, and with these new foreigners. As a nascent colonialism arrived on these shores, shipwrecks deepened, extended, and complicated networks that had already reached far along the coast and out into the Pacific. At the same time, shipwrecks in the early nineteenth century highlighted the fragility of colonial enterprise in the face of Indigenous territorialities and prerogatives. To echo Tleyuk's words, much that came ashore in those decades would become Indigenous.

———————

What makes a world? When do connections between places, movements of things and people, and the transmission of ideas translate into a space that we might call a "world"? Oceans and seas have been at the forefront of these questions, as the Mediterranean, Indian, Atlantic, and Pacific have each birthed their own specific sort of world, both in academic conversation and in the very real realms of coastline and open water.[11] The Pacific, with its vast distances ringed and networked by profoundly different kinds of societies over great swaths of time, is perhaps the most complex of all, and the coast was part of this maritime matrix, the enmeshments of which would become more pronounced in the late eighteenth and early nineteenth centuries. As historian Matt K. Matsuda has described, the appearance of colonial newcomers, like the things they carried with them, moved "from tidal rings to deep gyres, across the deep historical currents of shifting Pacific worlds."[12] But to say that that world—or as Matsuda puts it more accurately, *worlds*—began with these things would be far from the truth.

The ocean currents and upwellings of the Northwest Coast bring to the region great abundance, and that wealth interpenetrates both land and sea. Enormous runs of salmon—five species in all, each with their own geographies, ecologies, and, one might say, cultures—spawn in the upwaters of coastal rivers, circle out into the northern ocean, and return to die in their home tributaries, that word itself suggesting the gifts that they bring: deep-sea nutrients carried deep into the forests and mountains, fishy isotopes circulating in the xylem and phloem of cedar, hemlock, and spruce. All up and down the coast, deeply reverent First Salmon ceremonies continue today despite colonial attempts to end such practices and in spite of the diminishment of the runs through over-fishing, habitat destruction, and climate change.[13] Other porosities link continent and ocean here as well. Sediments from mountains and river valleys pour out onto the continental shelf; tiny seabirds called marbled murrelets nest miles inland, high on the moss-bedded branches of the re-maining ancient trees; and Indigenous communities have names for hali-but banks and other watery spaces beyond the deep green horizon. These connections between places also happen at hemispheric scales. All of the Indigenous peoples of what would become known as the Graveyard of the Pacific either actively hunted whales by sending canoes of physically and spiritually prepared men out onto the waters or at least harvested the great sea beings according to strict cultural protocols where they came ashore, alive or dead.[14] As with salmon, placing whales—their territories, their timescales—at the center of our story foregrounds the robust and fecund worldishness of the Indigenous Northwest Coast, reaching far out over the horizons into a burgeoning Pacific world made of both ecology and empire.[15]

To manage this abundance, many Indigenous societies of the North-west Coast built over millennia exceptionally complex ceremonial prac-tices that are most commonly known by a Nuu-chah-nulth word: *pała ̓č*, or potlatch. Simultaneously economic, political, and religious in nature, potlatches are great feasts held for many occasions—births, namings, marriages, deaths, political alliances, university degrees, and more—that build, foster, and strengthen relationships, privileges, and obligations through the redistribution of wealth according to strict protocols. Pot-latch is an expression of ancestry and peoplehood, which are in turn manifestations of relations to specific territories, whether terrestrial or maritime. Potlatch is also law, and that law is of the land and sea themselves; meanwhile, the relations built within nations through potlatch also reach between nations, weaving the coast together. This is the case now, even in the wake of attempts to eradicate the potlatch tradition on both sides of the US-Canada border that lasted late into the twentieth century, and it was certainly the case in the late eighteenth century.[16] Which is to say that when the newcomers arrived, wrecked or otherwise, they arrived in a world that was already whole and was hardly waiting for history to begin.

North of Grays Harbor, the coast becomes exceptionally rugged. From the Quinault River to the tip of the Olympic Peninsula at Cape Flattery, great headlands and bewildering and dangerous mazes of offshore islets and spires create a shoreline that has doomed many a ship. These are the territories of the Quinault, Hoh, Quileute, and Makah peoples, whose engagement with the newcomers' failed maritime voyages has left traces both in their own historical narratives and in the written documentary record. In the middle of the twentieth century, for example, Quileute knowledge keeper Arthur Howeattle offered a reminiscence of the first shipwreck in his people's territory:

> In the days of my great-grandfather, Chief Howiattle, there was a shipwreck on the beach during a heavy storm, about a mile north of the Indian village at LaPush. Most of the crew were drowned but three managed to swim to the shore. These were the first white men ever seen by the Indians at LaPush.
>
> The tribe extended the usual courtesies to these visitors, feeding and caring for them during the time they remained at the village, and see that no harm came to them. I do not know how long these men were with my

people, but finally they left the tribe, traveling south along the beach. The poor men could not understand our language, neither could we understand them. Mother used to mention the names of these men to me and I remember them yet. Their names were "Mo-lo-ko," "Ar-pu-nu-cha," and "Mar-sha." It may be that the old Indians did not pronounce their names correctly.[17]

Quileute elder Harry Hobucket carried similar stories; he told of his ancestors thinking that the strangers who had wrecked near the mouth of the river "lived in ships and drifted on the ocean as their home because no white men were ever seen on the continent for generations back." According to Hobucket, these members of the "drifting white race," or *hó·kwat'*,[18] "stayed with the Indians many years, but finally asked permission to leave the tribe. They took enough Indian food along to last them a while then went south along the coast. The Indians heard of them no more. The names of some of the Spaniards were Molloco, Arpanisha, Markisha, others being long ago forgotten. The shipwrecked sailors stayed with the Indians for a long enough time to learn the Indian language."[19] Whatever the differences between these two accounts of what appear to be the same event, each speaks to the memory of shipwreck and resonates with the discussions held with Isaac Ingalls Stevens in 1855 about the succor given to castaways by their Indigenous hosts.

South of Grays Harbor, meanwhile, the land is mostly flat, save for the prominence known as Cape Disappointment on the northern side of the mouth of the Columbia River. The great river's outlet is the heart of the Graveyard of the Pacific, where perhaps as many as a thousand ships have been lost trying to enter or leave the fresh water for open ocean. These are the territories of the Chinook and Clatsop peoples. At the south side of the river's mouth, Clatsop Spit reaches out into the weather, its dark green pines and silvery dune grasses holding pale golden sands in place. Near here, in the late nineteenth century, a Clatsop elder had told another story of shipwreck. After the death of her son, she had cried for a year. Now, back from a trip down the coast, she returned with a revelation: at first, she thought she had seen a beached whale, but it had instead turned out to be a monster of some sort, with two spruce trees rising from it. "Now she saw that its outer side was all covered with copper," the account continues. "Ropes were tied to those spruce trees, and it was full of iron. Then a bear came out of it. He stood on the thing that lay there. He looked just like a bear, but his face was that of a human being. Then she went home. She thought of her son, and cried, saying, 'Oh my son is dead and the thing about which we have heard in tales is on shore!'"

The people of her village, upon hearing of the strange thing, went to see it, now finding two bears with human faces. Maybe, the story goes, they were actually people; indeed, they offered the Clatsop two copper kettles and motioned that they needed water. One of the Clatsop men went into the strange vessel, discovering boxes and brass buttons as his companions set fire to the ship. According to the story, the strange thing "burned like fat," leaving behind only copper, iron, and brass. The two surviving crewmen were taken back to the Clatsop villages, and people came from all around the region to see them. Meanwhile, the foreign metals entered the trade networks that reached from the mouth of the Columbia far inland, brass traded for a servant, a nail for a deerskin, several nails for precious dentalium shells that might end up as far east as the Great Plains. "They bought all this," the account continues, "and the Clatsop became rich."[20]

Quileute and Clatsop stories of the first ships to arrive in their respective territories are only two of many along the coast that tell of the arrival of colonial presences. The nature of that arrival—as well as of the attitudes and perceptions of its Indigenous observers—can be seen in the many distinct languages of the coast. There was the Quileute term hó·kwat', for example. Among the Clatsop and their relatives the Chinook, the newcomers were tlon-hon-nipts, "those who drifted ashore."[21] And among the Makah, the strange foreigners were known as babaḷid, a name glossed as "those living on the water and floating around, like they have no land."[22] Taken together, terms like these highlight the precarity of the newcomers. The Spanish castaways at Quileute and the shipwrecked "bears" at Clatsop may have been part of a rising Pacific world of competing empires, but they were hardly in control of the situations in which they found themselves; rather, they were drawn into Indigenous societies and their trade networks by dint of being part of "everything that comes ashore." Two shipwrecks of the early nineteenth century would make this abundantly clear.

———————

In the first decade of the nineteenth century, a song was sung in Russian all around the great arc of the North Pacific. In English translation, it goes something like this:

> Buildings are raised on New World ground,
> Now Russia rushes to Nootka Sound,
> The Peoples wild are Nature's child,
> And friendly now to Russian rule.[23]

The so-called "Song of Baranof," named after the chief manager of the Russian-American Company, was the bracing refrain of an empire on the move. The Russians had been expanding their commercial activities from the east coast of Asia in the later eighteenth century and by the 1800s had begun to trade with the peoples of the northwest shores of North America, drawn above all else by the lushly pelted sea otters that rafted in the vast kelp forests garlanding the coast.[24] This expansion was a violent process, involving the regular kidnapping and conscription of Indigenous men (and sometimes women) from the Aleutian Islands, Kodiak Island, and elsewhere. These Indigenous people were among those who journeyed in tiny sailing vessels along the Northwest Coast, as were the mixed-heritage descendants of Russian-Tlingit relationships based in Novo Arkhangelsk, the capital of Russian Alaska.[25]

In October of 1808, one such vessel, *Sviatoi Nikolai* [*Saint Nicholas*], was traveling alone along the coast of what would, four and a half decades later, at least nominally become Washington Territory. Its crew was made up of Captain Ivan Bulagin; Bulagin's wife, Anna Petrovna; eleven Russian men; four Indigenous men; two Indigenous women; and—luckiest for us—a Russian supercargo named Timofei Tarakanov, whose account of the doomed voyage provides remarkable insights into the world of the early nineteenth-century Northwest Coast. En route in October 1808 to Grays Harbor to meet up with a sister ship before voyaging south to the

Almost immediately after wrecking in 1808, the crew of the Russian trading vessel *Sviatoi Nikolai* took violent action against local Quileute people. *From Charles Ellms,* The Tragedy of the Seas; or, Sorrow on the Ocean, Lake, and River, from Shipwreck, Plague, Fire and Famine *(1841)*

California kelp forests, *Sviatoi Nikolai* found itself alternately thrashed by storms and becalmed by still air. Finally, on October 31, the ship was caught on shoals, its anchor cables breaking during the night. The following morning, it was blown ashore in the territory of the Quileute people, just south of the river that now bears that people's name. All twenty souls on board easily gained the shore and quickly began setting up a camp. Tarakanov would later write, "Now it was necessary to think about our own safety. We had to save ourselves, and also to rescue our firearms, our only means to preserve our liberty. If captured, we would live out a miserable life as slaves to the savages, a consequence a hundred times more horrible than death."[26] Almost immediately, Quileute people arrived on the scene, and Tarakanov was invited to their leader's longhouse on the river. He refused. The locals began taking some of the newcomers' belongings—anything that came ashore was theirs—before being chased out of the camp. They threw stones back, and the Russians fired on them, killing three. The sailors then retrieved the dead men's cedar bark hats and capes where they had fallen. From there, the story of the crew and passengers of *Sviatoi Nikolai* would be one of fear, violence, and desperation and would include a shocking surprise.

Taking what they could from their beached vessel, the Russians destroyed everything else made of metal and threw it in the sea, then headed south toward Grays Harbor. The landscape was impossible to traverse, and they were loath to accept help; when two Hoh men offered to show them a path, the Russians fired on them. As the foreigners struggled along the shore in pelting rain and snow, they were showered with rocks from the cliffs above by unseen assailants. Finally, they reached the Hoh River, territory of the people of the same name who were close kin to the Quileute, where they were ferried across in two canoes. During the crossing, one of the canoes was captured, and a Russian, an Indigenous man, and most notably Anna Petrovna Bulagina were taken captive by the Hoh. Soon after, the bereft Captain Bulagin handed over leadership of the group to Tarakanov, who led them inland.

Hoh warriors followed with Anna and proposed a ransom for the Russian woman's return; Bulagin was even allowed to speak with his wife, but the ransom collapsed when the foreigners refused to give up their weapons to the Hoh. Crestfallen, the *Sviatoi Nikolai's* former crew continued inland, building a small fort and settling in for the winter. The conditions were terrible; the men and women fell to eating tree fungus, their sea-lion-skin gun covers, and even the expedition's dog. Despite trading occasionally for salmon with local people—sometimes at the point of a Russian gun—these strangers to this place experienced a deprivation that was profound.

By February 1809, the Russians had built a small boat, and early that month took it downriver to the mouth of the Hoh, where they took two women and a boy hostage. Anna Petrovna was brought out to meet with her countrymen, and here is where the story takes its most surprising turn: *she refused to be ransomed*, having been treated well by her captors and fearing the hardships of life deep in the forests of the upper Hoh watershed. At first, Bulagin made to shoot and kill her, but he soon realized the pointlessness and danger of this path of action and turned away in shock and grief. Then, inspired by Anna's choice, Tarakanov himself, along with four others, surrendered to the Hoh, hoping they would eventually be rescued by some other European ship. The rest of the group decided to head north in their homemade craft, but it soon wrecked, and all were taken captive. From there, the Russians and their Indigenous compatriots entered networks of exchange that stretched up and down the coast. Bulagin, for example, was eventually traded to the man who held Anna; later that summer, however, she died, and Bulagin followed her to the grave in February of 1810. As for Tarakanov, he ended up in the household of a Makah leader named Yutramaki, who treated him well due to the Russian's skills (which included building a kite, much to the enjoyment of his hosts). Finally, in May of 1811, Captain Thomas Brown of the American fur trading ship *Lydia* was able to ransom thirteen of the twenty crew and passengers of *Sviatoi Nikolai* (one Russian had disappeared forever into the exchange networks of the coast, while an Indigenous man had already been found on the Columbia River). The ordeal was over.

Tarakanov's account of his experiences ends abruptly: "On May 10th we set out on our way and sailed along the coast, often stopping at various harbors to trade with the savages; and on June 9th we arrived at New Arkhangelsk."[27] But as a document of early encounter, it provides a sharply focused and granular description of Indigenous geographies and protocols: an invitation to a longhouse, various attempts at ransom and other forms of negotiation, the harrowing harrying of the foreigners as they moved through Quileute and Hoh territories, and the lineaments of trade and diplomacy that reached from the homelands of the Makah in the north to those of the Chinook and Clatsop in the south. While it has historically been understood as a document of European travail in the face of a savage wilderness, Tarakanov's narrative is also a testament to the very sentiments that Isaac Ingalls Stevens would hear nearly half a century later: this land is ours, and so are those who come ashore here. A wreck like that of *Sviatoi Nikolai*, while representing an increasingly worlded Pacific with its links even to distant Saint Petersburg, also attested to the density and complexity of a world that already existed.

———

Before *Sviatoi Nikolai* wrecked, its crew members had been actively trading on the coast, and along the way, they had noticed something worth commenting upon: some people they met carried spears tipped with iron.[28] Indeed, the presence of iron at the end of those spears was strange, given that on the Northwest Coast, copper was the only metal traditionally mined and worked. So where had the Quileute obtained the black metal with which they threatened Tarakanov and his compatriots? The answer could be found in a river of seawater that crossed the North Pacific, darker than the ocean around it and thus named the Kuroshio

(Black Current) by the Japanese. On this flood, ships set adrift off the eastern coast of Asia sometimes ended up on the northwestern coast of North America, their fittings collected, modified, and repurposed for local use. This was a pattern established before the coming of Robert Gray or the Russians; in fact, when an eighteenth-century Makah longhouse that had been flattened by a mudslide was excavated in the 1970s, iron was found among the thousands of objects that had been perfectly preserved for more than two centuries.[29] In 1834, the workings of the Kuroshio would be apparent to Indigenous people and colonists on the Northwest Coast when three foreign men found themselves wrecked very near the site of that ancient buried house.

Their names were Kyukichi, Iwakichi, and Otokichi, or the "three Kichis" as they would become known, and they had come across the Pacific from Mihama in Japan aboard their vessel *Hojunmaru*, with its cargo of porcelain, rice, and cotton. They had been caught in a violent storm and lost their vessel's rudder, in doing so becoming beholden to the Kuroshio. Originally, there had been seventeen men aboard the *sengokubune*, a type of ship designed only for nearshore travel and trade. On the yearlong involuntary passage across the ocean, however, fourteen of the crew had died of scurvy, their bodies preserved on board in barrels. It is difficult now to imagine the fear, hopelessness, and boredom that must have filled the minds of those seventeen as they died one by one on the vast, seemingly empty, and featureless Pacific. When *Hojunmaru* at long last came ashore just south of Cape Alava in January 1834, the Makah immediately took the three survivors in and began salvaging materials from the vessel, including, almost certainly, iron.

Before long, word of the foreign strangers from Japan reached the ears of newcomers from another far-off land. In May of that year, Hudson's Bay Company factor John McLoughlin, based at Fort Vancouver on the Columbia River, would write to his superiors about surprising news from Makah territory: "Last winter the Indians informed us that a vessel had been wrecked somewhere about Cape Flattery and I sent a party along the coast to recover the crew from the natives but our people could not reach the place, and a few days ago I received through the Indians a letter written in Chinese characters and I have written to the captains of our vessels to do their utmost to recover those unfortunate men from the Indians."[30] The Hudson's Bay Company had been building forts throughout what would eventually become Washington and British Columbia, creating a regional trade network that built on preexisting Indigenous economic systems but linked them to places like London and Canton. In a matter of years, the HBC had become an important, if also fragile, force in the region's geopolitics. The company's men, many of Indigenous heritage themselves, already had some experience dealing with the Makah, if only at a distance, and so McLoughlin made a plan to ransom the three castaways. Eventually, they were brought to Fort Vancouver. After several months there, they were sent to England, and eventually to Macau. None of them ever returned to Japan. Meanwhile, porcelain purchased from the Makah would grace the tables at the HBC's Fort Astoria near the entrance to the Columbia, evidence of the Japanese men's passing through.[31]

By the 1830s, the tentative fur trade exemplified by *Sviatoi Nikolai* had burgeoned into a global fur economy in which the Northwest Coast played a central role. Manifest in iron and porcelain and sea otter pelts, the Pacific-ness of this increasingly interconnected world had as its foundation already-extant Indigenous territorialities and legal orders along which both furs and Japanese sailors now moved. Like the Russians of 1808, the shipwreck survivors of 1834 entered into networks that had existed for millennia. Unlike the crew of *Sviatoi Nikolai*, however, that of *Hojunmaru* would be relatively quickly redeemed by new colonial institutions that had come to play such an important part in local geopolitics. Things were changing. And the United States was just over the horizon.

Like *Valencia* in 1906, or like those mysterious first wrecks encountered by the Quileute and the Clatsop, *Sviatoi Nikolai* and *Hojunmaru* left wakes behind them in the memories of both Indigenous people and outsiders. Historian Josh Reid writes, for example, that accounts of powerful men like Tarakanov's host Yutramaki and their complex relationships with castaways shaped settler perceptions of the Makah for decades after these events took place.[32] In the later nineteenth century, meanwhile, observers of local history became fascinated with stories of Japanese ships washed up on Northwest Coast shores, which they theorized might explain phenotypic similarities they perceived between Asian people and the Indigenous peoples of the coast. This "admixture," the theory went, had its origins in lost vessels.[33]

Hojunmaru's wake extended even into the twentieth century. In 1983, for example, the film *Kairei/Adrift at Sea* debuted in Japan, telling the story of the three survivors' rescue from the Makah and their journey back to Asia. In it, a white-bewigged Johnny Cash plays John McLoughlin, and Japanese actors fill the roles of Makah people.[34] Six years later, in 1989, a monument to the "three Kichis" was installed on the grounds of the Fort Vancouver National Historic Site as part of Washington State's centennial. Then, in 1997, relations between Japan and the Makah people were rekindled. Having read a book about the life of Otokichi, Koichi Saito, the mayor of Mihama, began developing a program of commemoration that would see him and others from Mihama visit places where Otokichi had been: London and Singapore, for example, but also Makah territory. In September of that year, a delegation of almost one hundred residents of Mihama arrived in Neah Bay. They made a pilgrimage to the place where *Hojunmaru* had come ashore, building a small altar and chanting for the sailors' spirits before Makah tribal members offered songs. The question of captivity was not front and center in these events; rather, the emphasis was on building new relationships and thinking to the future.[35] Two days later, a group of actors from Japan and members of the Makah Nation performed a musical titled *The Tale of Otokichi* at a suburban theater near Seattle. The play had debuted in Mihama in 1993, but Indigenous actors participated in the 1997 performance, with Makah youth portraying their own ancestors.[36] Eventually, the world-renowned Makah Cultural & Research Center would place a large model of *Hojunmaru*, a gift from the people of Mihama, in its entrance hall.

The afterlife of *Sviatoi Nikolai* is less visible than that of *Hojunmaru*. In 1822, Tarakanov's narrative appeared first in serial form in both Russian and German newspapers, then in a loosely translated English version that was published in an obscure academic journal. Another Russian version was included in a collection of shipwreck stories printed in 1853 in Saint Petersburg, and other versions appeared in 1874 and 1884. Finally, a summary of the story, penned by a regional historian, appeared in the *Washington Historical Quarterly* in 1922. But unlike the ships that are the focus of the next chapter, the stories of which were widely known in the nineteenth century and after, the story of *Sviatoi Nikolai* remained relatively unknown in the region until the 1980s, when a full English translation with an editorial introduction was published in the United States.[37]

As for the Quileute, however, they continued to carry stories of the Russians and Unangax. In 1909, for example, elder Ben Hobucket shared his people's side of the story, confirming important details of Tarakanov's account:

The Hoh Indians had a village on the other side of the river, and from it Indians came over to take a look at the new people, appearing friendly. So the strangers got them to agree to ferry them across the stream. . . . The white people and their belongings were placed in several canoes the Hohs started to paddle them over; but, on reaching the middle of the stream, they suddenly opened up lightly plugged holes in the bottom of the canoes which they had intentionally cut and stuffed with cedar bark. Then, leaping from the crafts, they swam ashore, for could they get the new people adrift they could capture them single-handed without much trouble.[38]

Beyond Hobucket's offering, though, Quileute and Hoh accounts of the crew of *Sviatoi Nikolai* have not been shared with outsiders.

For some settlers, however, the story of the Russian ship continues to fascinate and elicit sympathy. On the Upper Hoh Road, for example, a wooden kiosk and shelter stands alongside the rural lane, surrounded by plantings and a pair of picnic tables. On the walls of the shelter, various plaques tell the story of *Sviatoi Nikolai*, along with cultural profiles of the Hoh, Quileute, and Makah Nations. Erected in 2015 by the Association of Washington Generals, the local post of the American Legion, the states of Washington and Alaska, and a local family, the kiosk is something of a shrine, if one that spends little time on Indigenous versions of the story.[39] Then, in 2018, British Columbia author Peggy Herring released *Anna, Like Thunder*, a novel written in the voice of the young Russian woman who chose to stay with the people of the coast. Here, the doomed Anna is an amateur astronomer with a gift for language. Of the wreck of *Sviatoi Nikolai*, she says, "Today my world has shattered, and its remnants have been strewn along a cold beach in a strange land. The order and the beauty of the constellations offer no comfort; instead, they only mock."[40] Worlds could be built or torn down on Indigenous shores.

In the years after the Chehalis treaty negotiations of 1855 that opened this chapter, shipwrecks in what would eventually be known as the Graveyard of the Pacific would remain very much on the minds of American officials, even if there was little that they could do about the realities of Indigenous control over coastal spaces and the accidents that happened there. For example, three years after the Chehalis council, Indian agent Michael T. Simmons had noted a distinct concern about the Makah and

Quileute further north. "It has so happened," he wrote in his 1858 report, "that whenever these Indians have come in contact with the whites, they have had the latter in their power. In most cases ships have been wrecked on their coast. The consequence is, that they do not appreciate our importance, and are very independent, and sometimes insolent."[41] We might in fact replace *independent* and *insolent* with *sovereign* and *jurisdictional* to more accurately portray what was happening on the beaches of so-called Washington Territory. Indeed, in 1862 another Indian agent described the Makah approach to both shipwrecks and territorial sovereignty:

> The location of the Makah tribe . . . enables them to be of service in res-
> cuing and aiding shipwrecked persons and in securing such property as
> may be cast ashore by the waves. Hitherto this tribe, in common with
> all other Indians on the sea-coast, have considered all waifs of the ocean,
> whether persons or property, that might be thrown upon their shores, to
> belong to them. Goods were indiscriminately appropriated to their find-
> er's use, and individuals thrown among them by the tempest, or strangers
> casually landing on their coast, were forced to ransom themselves or
> live a life of servitude till rescued by their friends. Although of late years
> this tribe has altered their behavior so as to have rendered assistance to
> distressed mariners in several instances, they still consider they have an
> undoubted right to everything cast ashore, and expect to be paid for
> every service they render in rescuing shipwrecked persons or property. In
> my opinion they are justly entitled to salvage on property saved, equally
> with white men; but all such adjustments of claims should be settled by
> the agent, and not by every person who may choose to interfere. The ter-
> ritorial law makes this duty devolve on the wreckmaster of the county;
> but that officer resides some seventy miles up the Straits of Fuca, and can
> render no assistance in case of emergency. In my judgment the agent is
> the proper person to arrange all matters relative to shipwrecks between
> the Indians and persons whom they may succor.[42]

Here were the limits of colonial infrastructure as they existed in the first decade after the treaties, as well as the simultaneities of succor and distress, hospitality and captivity, rescue and ransom.

In fact, relations of rescue dominate accounts of shipwreck on this part of the coast in the latter part of the nineteenth century. Indian agent G. A. Heney, for example, wrote this about the Hoh and Quileute peoples from his office on the Quinault Agency: "They are very peaceable, and in several instances have been of great assistance to individuals who have been wrecked and cast upon their coast, always treating them kindly."[43] This was a far cry from Tarakanov's terrible tale. Agent Charles Willoughby agreed in his annual report on the Quileute in 1879: "They have on several occasions been instrumental in saving the life and property of sufferers by shipwreck, who invariably receive the greatest care and attention from them, even when expecting no remunerative return. I would thus urge upon the government that the Quillehutes [sic] be permitted to remain in their present homes."[44] Willoughby no doubt had the story of *Southerner* in his mind as he wrote this, showing how Indigenous relationships with shipwreck could be a reason to leave people be.

———

In 1887, Sarah Willoughby, wife of Indian agent Charles, watched a ship founder in the surf at Taholah, site of the Quinault Agency and a traditional home of the Quinault people. Inspired by the spectacle, she made a drawing of it in colored pencil, in which two Quinault people watch the wreck. The first is a boy in pants and suspenders, who has climbed onto a massive drift log to get a better view as the wind tousles his hair. The second is an older woman, who carries on her back a load of firewood as she watches from the strand, the seawater curling around the end of the same log, behind which she stands. In the distance are the forested sea cliffs, and in the middle distance, a vessel lists dangerously, its masts nearly horizontal in the breakers.

This 1887 drawing by Sarah Cheney Willoughby shows *Sir Jamsetjee Family* caught in the breakers at the Quinault Indian Reservation. *University of Washington Special Collections NA4036*

This was the demise of *Sir Jamsetjee Family*, a Dundee-built ship once owned by Parsee merchants from India. First employed in the London-Bombay trade circuit, it had changed hands several times, eventually coming into the ownership of a Melbourne firm in 1884. Two years later, it was off the coast of Washington Territory, bound in ballast from Australia to Port Townsend in thick weather, when it foundered in the surf at Taholah. Its crew launched lifeboats, and Adeline Willoughby, daughter of Sarah and Charles, described what happened next:

> The night of the wreck my brother Charles . . . with a number of Indian
> men started with a lantern, some kindling and a can of petroleum to

the only short strip of beach where a boat could land. The night was very stormy and they had to climb along the rocky sides of the cliff. My brother and the Indians made the strip of beach after a hard climb in the darkness where a slip of the foot would mean plunging one on the rocks below. When they arrived at the beach a fire was started and my brother began to signal to the men in the boat to land there. It seemed they had launched all the boats but one and each one was swamped or crushed as soon as it was launched. Miraculously the last boat was launched and all the crew was aboard and they started for the shore through the terrible surf. When the boat gained the shore the Indians rushed into the surf to pull it up onto the beach and the men in the boat began to beat them off with their oars. My brother seeing what was happening called out to them in English and they stopped.[45]

At great risk to themselves, members of the Quinault Nation had participated in the rescue of *Sir Jamsetjee*'s crew, all of whom survived the ordeal. The wreck of *Sir Jamsetjee Family* was emblematic of two patterns. First, it highlighted the growing and widespread tradition of Indigenous rescue in what was by that point in time becoming known as the Graveyard of the Pacific. Meanwhile, with its connections to the Indian and Atlantic Oceans, as well as to the wide Pacific, the ship was empire afloat. In many ways—technologically, economically, and materially—the square-rigged and doomed vessel was a microcosm of colonialism itself: it used wind power as had the first visitors to the coast, it linked places like India and Australia within networks of the British Empire, and the cargo it was intended to pick up in Port Townsend was the stuff on which settlers in many places depended. And yet here it was in Quinault space, turning over and coming apart in the pounding and crashing surf.

Quinault men had rescued shipwrecked sailors before, and they would do it again. In December 1886, for example, the leaking Chilean bark *Lillie Grace* was deliberately grounded just north of Grays Harbor near the home of Sampson Johns, who paddled his canoe out to the wreck with several other Quinault men and brought off all the crew. Two years later, Johns cared for the three survivors of the fatal wreck of *Abercorn*, receiving thirty-five dollars for what a local newspaper called "humane services." Ultimately, Johns earned congressional medals for his efforts and was known for wearing them publicly. He now lies buried in the same cemetery as those who did not survive the wreck of *Abercorn*.[46]

By the late 1880s, much had changed for the peoples of the coast since the treaty negotiations of thirty years earlier. While some Clatsop people still lived in their traditional territory at the mouth of the Columbia, many had moved down the coast to an enclave at Seaside, Oregon, alongside members of the Nehalem and Tillamook Nations.[47] The Chinook, whose treaty negotiators included Nah-kotti and Moos-moos, had not received a reservation and found themselves mostly having either to enter into settler society or to move to reservations far from home.[48] For the Chehalis, on whose land the council had taken place and whose leader Tleyuk had said that everything that came ashore was his, a reservation had been established in 1860, some distance up the Chehalis River and far from the coast.[49] The Quinault, meanwhile, had retained the largest reservation in western Washington Territory, centered on the settlement where the Willoughbys were living when *Sir Jamsetjee Family* went to pieces in the surf.[50] The Quileute and Hoh, for their part, managed to continue to live at the mouths of their respective rivers.[51] Lastly, the Makah had signed their own unique treaty in 1855 that protected the practice of whaling but ended the system of captivity that had helped save the crews of *Sviatoi Nikolai* and *Hojunmaru*, even as the Makah would continue to insist on salvage rights to wrecks in their homeland. On their reservation at the northwesternmost point in the contiguous United States, the Makah were also becoming active participants in the sealing and commercial fishing trades, translating their maritime expertise for a new economic system.[52]

In other words, by the time *Sir Jamsetjee Family* foundered at Taholah, the peoples of the central stretch of the Graveyard of the Pacific had experienced, if in differing ways, the brunt of American federal Indian policy, the pressures of settler colonialism, and the economic and cultural changes that emerged from both. And yet, the Melbourne-based vessel wrecked on a shore that was still Indigenous, just as others before it had as well—and just like the Pacific world itself had over the course of a century. More than mere observers to maritime disaster, Indigenous people had profoundly shaped the experience of shipwreck, just as shipwreck had transformed relations between the newcomers and the peoples and nations whose ancestors had lived in these places since time immemorial.

Peter Iredale newly wrecked on Clatsop Spit
in northern Oregon, where it soon became
a tourist icon—and has been ever since.

*Image courtesy of Columbia River Maritime
Museum, Astoria, Oregon*

TWO

Troublous Days

Colonial Fear and the Wakes of Maritime Violence

AT THE TURN of the twentieth century, Portland had arrived, and a modern city needed modern history. All across the American West, civic leaders founded pioneer associations and historical societies to capture the past before it died with the first generation of settlers and to create a story of belonging in place. When the Oregon Historical Society was founded in 1898, it built upon the earlier work of the Oregon Pioneer Association to establish a powerful historical narrative that would serve the city, not just by looking backward but also by gazing forward. While the pioneers had achieved the "pre-empting and subduing of an adequate dominion and home for a civilization," according to OHS founding member Frederic George Young, the University of Oregon economist and sociologist also argued that attention to the state's colonial history would provide a foundation for a good future. One of the organization's early directors, James Robertson, argued similarly that "although we have been engaged upon a theme of local history, we have beheld at the same time . . . a steady progress toward greater things." Indigenous people, all too often portrayed as relics of a vanishing past by historical societies, would nonetheless appear in this story of progress. The original seal of the OHS, for example, featured two hands grasped in friendship beneath a peace pipe, referring back to the peaceful encounter between local Indigenous people and the United States' Corps of Discovery, better known as the Lewis and Clark expedition and seen by many Portlanders as the founding moment of their city's American trajectory. But the seal occluded more than it revealed. It hid a history of violence, and at the Oregon Historical Society's gathering in December of 1900, that violence would be surfaced through the words of one Indigenous woman.[1]

She had been invited to come and tell stories, and this she did. "I, Tsin-is-tum, otherwise known as Jennie Michel, say: I am a Clatsop Indian," she began before turning to her genealogy and to a story that must have been difficult to share. "My mother was named Wah-ne-ask. My father was killed in the bombardment of the Clatsop village by the ship sent by Dr. McLoughlin; I do not remember his name. I remember well when the village was bombarded. I was a small girl then. All the Indians ran to the woods. I ran with my mother and she carried my younger sister on her shoulders. In running through the woods a stick caught one of my sister's eyes and tore it, so she was called 'Squint-Eye.'"[2]

The community that she described was *tłác'əp*, from which the term *Clatsop* derives, once located where the small settlement of Hammond now squats on the inland side of the spit. To tell her story, Tsin-is-tum had traveled to Portland from the small town of Seaside, Oregon, where she lived in an enclave of Indigenous and mixed-heritage people who had managed to remain in their homelands.[3]

In sharing the story of the destruction of *tłác'əp* with her settler audience, Tsin-is-tum was confirming an account that had lain in colonial archives for decades. John McLoughlin, factor of the Hudson's Bay Company fort at Vancouver, had written of the same event in 1829. Hearing that a British ship called *William & Ann* had wrecked on Clatsop Spit, and that the captain and six crew members had made it to dry land before being killed by Clatsop warriors, McLoughlin had directed his employees to go to *tłác'əp*. On arriving, they saw hundreds of Clatsop people there and decided to withdraw. As McLoughlin learned more, he realized that the crew of *William & Ann* had likely all drowned, and yet he instructed his men to return and attack *tłác'əp* and its residents

At a 1900 meeting of the Oregon Historical Society, Clatsop knowledge keeper Tsin-is-tum gave an account of surviving a Hudson's Bay Company attack on her community after the 1829 wreck of *William & Ann. Oregon Historical Society*

anyway. "In regard to this melancholy event ... I am of [the] opinion the Crew were not murdered," he wrote to his superiors, and yet he called for an attack to force the Clatsop to return any goods they had retrieved from the wrecked ship and to terrorize them into submission. The British men fired on the village with cannons, resulting in the deaths of Tsin-is-tum's father and an unknown number of Clatsop people.[4]

The attack on *tɬác'ǝp* took place in part because of stories that white people had heard about their Indigenous counterparts and that they amplified as they repeated those stories among themselves. For example, the fur trader Gabriel Franchère, who had visited the mouth of the

Columbia in 1811, recalled how local accounts of Indigenous violence stretched back into the dim past, long before the Hudson's Bay Company and other fur trade companies had established themselves in the region:

> We found here an old blind man, who gave us a cordial reception. Our guide said that he was a white man, and that his name was *Soto*. We learned from the mouth of the old man himself, that he was the son of a Spaniard who had been wrecked at the mouth of the river; that a part of the crew on this occasion got safe ashore, but were all massacred by the Clatsops, with the exception of four, who were spared and who married native women; that these four Spaniards, of whom his father was one, disgusted with the savage life, attempted to reach a settlement of their own nation toward the south, but had never been heard of since; and that when his father, with his companions, left the country, he himself was yet quite young.[5]

This story and others of alleged Indigenous rapacity were propagating and migrating along the northwestern coast of North America in the early nineteenth century, with consequences for Indigenous people and newcomers alike.

Some thirty years after Tsin-is-tum's death, the prolific regional historian F. W. Howay described the early years of the fur trade on the coast as "troublous days," and he was accurate in his estimation.[6] Over the course of her life, Tsin-is-tum, like other Indigenous people living on the coast, had seen great violence done to her people and community, often as a result of colonists' fearful accounts of supposed Indigenous bloodthirstiness. She had also, in her long life, seen the transition from the maritime fur trade to the ascendancy of something entirely new in the region: settler colonialism. This was a hinge in the history of the Northwest Coast, in which stories and actions turned back on each other recursively: older stories influenced violence, which in turn inflected the stories told by settlers and Indigenous people alike. The loss of Tsin-is-tum's sister's eye and their father's life would be but two casualties out of many. At the same time, the persistence of these stories would also point toward continued survivance of Indigenous families and nations on the coast.

_____

On the evening of Tuesday, May 12, 1812, Manhattan financier John Jacob Astor received bad news while dressing for a night at the theater. A "melancholy report" had appeared in that day's *New York Gazette and General Advertiser*, written by a Massachusetts sailor named Nathaniel Woodbury the previous September. In the reprinted letter, Woodbury announced that he had learned of the destruction of a trading ship called *Tonquin*, owned by Astor, on the far northwestern coast of North America. Given that the vessel had been the flagship of Astor's ambitious trading enterprise based at the mouth of the Columbia River, the news was necessarily devastating. But according to one account, Astor was described as having said before leaving for the theater, "What would you have me do? Would you have me stay at home and weep for what I cannot help?" The show, it seemed, must go on.[7]

Nearly five years later, at six o'clock on a Friday evening in March 1817, the curtains rose at the Philadelphia Theatre to reveal a gaslit scene from a distant land. Deep forest framed the stage, where an American ship was seen lying at anchor in a sheltered bay. Over the next short while, audience members, who had paid fifty cents to a dollar for their seats, would catch glimpses of this far-off place: more forest, a village along the saltwater shore, the interior of a vast house made from great cedar logs. The performance was punctuated by moments of great excitement: the deaths of most of the ship's crew, a great chief's funeral, a lunar eclipse. At the center of all this was a single white man. Lanky and with a noticeable scar across his forehead, blacksmith John Rodgers Jewitt was the star of this world premiere of a two-act spectacle he had titled *The Armourer's Escape*. As he proceeded through the story of his captivity and eventual liberation, Jewitt offered two musical numbers as part of the show. The first was, he claimed, a "Nootkian" war song. The second, which brought the performance to a close, was called "Song of the Armourer Boy" and captured the deeply emotional nature of his travail. "No thrush that e'er pip'd its sweet note from the thorn / Was so gladsome and lively as me," it began, "Till lur'd by false colours, in life's blooming morn / I tempted my fortune at sea." Jewitt sang on, ending on a note of both trauma and piety:

> From slav'ry escap'd, I, joyful, once more
>> Hail'd a civiliz'd land, but alone
> And a stranger was I on a far-distant shore
>> From that which my childhood had known.
> "If such be life's fate, with emotion I cried,"
>> Of sorrow so great the alloy;
> "Heaven grant that sole blessing that ne'er is denied,"
>> To the friendless Poor Armourer Boy![8]

And with that, the evening's entertainment ended, and the audience filed out into the Pennsylvanian spring.[9]

Astor's misfortune and Jewitt's trauma made for compelling stories. Indeed, they would become origin stories for the Graveyard's colonial history. As Māori Indigenous studies scholar Linda Tuhiwai Smith argues in her now-canonical work *Decolonizing Methodologies*, one task at hand for scholars is to critically examine and then pull apart colonial origin stories to better understand the narrative and material machinations of empire. "The genealogy of colonialism," Smith writes, "is being mapped and used as a way to locate a different sort of origin story, the origins of imperial policies and practices, the origins of imperial visions, the origins of ideas and values."[10] On the Northwest Coast, two maritime disasters—the loss of the American trading ship *Boston* and most of its crew in 1803 and the destruction of the bark *Tonquin* in 1811 with scores of lives lost, both foreign and Indigenous—have served as especially

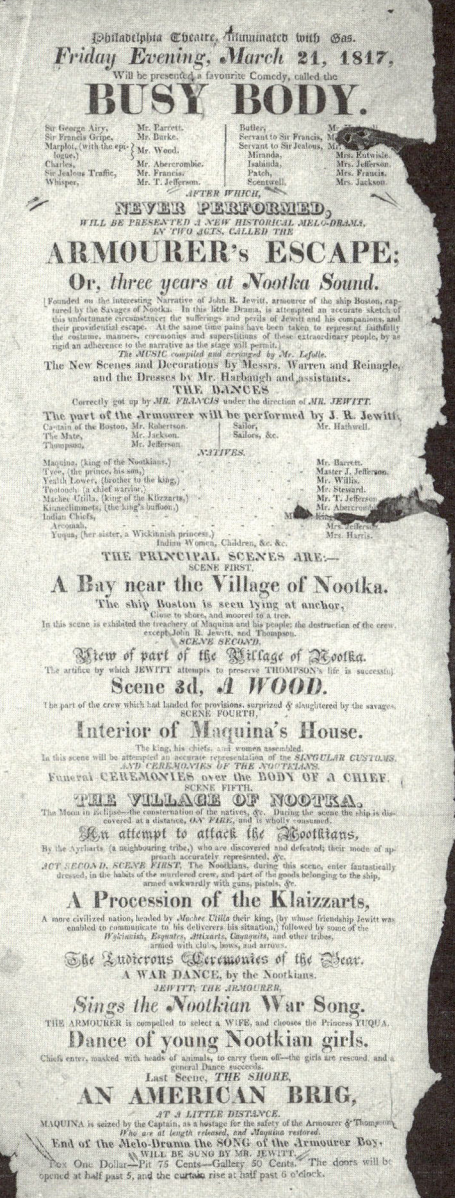

After returning from three years among the Mowachaht Nuu-chah-nulth, British blacksmith John Rodgers Jewitt made a short career out of performing his travails on stages far from the Northwest Coast. *Collection of the Historical Society of Philadelphia*

potent origin stories of colonialism in the region, reflecting and refracting long-standing and persistent imperial narratives of settler innocence and justifications for violence against Indigenous people. These two episodes and the stories told about them by non-Indigenous people both prefigured and configured further violence along the coast after white settlers and their institutions began to permanently establish themselves in the region in the mid-nineteenth century. Although neither event was exactly a shipwreck, their echoes would shape how wrecks would be understood in the decades to come, with deadly results. Indigenous people were scapegoated, targeted, and in some cases killed because of the kinds of stories that white people told about lost ships and their crews. Meanwhile, *Boston* and *Tonquin*, along with other maritime disasters, remain relevant for both settler and Indigenous communities along the coast today. Two centuries and then some since their destruction, these ships continue to sail the fraught waters of the coast, their wakes ironically refusing the very colonialism that they embodied.

Boston sailed into the waters of the Northwest Coast in 1803. Its captain was John Salter, but the crew member whose name would be most widely remembered was John Rodgers Jewitt, a twenty-year-old blacksmith from Boston, England, who had boarded *Boston* in the *other* Boston, in Massachusetts. After a trip round Cape Horn, *Boston* arrived in 1803 in Nootka Sound, where its crew began trading with *hawiilth* (chief) Maquinna's people, the Mowachaht Nuu-chah-nulth. Before long, though, the encounter soured badly and ended when Mowachaht men killed all but two of *Boston*'s crew, Jewitt and another man named McKay. The two would spend nearly three years in Mowachaht territory, and Jewitt's account of his time there would ultimately fascinate and titillate generations of readers, all the way into the present.[11]

Eight years later, in 1811, another ship, *Tonquin*, sailed north from

The *Tonquin* disaster, in which the American Fur Company's flagship was destroyed and dozens of Tla-o-qui-aht people were killed, shaped foreigners' ideas about the Northwest Coast and its peoples for decades. *From Edmund Fanning, Voyages to the South Seas, Indian and Pacific Oceans, China Sea, North-West Coast, Feejee Islands, South Shetlands, &c. &c. with an Account of the New Discoveries Made in the Southern Hemisphere, Between the Years 1830–1837 (New York: William H. Vermilye, 1838)*

the American Fur Company outpost Astoria, at the mouth of the Columbia River, en route to the west coast of Vancouver Island and the Nuu-chah-nulth homelands and homewaters. Along the way, it picked up a young Quinault man named Joseachal, who had relatives among the Tla-o-qui-aht Nuu-chah-nulth and could serve as an interpreter. Indeed, Joseachal's kinship with the Tla-o-qui-aht likely saved his life; he would be the only survivor when the ship's magazine was deliberately detonated during a bloody melee that erupted when negotiations went south. All the non-Indigenous crew members were killed, as were up to two hundred Tla-o-qui-aht people on board and in surrounding canoes. Joseachal eventually returned to Astoria and gave a detailed account of a disaster that, like the travails of John Rodgers Jewitt, would inspire settler nightmares for centuries to come.[12]

Historian Joshua Reid has called this land- and seascape a "geography of fear" and offers us the best interpretation of what was happening on this coast during the late eighteenth and early nineteenth centuries: "When imperial actors entered the region, they exacerbated older lines of tension, added new opportunities for conflict, and applied their own tools of violence and terror. In this Indigenous borderland where distinct peoples shared and contested spaces and resources, violence was not anomalous or the result of miscommunications: threats and violence were central to both the borderlands and imperial processes of this period."[13] But what Reid calls the geography of fear stretched further than the territories of the Clatsop, the Quinault, the Nuu-chah-nulth, and other Indigenous peoples of the coast. It could also reach as far in space as Manhattan and Philadelphia and beyond, and as far in time as the twenty-first century.

––––––––

Of the two ship-stories, Jewitt's is the most famous by some measure. Its original 1807 version, *A Journal Kept at Nootka Sound*, sold some nine thousand copies within two years in North America and Britain.[14] Indeed, as one twentieth-century historian of the region would argue in 1940, "There are few tales of Indian captivities which enjoyed so extensive an audience, for by a combination of timely chance and Jewitt's own restless showmanship his story obtained widespread currency along the eastern seaboard of the United States upon his return to civilization."[15] Working with Connecticut editor Richard Alsop, and in the same year he appeared on that Philadelphia stage, Jewitt published an extended version of his account in 1817: *A Narrative of the Adventures and Sufferings of John R. Jewitt, the Only Survivor of the Crew of the Ship* Boston, *during a Captivity of Nearly Three Years among the Savages of Nootka*

Sound, and an Account of the Manners, Mode of Living, and Religious Opinions of the Natives. Meanwhile, early accounts of the region and its early colonial history commonly made explicit references to Jewitt's account, often excerpting it substantially or printing it in its entirety.[16]

As for Jewitt himself, he would have a family and return to American society, but his later life was marked by poverty, transience, and misfortune. "I exerted myself this Cold winter in the public streets when the Snow was verry deep and I was doeing well," he wrote to his wife in 1817, "but some evil minded disposed person or persons, in the night, when I had just received four Hundred Dollars worth of my Books, went and broke open the barn which was verry secure, and picked the locks of my Boxes and stole all my books did not leave me a Single One." He also regularly endured "a violent pain in the head, right where I was wounded," and he died in 1821 at the age of thirty-seven in Hartford, Connecticut, even as his narrative continued to proliferate.[17]

The story of *Tonquin* was similarly widespread, and like Jewitt's narrative tapped into long-standing trends in popular literature. As geographer Daniel W. Clayton has argued, "Contemporaries saw this event as a leitmotif of Indian savagery . . . and American and Canadian journalists, collectors, and scholars have written more about the *Tonquin* disaster than any other single event in early British Columbian history."[18] That writing began in earnest in the 1830s, when versions of the account appeared in the British *Atheneum* magazine and in a narrative of western journeys published by fur trader Ross Cox in 1832.[19] But it was Washington Irving's magisterial *Astoria*, written through a close working relationship with Astor himself, that truly brought *Tonquin* to popular audiences and was reviewed favorably by figures as notable as journalist Edgar Allen Poe.[20] Irving had managed to turn the failed Astorian project into a compelling account that included the *Tonquin* incident as one of its most exciting moments—so much so that even James Fenimore Cooper incorporated a fictional version of the disaster into his own popular published work.[21]

The stories of *Boston* and *Tonquin*, while full of their own particular-
ities and idiosyncrasies, were also exemplars of two sorts of narratives
that animated popular consciousness in the nineteenth century: the
captivity narrative and the maritime adventure. Captivity narratives, in
which settlers are abducted and (usually) redeemed back to "civilization,"
had been a distinct and immensely popular genre since the seventeenth
century in colonial North America and beyond. Numerous scholars have
argued that captivity narratives were, in fact, the first North American
literary genre, and Jewitt's account of his time with the Mowachaht
was a prime example.[22] The second genre within which accounts of
both *Boston* and *Tonquin* sat squarely was the maritime adventure, with
its exotic locations, strange peoples, and constant danger. As historian
Robin Miskolcze notes, by the early nineteenth century, "ships and the
sea became part of the fabric of U.S. national narratives because they
contributed to America's efforts to imagine herself as a viable, if not exceptional, community in relation to the rest of the world."[23] And as Jason
Berger has argued, that relationship had manifest destiny at its center.[24]
Meanwhile, children were among the most important consumers of
maritime adventure. "The sea," historian John R. Gillis writes, "became
the prime locus of danger and adventure, the ultimate rite of passage for
inland boys," and of Jewitt's narrative specifically, one reviewer wrote
that the blacksmith and his editor had created a work that "may com-
municate a good deal of entertainment and information to all classes
of readers, is peculiarly fitted for the young; it forms, in fact, a very
appropriate companion to Robinson Crusoe."[25] *Tonquin*, meanwhile,
became a meditation on mortality. "Such was the fate," went one 1849
rendition, "and such the melancholy end of the ship *Tonquin*," slipping
neatly into broader colonial narratives of melancholy in which violence
was inflected, and sometimes masked, by mourning.[26]

Melancholic meanings aside, the violence with which the creators of
these narratives were obsessed often emerged, at least in settler minds,

out of supposedly inborn traits of Indigenous peoples, whom one early visitor to the coast described as "sensible of the slightest attention, and . . . prone to revenge at the slightest insult."[27] Indeed, given the often-overdetermined nature of both captivity narratives and maritime adventure stories, it would be tempting to assume that accounts of *Boston* and *Tonquin* were unalloyed narratives of colonial victimhood in which seamen found themselves at the sharp end of deadly Indigenous bellicosity. After all, as historian Boyd Cothran has shown, the construction and articulation of settler innocence is a central element of many accounts of Indigenous-colonizer conflict, just as Emilie Cameron, in her work on an alleged massacre in the Arctic, has accounted for the seemingly endless settler appetite for tales of Indigenous violence.[28] But that assumption would be wrong.

From the very first written accounts of both events, chroniclers pointed toward the behavior of the ships' captains as the proximate cause of both disasters. Astor himself referred to *Tonquin*'s captain Jonathan Thorn as a "gunpowder fellow,"[29] and virtually every account of that ship's destruction points toward Thorn's behavior as the reason he and so many others died. Fur trader Gabriel Franchère wrote at the time of Thorn's "abrupt manner and passionate temper," and explorer and botanist John Scouler placed the blame on Thorn in the 1820s.[30] Trader Ross Cox joined the chorus in 1832 and added a flourish of nationalism: "His [Thorn's] manners were harsh and arbitrary, with a strong tincture of that peculiar species of American *amor patriae*, the principal ingredient of which is a marked antipathy to Great Britain and its subjects."[31] Washington Irving called the captain of *Tonquin* "dry and dictatorial," while reverend Samuel Parker wrote in 1846 of Thorn's "great want of prudence," which had also cost the lives of eight men at the Columbia River's powerful and deadly bar.[32]

Later historians would sometimes look beyond the actions of bad apples such as Thorn to make critiques of the inherent violence of the fur trade as a whole. "There was no cohesion or cooperation in the maritime fur trade," wrote F. W. Howay in 1928. "It was a congeries of individual efforts. Each trader strove to seize the present advantage, regardless of the future. Neither ship nor trader might return."[33] Elsewhere, Howay would simply call the trade "predatory."[34] Even as early as 1817, writers could use the story of Jewitt's captivity not just to level criticism at the fur trade but to draw attention to a hypocrisy at the heart of colonialism, such as when the *Analectic Magazine* printed a review of Jewitt's account. "It is by bloody atrocities such as these, and by the propagation of vice and disease," offered the editors, "that civilized man has hitherto delighted to display his superiority over the savage. Shall we then wonder that the christian name has become a reproach and an abomination among the heathen—that the missionary labours in vain, as long as christian faith is thus contradicted by christian practice?"[35] Even this trenchant critique, however, was an aspiration toward the wholesale transformation of Indigenous societies; it was just that venal fur traders had been getting in the way of the civilizing mission. As historian Traci Banivanua-Mar writes, "As the individualized acts of the unscrupulous, frontier violence was dislocated from its enabling colonial context as the unfortunate product of the very conditions of savagery that regularly justified and necessitated colonial intrusion."[36] Bad apples or predatory trade relations notwithstanding, the conditions that led to the violence of *Boston* and *Tonquin* would thus require further imposition of foreign beliefs and practices in the form of missionaries and other "civilizing" policies and practices.

Along with a deep conviction that the dispossession of Indigenous peoples was inevitable, there was, underneath all this ambivalence, a bedrock of fear with a long pedigree that reached back to earlier colonial histories. That fear was expressed in a ballad that was reported to have been in wide circulation among ships' crews by the 1830s and that referred to both the horrors of "savagery" and the imagined, seemingly necessary terrors of future settler retaliation on the Northwest Coast:

I'd have you all take warning and always ready be,
For to suppress those savages of Northwest America;
For they are so desirous some vessel for to gain,
That they will never leave it off, till most of them are slain.[37]

The "Ballad of the Bold Northwestman" is an anticipatory document. It looks toward the future, using stereotypes of Indigenous savagery and greed that emerged from the fur trade to gesture toward what would ultimately be required to end violence on the Northwest Coast: more violence. As it had at *tłác̓əp* in 1829, this old logic would have new consequences for Nuu-chah-nulth and other Indigenous nations once it was fused with the imperatives of settler colonialism along the Northwest Coast.

———————

In his 1902 account of the fur trade in the far northwest of North America, government engineer Hiram M. Chittenden located the origin of "the Indian Question" in the fur trade. "It was in this intercourse that the Indian Question had its origin," he wrote, "and here began, for better or for worse, that process which must eventually result in reducing the Indian to a civilized order of life."[38] Stories about fur trade–era violence, then, are origin stories of a sort. In the case of *Boston* and *Tonquin*, they would become a foundational layer of colonial narrative over which a new set of stories—and actions—would be sedimented as settler colonialism began to take hold along the Northwest Coast in the middle of the nineteenth century. What would bind those two layers of colonial history together was fear.

One place where this fear can be seen is in the rapidly expanding print culture of places such as Victoria, at the southern tip of the colony of Vancouver Island. Historian Kenton Storey has used local newspapers to examine settler attitudes toward local Indigenous peoples, noting that the papers "offer the best evidence of settler fears." These fears were not just of Indigenous violence; they could also focus on settler violence, which was in Storey's words "intrinsic to the colonial project," and such stories "bred fear."[39] Storey goes on to note that editors in Victoria "intentionally and strategically emphasized First Nations antipathy towards the region's white residents in order to mobilize popular support for the confiscation of Aboriginal reserve land in Victoria and to eliminate Aboriginal participation in the local economy."[40] In other words, the stories white settlers told about Indigenous people and about themselves were inextricably linked to dispossession.

For example, on April 25, 1860, the *Victoria Gazette*'s editors printed a piece in which they simultaneously affirmed and whipped up fear of Indigenous violence.

> Everybody must be fully convinced, by observation of the gradual increase of Indian depredations, that the leniency which has been exercised toward them hitherto, is of no avail, and if persisted in, will only succeed, by inspiring them with a false confidence, in rendering them still worse; until at length the day will come, when, perhaps for our very lives, we shall be forced to arms, with or without the consent of our Rulers; all the wild passions of our nature will be let loose, and we shall only feel a sense of security in the extermination of the tribes.[41]

Meanwhile, John Gowlland, master of HMS *Hecate*, focused on the threat to maritime crews presented by Nuu-chah-nulth people: "They would be only too glad to murder all the boats [*sic*] crew for sake of the utensils in her; only knowing us to be a man of war—of which they have a wholesale dread, are afraid of the consequences."[42] In this way, Indigenous violence (or threat of it) became criminalized, even as settler influence expanded throughout the region with almost no legal processes of expropriation such as treaties. In this sense, the colony of Vancouver Island was what Indigenous studies scholar Heidi Kiiwetinepinesiik Stark has called a "criminal empire."[43] In this social, cultural, political, and legal milieu, the accounts of *Boston* and *Tonquin* continued to circulate. Indeed, according to historian Barry Gough, accounts of the two ships were "celebrated stories" in Victoria.[44] Even if, as historian Laura Ishiguro has shown, settlers who were not part of the publishing class in Victoria rarely made references to Indigenous violence—or to Indigenous people at all—in their letters home to Britain, those settlers still lived in a place that was saturated with fear.[45]

That fear all too easily led to violence. In late summer of 1864, the editor of the *Victoria Daily Chronicle* warned that the colonial town and British settlements all across the island were "seated as it were on a powder magazine," almost certainly invoking *Tonquin* in doing so.[46] In August of that year, reports had arrived in Victoria that the three-man crew of the small trading vessel *Kingfisher* had been killed by Ahousaht Nuu-chah-nulth men under the leadership of a man named in the colonial record as Cap-chah, and the cargo had been taken off the ship and *Kingfisher* burned to the waterline. Oral tradition attests that the attack was in response to the sexual assault of an Ahousaht woman by the *Kingfisher* crew,[47] but to colonial authorities, the act was wanton murder and rapacious piracy. In response, officials in Victoria sent HMS *Devastation* and HMS *Sutlej* north to Ahousaht territory. Under the leadership of Rear Admiral Joseph Denman, the gunboats loosed their weapons on Ahousaht communities, killing more than a dozen people, destroying houses and canoes, and forcing the survivors to disperse to relatives' communities in order to survive through winter. At the same time, the fact that Denman never returned to Ahousaht territory as he had threatened apparently led Cap-chah to claim victory, with a resulting increase in his social and political status.[48] Whatever its outcomes for Ahousaht people, a Victoria newspaper crowed that the gunboats had offered a "wholesome" lesson.[49]

Then, in February 1869, the bark *John Bright*, outward bound with lumber from Port Gamble in Washington Territory to Valparaiso, Chile, wrecked in Hesquiaht Nuu-chah-nulth territory during a southeast gale. All aboard perished, including the captain's wife, their child, and a servant girl. News of the wreck was brought to Victoria in March, and a story quickly developed that *John Bright*'s crew and passengers had been murdered. HMS *Sparrowhawk* was dispatched to the scene, where Hesquiaht people insisted that the dismembered bodies of which newspaper editors made such horrifying hay had in fact come apart in the violent surf and among the sharp rocks of the shore. Nevertheless, seven Hesquiaht people were brought to stand trial in Victoria, and ultimately, two men, the *hawiilth* Anietsachist and the commoner Katkinna, were sentenced to death for the alleged murder of an unidentified white woman.[50] They were returned to Hesquiaht territory and hung in front of their relatives on gallows erected near the site of the wreck. A priest then walked through the crowd offering to serve as a minister to the people, to no response, and the gallows would stand there for five more years. *Colonist* editor D. W. Higgins would later write that this lesson was "salutary."[51]

Four years later, Higgins appeared—at least superficially—to be correct in his estimation of the positive effects of such violence. When the waterlogged American bark *Edwin*, weighed down with lumber and headed for Australia, began to break apart off Vancouver Island in December 1873, the captain's wife was crushed by falling timbers, and the couple's children were washed overboard. Some of the crew managed to clamber aboard a makeshift raft and make for shore, but with little hope of surviving the cold water and pounding surf. Soon, however, a cadre of Hesquiaht men under the leadership of a *hawiilth* named Matlahaw came to the rescue in their massive seagoing cedar canoes. Missionary August-Joseph Brabant, ministering among the Hesquiaht at the time, noted that "the Indians had treated the sailors and captain . . . with much kindness. They appear, however, to have been a rough crowd. . . . Later they began quarreling in the chief's house, fought and wounded each other to such an extent that they had to be separated and made to lodge in different houses." In the end, Brabant led the retrieval of *Edwin*'s spilled cargo to build his mission church, while Matlahaw received a silver medal from the Dominion of Canada, and he and his men were given cash rewards by the American government.[52] Two years later, the *hawiilth* visited Victoria to much acclaim, wearing the medal he and his men had earned for their brave efforts.[53]

What seems clear from the archive is that the stories of men like Matlahaw vastly outweigh what some settlers liked to imagine as wanton murder. Indigenous rescue of shipwreck victims was an important tradition in the Graveyard of the Pacific, based on territorial protocols, intimate knowledge of the sea and shore, and a basic capacity for compassion and hospitality in the face of disaster. The evidence of this tradition, which had begun before *Kingfisher* and lasted long past *John Bright*, lies in a source that was not much concerned with Indigenous peoples at all. *Lewis & Dryden's Marine History of the Pacific Northwest*, published in 1895, is a magisterial and almost overwhelming accounting of shipping and its perils beginning with the first foreign presences in the region. It includes regular—if usually vague and brief—references to the Indigenous rescue of crews and passengers of doomed ships, all up and down the coast. When the French bark *Morning Star* began coming apart on the Columbia Bar in 1849, for example, a river pilot brought with him some Chinook people who helped with the rescue. Six years later at Cape Perpetua on the Oregon coast, the crew and three passengers of *Fawn* were "rescued by Indians [likely Alsea people] before she struck" according to the *Marine History*. In 1875, *Emily Farnum* wrecked at Destruction Island in Quileute territory, and its crew members "were taken to the mainland by the Indians." In Huu-ay-aht Nuu-chah-nulth territory in 1879, the crew of *Becherdass-Ambiadass* was rescued by local people after a bleak and terrifying night on the rocky shore. Nearby the next year, the men of *General Cobb* came ashore, and "after remaining there two days and one night . . . were rescued by some Indians." Port San Juan on Vancouver Island, home to the Pacheedaht people, saw *Revere* wrecked there in 1882, but "the crew and passengers were brought to Victoria by the Indians the next day." The crew of the Hawaiian bark *Thomas R. Foster* was also rescued by local Indigenous people, living with the Kyuquot Nuu-chah-nulth for two months. And when *Woodside* was destroyed near Pachena Point in 1888, the crew was "taken to Victoria by the Nitnat [*sic*] Indians." Two years later, two storm-battered boats from *Atalanta* came ashore in Clayoquot Sound, where "the Indians were very kind to us" despite the long-standing stories about Tla-o-qui-aht savagery associated with *Tonquin*.[54] From Vancouver Island in the north and far south to Oregon, and until the establishment of US and Canadian lifesaving stations in the late nineteenth and early twentieth centuries, Indigenous people were the primary saviors of shipwrecked sailors in the Graveyard of the Pacific, never mind the stories that white people told about them.

Sometimes, these rescues were remembered by settlers and Indigenous people alike. Ditidaht tour boat operator Carl Edgar Jr., for example, tells a story about descendants of the survivors of one shipwreck coming to visit the reserve where he lives: "The descendants of the survivors came to Nitinat about five years ago with handwritten notes of the stuff they experienced and endured, and everything lined up with our oral history. Same thing, it was just on the other side."[55] According to one locally published history, this was the wreck of *Skagit*, which went ashore in 1906, not long after *Valencia*.[56] In both Ditidaht and settler accounts of *Skagit's* demise, the sole death caused by the wreck was that of a Jamaican cook, notable for being the first Black person to be encountered by the Ditidaht. Small tragedies such as this one could echo into the present and serve to foster relationships between Indigenous people and settlers—and their respective archives—more than a century later.

———

Both *Boston* and *Tonquin*, meanwhile, continued to sail into the twentieth century, long after *Kingfisher* and *John Bright* were likely forgotten by most settlers. In 1912, a writer for the *Victoria Colonist* described Jewitt's narrative as "one of the classics of western America," and by the early twentieth century, it was familiar enough in the region that F. J. Howay wrote in 1925 that "the circumstances of this case are so well known, as set forth in Jewitt's *Narrative*, that I shall not repeat them."[57] Across the twentieth century, local newspapers regularly ran retrospective articles about Jewitt, keeping his story alive for new generations of settlers.[58] Once again, Jewitt's "adventures" seemed particularly well suited for children; "John Jewitt was a real boy," said one article, and his narrative was "one that can't help but appeal to youngsters where this exciting story actually happened."[59] *Tonquin* stories, meanwhile, appeared regularly in newspapers in the late nineteenth and early twentieth centuries and showed up in venues ranging from *Harper's Monthly* to regional histories.[60] Together, the two stories were so ensconced in local settler mythology that they hardly needed retelling. In his 1926 reminiscences of life on Vancouver Island, for example, Charles Moser told his readers that "I confined myself to adding what had not been published before. Hence in my chapter of Nootka I only alluded to the Jewitt case, and omitted entirely the murdering of the crew of the ship *Tonquin*, and its subsequent blowing up with great loss of life, in Clayoquot Sound, because this has appeared in print times and again."[61] That same year, the city leaders of Astoria, Oregon, erected a 125-foot column funded by the Great Northern Railway and John Jacob Astor's great-grandson that celebrated the early history of the region, including the arrival and eventual destruction of *Tonquin*, and that overlooked the estuary of the Columbia, literally cementing the story into official civic history. At the same time, though, some newspaper accounts of *Tonquin* lamented that not enough people knew the story, which suggests that it was part of a vernacular settler curriculum of belonging, something that colonists and their descendants needed to know in order to claim status as locals.[62]

Stories of *Tonquin* continued to multiply as the century proceeded. In 1941, a film based on the disaster played at the Dominion Theatre in

Victoria, while in 1943 the children's page in the *Colonist* featured the ship's demise.[63] A fictional treatment of Jewitt's experiences also found audiences in the 1940s.[64] Then, beginning in the 1960s, professional and amateur marine archaeologists and divers began searching for the remains of *Tonquin*, which they called "the Mayflower of the Pacific northwest," clear evidence of the ship's iconic status.[65] As for Jewitt's narrative, by the 1970s it was being used to inform discussions of a national park along the island's coastline, capitalizing on the rescue trail cut through the forest in the wake of the *Valencia* disaster. Both *Tonquin* and *Boston* remained critical touchstones—origin stories—for regional history. They were a far cry from "dead" or "lost" objects; rather, they were together an animating force in settler historical consciousness in the Graveyard of the Pacific.

————

In 1868, British Columbia colonist and Indian reserve commissioner Gilbert Malcolm Sproat noted that the destruction of *Tonquin* was "an occurrence which to this day is spoken of among the tribes."[66] Similarly, one explorer noted the tale of the disaster was also kept alive among the descendants of the translator and survivor Joseachal, and one other *Tonquin* witness, later a resident at Fort Langley on the mainland, enjoyed regaling listeners with his account of the events of 1811.[67] In the many decades since, meanwhile, Nuu-chah-nulth and other Indigenous communities along the coast have insisted on maintaining connections to these stories and engaging with settler society around the unfinished business of maritime violence—and sometimes settlers have engaged in return.

In the late 1980s, for example, a man named John R. Jewitt VI, a direct descendant of the man who had performed onstage in Philadelphia, made two visits to Mowachaht territory to retrace the steps of his ancestor. There, he was welcomed by the descendants of *hawiilth* of the early nineteenth century, including Hawiilth Yathloua Mike Maquinna. Arriving with several family members, Jewitt recalled having received a copy of his kinsman's narrative in the eighth grade, noting that "I really had no idea at all where Nootka or Vancouver Island was—it was just way off, far away somewhere." Having ultimately come to live on the West Coast, Jewitt became fascinated with seeing the places where his ancestor had stayed. "It feels great to be here. . . . It's like walking in my forefather's shoes." As for Maquinna's descendant, Yathloua told a reporter that "it's a warm feeling to reconnect with our past. . . . We share a very important history here between our families and our peoples. You and your family are always welcome in our houses, just as it was 200 years ago." Similar in some ways to the relationships built between the Makah and their Japanese guests in the 1990s, the *hawiilth* simultaneously emphasized familial relationships between Ahousaht people and Jewitt's descendants and asserted territorial rights through the extension of hospitality.[68]

Revisiting the story of *Tonquin* in the twenty-first century, perhaps unsurprisingly, proved more complicated. When investigators retrieved a ship's anchor encrusted with trade beads from Clayoquot Sound in 2003, Tla-o-qui-aht Nation member Nupit-Tu-Chilth Joe Martin—whose father carried the name of the *hawiilth* who had been so offended by Thorn in 1811—argued that "we have a very big interest in this anchor" and described it and the beads as "war spoils," echoing Indigenous attitudes toward ships' resources elsewhere on the coast. Meanwhile, marine archaeologist James Delgado described *Tonquin* as "one of those great sea stories that has staying power" and one that held tourist potential.[69] Such positive outlooks were matched, though, with reminders of conflict and environmental devastation: one local First Nations member, Gisele Martin of Esowista, told a reporter, "Maybe we should blow it up again! A replica's okay as long as it's not glorified, and our canoes escort it. It's still ours. The whole story needs to be told. Who's commemorating the sea otters? The whole history is about otters. Maybe we should have a *Tonquin*athon to raise money for otters."[70] But for other local Indigenous people, *Tonquin*'s resurrection could have positive ramifications, even for their own communities; Nupit-Tu-Chilth argued, for example, that "I think that building the replica of the ship would help promote education of youth in the community."[71]

If *Boston* and *Tonquin*, as colonial origin stories, could serve many purposes in the minds of local people and the descendants of those involved, the cases of *Kingfisher* and *John Bright*, which had been so shaped by those earlier events, were far more pointed and complicated. In the case of *Kingfisher*, HMS *Sutlej* crew members had abducted a young girl after the shelling of her village in 1864 and renamed her after the ship that killed her relatives. "Maggie Sutlej" was given to a naval officer's wife before dying and being buried at sea two years later.[72]

In 2018, the girl's story came to the attention of the British Columbia Sikh community, who noted that the ship's name, *Sutlej*, commemorated a violent conflict with the British in their own homeland. Appalled by the Ahousaht child's fate, the Sikh NGO Khalsa Aid reached out to her community, where shells from *Sutlej* and *Devastation* had continued to be found well into the twentieth century. New relationships were built, not just between Ahousaht and Sikh communities, but between the present and the past. As Khalsa Aid representative Jatinder Singh noted, the story of the stolen child was an "early example of children kidnapped from their families and westernized," linking the events of 1864 to the longer history embodied by genocidal institutions such as the so-called residential schools that operated in Nuu-chah-nulth territories into the late twentieth century.[73]

Reconsiderations of the *John Bright* incident garnered much wider attention. In 2018, more than four hundred people gathered in a gymnasium in Port Alberni to participate in an event that brought together representatives of the federal and provincial governments, members of the Hesquiaht and other local nations, and the media. The road to that gathering had begun in 2004, when Hesquiaht leaders including Victor Amos began seeking redress for the hangings of Anietsachist—Amos's five-times great-grandfather—and Katkinna. "We didn't want the history books to show that my grandfather was a murderer," Amos said. "Using oral history and songs we have kept the story of Anietsachist alive for 143 years and counting, we have never wavered or doubted his innocence."[74] The event also included the performance of a song Anietsachist had composed on the gallows, protesting his innocence and predicting the ongoing strength of his family. To all this, British Columbia Aboriginal Affairs minister Ida Chong responded to the event by formally announcing, "I wish to express our sincere regret that your homeland was forced to bear witness to such violence."[75]

Among the participants that day was Erik Kiaer of Portland, a descendant of HMS *Sparrowhawk*'s captain, who had this to say: "Other people have ancestors who were sea captains and they create their own myths about them. I didn't exactly brag about mine ... it's an eye opener that the actions of your ancestors can have such an impact on others." Of Anietsachist's song, Kiaer noted that "Captain Mist would have heard it the first time it was sung and didn't understand it ... now we're at a place where we understand its meaning, and where amends are being made for what happened."[76] Both Amos and Kiaer spoke eloquently of the power of family stories, only some of which had been shared with outsiders. Amos, for example, told a reporter that "prior to this last little while here, the only people who really knew that he was innocent was the family, the tribe. . . . For us, it clears his name. Maybe not in a legal way, but at least now, it's being talked about by the general public. That he was innocent, it was a wrongdoing." Chong, meanwhile, noted that the event in Port Alberni was "about some closure to the pain they have been feeling. Every generation hereafter, when they hear the story about what happened, now they can plug in this chapter and say, 'But on this day what took place was an offer from the province of regret and an offer from the Hesquiaht of forgiveness.'" Later, a cleansing ceremony was held at the site of the gallows.[77] According to one Hesquiaht elder who participated in the ceremony, Anietsachist's death song had proclaimed,

"I'm innocent and from this day forward my family will flourish to prove my innocence," and the very nature of the ceremony proved it to be so.[78] If *Kingfisher* and *John Bright* represented pain, their stories also carried within them the possibility of long-awaited reconciliation.

———————

In the last decade of the nineteenth century, the famed anthropologist Franz Boas visited Seaside, the town where the elderly Tsin-is-tum lived with her husband. He was looking for stories, but he complained that he didn't find any:

> I first went to Clatsop, where a small band of Indians are located near Seaside, Clatsop county, Oregon. Although a number of them belonged to the Clatsop tribe, they had all adopted the Nehelim language, a dialect of the Salishan Tillamook. This change of language was brought about by frequent intermarriages with the Nehelim. I found one middle-aged man and two old women who still remembered the Clatsop language, but it was impossible to obtain more than a vocabulary and a few sentences. The man had forgotten a great part of the language, while the women were not able to grasp what I wanted; they claimed to have forgotten their myths and traditions, and could not or would not give me any connected texts.[79]

Boas's account seemed a familiar one: in the wake of disease and dispossession, Clatsop historical consciousness had been eroded almost out of existence.

Thirty years later, another researcher, May Mandelbaum Edel, visited Seaside and asked the people living there questions about Clatsop history and culture, and it became very clear that Boas had simply been given the cold shoulder. Talking with elders in the small town, Edel heard a story of violence that resonated with the one that Tsin-is-tum told to the Oregon Historical Society more than a generation earlier:

A sailing ship drifted along this coast. It wrecked and it came ashore. Blankets, food, bread, sugar, rice, poison—everything washed ashore from that ship. . . . One boat of white men came to fight. That main white man wanted furs. One Indian, a Nehalem, tried to trade away his beaver skins. Those Clatsops from Point Adams village [*tɬác'ɔp*] said "No."

They prepared to fight. These white men didn't strike first. They landed on shore. The Indians shot at them. Then this ship shot back. They shot a big gun, a cannon. These Indians ran for the brush. The white men came ashore and set fire to the town. They killed people.

They killed an Indian man. His mother and father were killed with the rest. He himself hadn't taken anything from the wreck. He had been visiting the village at Newport when it had come ashore. His young son cut the [child carrier?] strap, freeing himself. The boy ran away on the beach.[80]

Here, another Clatsop historical account serves as evidence of a second episode of violence precipitated by shipwreck, recalled and shared by someone whose parents likely experienced it firsthand. And despite the challenges of all those years, when Indigenous people living on the coast had almost all been pushed off their lands and forced to distant reservations, or had succumbed to foreign illnesses, this was still a story worth telling.

Today, Clatsop descendants with roots in the territory near the mouth of the Columbia have confederated with descendants of their southern neighbors the Nehalem people, with whom they had built a community in Seaside. Although unrecognized legally by the United States federal government, the Clatsop-Nehalem have continued to maintain their histories and a distinct identity—distinct even from their relatives, the also-unrecognized Chinook of the lower Columbia. These Indigenous communities have survived the violence of the past for two centuries and then some. Some of that violence was swift and sharp, some of it slow and plodding. Still, the First Peoples of the Graveyard of the

Pacific—including the Clatsop, Ahousaht, and Hesquiaht—insist on their connections to place and past despite the depredations of colonialism. The accounts of *William & Ann* and *Boston* and *Tonquin* and *Kingfisher* and *John Bright* and so many others are evidence that the wakes of colonial violence that continue to disturb the waters of everyday life are not endings; rather, they are proof of Indigenous survivance.

A lantern slide of *Peter Iredale*, ca. 1910.

THREE

All Lost

The Making of a
Settler Graveyard

TILLAMOOK ROCK STANDS ALONE. The basalt outcropping rises out of the Pacific off the northern Oregon coast, some eight stories above the crashing waves and the rocky platforms where sea lions bask. It has been known as Terrible Tilly since the late nineteenth century, when nigh-superhuman efforts were required to dynamite its top and build a lighthouse there. The rock is the only offshore island of any note in Oregon, swarming with seabirds and battered by enormous breakers in the great storms that so often tear across the fetch here. Today, the lighthouse is dark, serving only (and strangely) as a columbarium for a few dozen human dead. But Tillamook Rock is a graveyard in other ways as well.

One foggy night in January 1881, during the lighthouse's construction, workers on the rock heard voices out in the darkness. "Hard to port!" cried out a man's terrified voice, and the workers could hear the straining of pulley blocks. They also noticed a red beacon of some sort, hanging in the mist. They lit lanterns and quickly built a bonfire, and in the glowing light, they saw the source of the sounds and light: a sailing ship struggling just beyond the shoals surrounding the rock. It was *Lupatia*, a British bark traveling from Japan to the Columbia River in ballast. Soon, however, the red light disappeared, and silence but for the waves returned. In the morning, the lighthouse construction crew saw only the destroyed topmast and some of the riggings above the surface of the roiling sea, and worse yet, they saw twelve bodies on the rocks, with a black shepherd dog, the only survivor of the wreck, running and whining amid the corpses. Of *Lupatia*'s crew of sixteen, four would never be found. The twelve men would be interred in the rocky soil of Terrible Tilly, seven in one shallow grave and five in another. Seventeen days later, the Tillamook Rock Lighthouse would send its inaugural light out into the darkness of the Pacific.[1]

Doomed *Lupatia* was only one of hundreds of shipwrecks to take place along the coasts of Oregon, Washington, and Vancouver Island in the late nineteenth and early twentieth centuries. As settler society burgeoned in the region, the density and frequency of shipping meant that maritime disaster became almost quotidian: only the very worst instances, usually involving significant loss of life, merited much attention from the robust press of the era. For the most part, shipwreck was simply the cost of doing settler business. Indeed, those who wrote about marine affairs in the period linked contemporary oceangoing activity to the much longer history of empire and expansion, even if stories of shipwreck also disoriented and eroded settlers' confidence in the colonial project. As the notion of a "graveyard of the Pacific" began to take shape, observers recorded the ways in which maritime misfortune could break local economies and livelihoods. To call the region by such a name spoke to the very real costs of building a new society in this place. In wood and canvas, steel and copper, the nearly countless lost ships of the late nineteenth and early twentieth centuries together tell a story of colonial failure that, ironically, would deepen settler claims to territory.

———

Winter often brings misfortune on the coast, but spring can be a bastard as well. On the fourth of May, 1880, a rogue squall bore down on the mouth of the Columbia, where dozens of fishermen from Astoria, Ilwaco, and other nearby communities were busy catching salmon. Almost all of them worked for one of the many canneries that lined the shores of the great river's estuary. As the brief but violent storm overwhelmed them, many of their small boats either capsized, sank, or were at the very least swamped, and the men began to drown in the cold waters. Over the next few weeks, the *Daily Astorian* would print notices of bodies found on local beaches: twenty-three in total, a devastating loss to these small communities. More were almost certainly lost, their deaths—like their lives—poorly documented in this newly resettled place. Indeed, as the story of the disastrous storm traveled far from Astoria, as far even as the *New York Times*, the number of dead was claimed by surviving local fishermen and by cannery employees as being as high as two hundred, three hundred, or more. If these numbers are correct, it was the deadliest tragedy in the history of the Graveyard of the Pacific, if one that appears only briefly and partially in the archive.[2]

If a single spring squall could bring so much death, a single days-long winter storm could wreak havoc on the entire region. In early December 1894, for example, a sequence of massive gales struck the whole of the coast. The collier and barkentine *John Worster*, having left Seattle on the first, found itself leaking off Oregon's aptly named Cape Foulweather, despite being described as "staunch, stout, and strong." Ultimately, it was abandoned by its crew, who saved only the ship's chronometer. Others were concerned about the whereabouts of the schooner *James Russ*, which had left the mill-side wharves in Fairhaven, Washington, loaded to within seven inches of the water, and which hadn't been heard from since. Four other ships had likewise gone missing in the storm: the barks *Columbia* and *Germania* and the colliers *Montserrat* and *Keweenaw*. The *Seattle Post-Intelligencer* reported on December 17 that the ships were six days overdue and noted that "if any vessels should be in distress off the Oregon or Washington coasts the present storm would doubtless send them to the bottom." One captain who had made it back to port—albeit after losing forty thousand feet of lumber—described the storm in harrowing detail: "Never in my life have I seen such terrific lightning, dancing all around us and covering the sea with forked streaks. There was no thunder, but lots of rain. . . . I had expected the gale, as the barometer had crept as low as it could, and we made things snug. In spite of all we could do, however, the storm took us along like a cockleshell, and tremendous seas broke over the heavily laden vessel. The strain was great and finally she sprang a leak. . . . The wind was something frightful, stronger and longer in duration than anything I have ever seen. . . . The lightning, wind, and rain seemed to conspire to send us to the bottom." In all, ten vessels went missing in this single storm, having left ports like Nanaimo and Port Blakely with loads of lumber or coal, or having been headed to the sealing grounds. "Grave fears are entertained," fretted the *Post-Intelligencer*, and those fears seemed to come true in the days after the storm as wreckage would be found both off and onshore. Ship's timbers painted black and white were found floating off Cape Flattery, and thousands of board feet of lumber littered the beaches south of there. As late as the following May, pieces of *Keweenaw* would be found on Haida Gwaii, hundreds of miles to the north. Indeed, only *Columbia* and a sailing vessel called *J. B. Brown* appear to have made it home safely after that December tempest. The others, a maritime history published in 1895 would describe, were simply "blotted out of existence." The dangers of maritime life were common, quotidian, and indeed expected—even in a "new" Northwest—and their recitation in the press served as an archive of the region's almost-daily perils.[3]

Across the decades in which Oregon, Washington, and British Columbia took shape as settler societies, accounts of shipwreck provided readers with evidence of the precarity of the maritime colonial project. Often recounted in grisly detail in local newspapers, these accounts were filled with the horror and pathos of marine disaster, and such stories became part of everyday life across the region in the late nineteenth and early twentieth centuries. In January of 1852, for example—in the early years of settler colonialism, as opposed to the extractive colonialism attendant to the fur trade—a ship called *General Warren* attempted to cross the Columbia Bar on its way to San Francisco. As *General Warren* struggled through the huge waves where river met sea, its foretop mast was torn away, and the captain decided to turn back. Meanwhile, the loose wheat in the hold had blocked the pumps, so the ship began taking on water. The river pilot aboard advised the captain not to cross the bar, but a committee of passengers demanded they be returned to Astoria and accused the pilot of cowardice. Eventually, the ship was intentionally beached on Clatsop Spit as a last-ditch measure. There, *General Warren* began breaking apart almost immediately, and the captain sent a boat to Astoria to call for help. By the time the boat returned in the morning, *General Warren* was gone, and the beach was littered with bodies. With the help of local Indigenous people, Clatsop County settlers buried the victims, most with neither shroud nor coffin. And two years later, settler James Swan discovered the stern frame of *General Warren* on a beach north of the river's mouth. Around the mouth of the Columbia, the deadly waters left marks both on the bodies and minds of settlers and on those of their Indigenous neighbors alike.[4]

The physical remainders of wrecks could also serve as potent reminders of the danger. Four years after the *General Warren* disaster, in 1856, a ship called *Desdemona* crashed onto a sandbar just off Astoria and stuck fast. All aboard but one disembarked with their lives, but the ship remained in place for many years, to the extent that the site where it had grounded became known as the Desdemona Sands. As maritime historian Jennifer Kozik writes, the wreck of *Desdemona* "occurred during important formative years of the American Northwest. It was before the borders recognized today as the western states were in place, and it was less than five years before the Civil War consumed the United States. Missionaries, retired fur trappers, and other settlers were deciding which dreams and values of American Culture they wanted to extend to the region. . . . A ship bringing the goods to help build those dreams had wrecked in a highly visible spot, with the remains left behind as if on display." Meanwhile, the name Desdemona was given to Astoria shops, to labels pasted onto cans of salmon filled in local canneries, and even to a tavern, which still exists today, where the back wall is ornamented with a painting of the lost vessel. Shipwrecks, then, could help anchor settlers in place even as they threatened the future.[5]

The spectacle of shipwreck could inspire horror among the settler population even as steam took over from sail and as shipping became ever more prominent in the local economy and the everyday lives of settlers. In 1896, for instance, when the steamer *Arago* smashed into the newly built north jetty at the entrance to Oregon's Coos Bay, crowds gathered on the beach to observe the disaster. They watched as lifeboats overturned in the surf, pitching their occupants into the cold, churning water. In all, fourteen of *Arago*'s crew and passengers would be killed, and as the remains of the ship began digging themselves into the sand, a man's drowned body could be seen hanging head-down in the forward rigging, a grim token of the disaster. Such graphic descriptions of death filled newspaper accounts of wrecks on the Northwest Coast, and as they circulated, they began to cement the reputation of the region as a particularly dangerous place.[6]

Twelve years after *Arago*, in 1908, the *Morning Astorian* warned that the American ship *Emily G. Reed*, carrying coal from Australia to Portland, was overdue from Australia. Three days later, *Emily G. Reed* was found wrecked at the mouth of the Nehalem River. Three survivors in a small lifeboat eventually came ashore some two hundred miles north on the Makah Reservation, but twelve crew members were lost. The *Morning Astorian* reported that the destruction of *Emily G. Reed* was "one of those sad messages from the ever treacherous sea that come, always without warning, and laden with bitterness. The ship was well known in these waters and by every mariner who made the farther reaches of the globe, and there was many a story afloat anent her long service and the conspicuous incidents of her career, each and all of which are now in the process of eager reiteration."[7] Passenger ships were, of course, the worst to be lost; sailors might be expected to face the dangers of the sea, but average, everyday settlers often died as well when ships went down. In the early fall of 1914, for example, the steamer *Francis H. Leggett* sank in a storm off the Oregon coast, killing at least fifty-eight people. Local newspapers printed reports of bodies buoyed up by life preservers being found for days afterward, once again a graphic testament to the power of the sea.[8]

More than costing human lives, shipwrecks also could damage livelihoods, threatening the very process of establishing settler society in the Pacific Northwest. Sometimes, the economic price of shipwreck could happen at small scales. When early settler John M. Shively chartered a small vessel in San Francisco and headed for the Rogue River goldfields in southwestern Oregon in the 1850s, little did he know his voyage would be cut short, as would his prospects: he recalled how he "got out of provisions and water in the attempting to land at the mouth of Rogue River [and] was wrecked and lost all."[9] Misadventures like these were no doubt common, but they paled in comparison to the effect one large shipwreck could have on the region's economy.

For example, when the steamship *Great Republic* ran aground just inside the Columbia Bar in 1879, the mouth of the "great river of the west" was a bustling threshold between the Pacific and the interior. But the grounding was a disaster for local communities, and newspaper accounts provide a window into the ways in which settler fortunes could be made or unmade based on the fate of a single ship. As the side-wheeler—at the time, the largest ship on the Pacific coast—quickly began to disintegrate in the endless tides and surf, its $300,000 worth of cargo attracted both "pirates" and a force of policemen, who guarded the site against even the "most respectable" citizens of Astoria. One immigrant farmer with nine children lost all of his family's possessions, while in Portland and Vancouver, Washington, dry goods businesses, milliner's shops, and clothing stores were forced to close as their shipments were lost to the waters. Astoria, meanwhile, was burdened with the hundreds of passengers who needed a place to sleep. One shipwreck, then, could have dramatic effects

"The Alice" At Sundown

Shipwreck was a quotidian feature of life on the Northwest Coast. Here, the French bark *Alice* rests in the sands of the Long Beach Peninsula in 1909. *North Olympic Library System*

on an entire region's economic and social life, underlining the precarity of settler society at the beginning of the fourth quarter of the nineteenth century.[10] When the ship *Kate L. Heron* wrecked while crossing the Columbia Bar, for example, one newspaper quipped sardonically that it was "another feather in Portland's cap."[11] Meanwhile, when *Harvest Home* ran aground on the Long Beach Peninsula in 1882, it was carrying more than two hundred tons of merchandise for Seattle establishments, including that of the unlucky business partners Waterman and Katz, who lost 285 packages of materials they had intended to sell in their shop.[12] The vicissitudes of Pacific Northwest shipping and economy were such that a single shipwreck could alter the fortunes of more than a few settlers.

Whether in loss of lives or livelihoods, shipwreck had become a common and particularly potent element of regional experience in the late nineteenth century. As settler societies established themselves along the coast, up the Columbia, and on the Salish Sea, they had to contend with the material limitations placed upon them by the very nature of the region. The coast was where things could go horribly wrong: the ship in the sand with its lost cargo, the flotsam out on the open water signaling the death of a vessel, the dead body in the riggings. All of these would challenge the optimism and futurity of settler life on the Northwest Coast. And nowhere would that be more apparent than one of the worst maritime disasters in the history of what was becoming known as the Graveyard of the Pacific, second perhaps only to the 1880 spring squall event. This wreck would be devastating for people throughout the region.

―――――――

When the missionary August-Joseph Brabant, who had been attempting to spread the gospel among the Nuu-chah-nulth Nations of Vancouver Island's west coast, arrived in Victoria in early November of 1875, he found the colonial capital abuzz:

> At the time of our landing an immense crowd of people were on the wharves. The city was indeed in great excitement, for the news had just reached the people that the steamship Pacific with 260 passengers— quite a number of Victorians—had foundered at sea and that thus far only one passenger had reached shore alive. As we came from the very coast where the wreck had taken place, the people were all in hopes that a number might have been picked up at sea. We had seen nothing of the wreck, and the crowd, looking for friends and good news, were doomed to return home disappointed.[13]

Disaster had struck Victoria in the form of shipwreck. The loss of SS *Pacific* off Cape Flattery would shake the city—indeed, the entire colonial endeavor—to its foundations. Taking the largest toll in lives of any single wreck on the Northwest Coast, the sinking of *Pacific* best epitomized the potential for shipwreck to nearly capsize settler ambitions, while simultaneously, and somewhat paradoxically, to further strengthen newcomers' connections to place. In other words, the tragedy of *Pacific* helped make colonialism stick.[14]

The story of *Pacific* begins in New York City's East River, where the oaken side-wheeler was launched in 1850. After servicing ports in Cuba, Panama, and Nicaragua, it began plying Pacific waters in 1858. Its duties included ferrying gold-crazed passengers from California who were headed to British Columbia's Fraser Canyon, meaning that the ship played a central role in the war that erupted between American prospectors and the Nlaka'pamux people who called the canyon home. By the 1870s, *Pacific* was making regular trips between Puget Sound, Victoria, and San Francisco. And on the night of November 5, 1875, it sank.

Four days later, Victoria's *Colonist* newspaper broadcast the horror that had shaken the colonial capital to its core:

> We have no heart to dwell to-day on the disaster that has hurried into eternity so many of our fellow-citizens with whom only a few brief hours ago we mingled on the streets or met in the social circles as full of life, hope and energy as any who may read the Colonist today. The catastrophe is so far-reaching that scarcely a household in Victoria but has lost one or more of its members, or must strike from its list of living friends a face and form that found ever a warm greeting within their circle. A bolt out of the blue could not have caused more widespread consternation than the awful tidings spread far and wide yesterday. In some cases entire families have been swept away, in others fond wives returning from a visit to their childhood's home to meet husbands and children in San Francisco have gone—down to an early grave. In others, the joyous, happy maiden, the sweet, innocent, prattling babe, the banker, the merchant, the miner, the public officer, all, all have found a common grave.[15]

Meanwhile, newspapers in Washington Territory spoke to similar outpourings of grief. "The awful calamity," wrote the *Puget Sound Dispatch*, "calls forth a wail of mourning from every house on the coast, and the eyes of the beautiful are still wet for the unreturning brave."[16]

And indeed, many of the men and women aboard *Pacific* had played significant roles in the region's public life. Mill owners from places like Port Discovery and Utsalady and what would become North Vancouver, merchants from Walla Walla and Puyallup, Victoria bankers, a Fraser River steamboat captain, well-known actors, a territorial postal agent, even the commissioner for the Cassiar goldfields in the interior of British Columbia: these dead, along with scores of victims of lower standing or esteem—including forty-one unnamed Chinese travelers—highlighted the regional scope of this single disaster's reach.[17] However, exactly how many passengers had been lost aboard *Pacific* would always remain unclear. In the investigation that would come soon after the wreck, a Victoria agent testified that he had sold 132 tickets locally, in addition to the 35 tickets sold to passengers who had boarded in Puget Sound ports. The ship's purser, meanwhile, had booked another twenty passengers without taking their names, and most confusingly, others—including many miners fresh from the Cassiar District—rushed on board as the ship prepared to pull away from its moorage.[18] Ultimately, it is impossible to know how many people died with *Pacific*, but observers at the time and historians in the decades since have put the number at between 250 and 300. Given that there were only about 4,000 people living in Victoria at the time, the loss of so many people was a trauma that gutted the town's young society.

That we know anything about what happened aboard *Pacific* during its final voyage comes down to the testimonies of two survivors. One, *Pacific*'s quartermaster Neil Henley, had been picked up some eighty hours after the sinking, clinging to a piece of debris. The other, Henry F. Jelley, was the only passenger to survive; he had been in British Columbia to survey routes for the Canadian Pacific Railway. Together, the accounts given by the two men about what they had experienced on the night of November 5 crafted a narrative that horrified those who read about it in the region's newspapers. Both Henley and Jelley had been asleep in their bunks when a great and violent shudder moved through *Pacific*. Awakened abruptly, Henley saw water rushing into the hold and quickly went on deck, where all was in chaos. Off the starboard side of *Pacific* stood a large sailing vessel that had apparently just collided with the side-wheeler. In his testimony, the young quartermaster described what happened next:

> The captain and officers of the steamer were trying to lower the boats, but the passengers crowded in against their commands, making their efforts useless. There were fifteen women and six men in the boat with me, but she struck the ship and filled instantly, and when I came up I caught hold of a skylight, which soon capsized. I then swam to a part of the hurricane deck, which had eight persons clinging to it. When I looked around the steamer had disappeared, leaving a floating mass of human beings, whose cries and screams were awful to hear and the sight of which can never be effaced from my memory. In a little while, it was all over.

From there, it was a matter of hoping for rescue—a hope that began to fade as the ship that had rammed *Pacific* shockingly and incomprehensibly moved off into the darkness. On the makeshift raft, Henley's companions were Captain Jefferson Davis Howell, *Pacific*'s second mate and cook, and four passengers. Over the next few hours, four of the raft's occupants would be washed away by heavy seas, while the other three would die of exposure. Seemingly interminable hours later, Henley was found by a revenue cutter. Henry Jelley, meanwhile, gave more confused and conflicting reports of the last moments of *Pacific*, although what he did tell only confirmed the sense of utter mayhem reigning aboard the ship as its crew and passengers tried to escape their fates.[19]

As investigations began in Victoria in the days after Henley and Jelley

The 1875 sinking of SS *Pacific* after a collision with *Orpheus* was the single most lethal shipwreck in the Graveyard of the Pacific, devastating the town of Victoria. *From D. W. Higgins,* The Mystic Spring and Other Tales of Western Life *(Toronto: W. Briggs, 1904)*

arrived in the city, they quickly came to focus on the actions of the captain of that other ship, which was soon identified as *Orpheus*, on its way from San Francisco to take on a load of coal at Nanaimo. Charles Sawyer would become the disaster's chief villain as grief-stricken Victorians sought blame for *Pacific*'s loss. That *Orpheus* had struck *Pacific* was never in question; it was what had happened next that so inflamed public anger. Sawyer claimed that once the emergency aboard his own ship had been addressed—riggings torn away, a possible leak in the hold—he noticed that *Pacific* could no longer be seen. He and his crew assumed that the steamer had retreated into the night, not knowing it had in fact sunk. Newspaper accounts of the investigation noted that Sawyer, who was arrested, might even face the death penalty. At the same time, rumors abounded that there might be other factors in the sinking: the *Colonist* reported that *Pacific* was "rotten and unseaworthy and known to be such by her owners [and] not properly equipped for a voyage at sea," while others claimed that *Pacific*'s Captain Howell had been drunk at the time of the collision. In the end, Sawyer was exonerated by a San Francisco inquest of deliberately ramming *Pacific* or knowingly abandoning the dying steamer's passengers and crew.[20]

Meanwhile, the bodies of *Pacific* kept coming. As the investigations continued, the corpses of men and women—and even those of horses that had been on board—washed ashore seemingly everywhere: at the mouth of the Elwha River on Washington's Olympic Peninsula, at Kyuquot on Vancouver Island's central coast, and, most horrifyingly, at Victoria's very doorstep. As regional newspapers tracked the progress of victims' bodies back to their home communities, and as the transcripts of coroner's juries appeared one after the other in the *Colonist*, often with graphic details of the state of victims' bodies, *Pacific* sank into the affective sediments of Northwest Coast settler society.[21]

One document above all speaks to the emotional trauma of *Pacific*'s loss. Its author, George Mason, was a successful Victorian brickmaker and society man, and his response to the disaster was to pen a long ode to the ship itself, in language simultaneously florid and deeply moving. Victorian in both senses of the word, Mason's paean is remarkable for its depth of feeling and for the tropes of civilization in which it traffics, qualities that would have implications for the place of *Pacific* in regional settlerist mythology. "Speed on thy course, Leviathan of art! Thou boast of modern science!" it begins, followed by a description of "crests of angry foam" that rise in vain against "guarded bulwarks" and the destiny of "careful pilots." Then comes a stanza that accounts for those about to become victims—happy children, merchants and maidens—followed by one that warns "a day of sorrows awaits you!" that will require much prayer. The penultimate stanza is a refrain of a community's collective grief:

But—hush—again! the news! the dreadful news
Has reached our shores! has paralyzed the hearts
Of all! Oh! say; it is not true! What! Lost!
All lost! All! All! but one snatch'd from the deep,
A solitary messenger of woe,
Left on the cruel waters to recount
His tale of misery, the fatal crash,
The rush, the panic—accents of despair,—
The infant's wail,—the Mother's piercing cry,—
The brave man's fight with death, and chivalry
Unselfish even to his latest gasp.
And now another, rescued from the waves
But to confirm the tidings of their fate
Pants forth fresh horrors from the awful wreck.
All lost! No! No! the agony is o'er,
The dark, cold waters of destruction past,
And on the tearless shore they rest. God grant,
In peace awaiting now perennial bliss,
Purg'd from all earth-stains in the o'er whelming tide
By God's consuming Love, washed in the blood
Of Him whose dying pangs outweigh'd the sum
Of mortal agonies, who tasted death
For all, that all, who will, might never die,
But only sleep—Mother! she is not dead,
Tho' she return not, thou shalt go to her
In the far land; when sea shall be no more
And from its depths are yielded up the dead—
Pitiless Ocean! thou has done thy worst!

Mason continues by bemoaning how the wreck of Pacific was "harrowing our souls with hideous spectacle / Or marr'd remains," and yet "beyond the u'most fury of thy storms / The Spirit soars, and holds Communion still / With kindred hearts in voiceless sympathy." After a long reference to the travails of Shakespeare's Hamlet, the brickmaker-poet offers a warning:

> Ye launch your monster vessels on the deep,
> With scarce a thought of the Omnipotent,
> The forces of the Universe obey
> The magic sceptre science proudly wields,
> Flush'd with your triumph Nature is defied—
> Danger despised, till danger's self has come,
> And finds you unprepared with all your arts
> Against the common accidents of life!
> The untamed billows mock your pigmy toys,
> When mercilessly rushing on their prey
> They gain their vantage, and the striken [*sic*] ship
> Sinks 'neath the pæan of their road, an [*sic*] hopeless wreck.

Here, the author—one of Victoria's early colonists, having arrived in 1851—offered simultaneously a jeremiad against modernity and an assertion of Christian faith against the violent powers of nature. In doing so, Mason articulated the mix of horror and grief experienced in Victoria and beyond. Indeed, the fact that his work was printed and distributed attests to the ways in which it spoke to his contemporaries' sense of loss.[22]

George Mason's long ode was not the only emotional artifact inspired by the destruction of *Pacific*. In 1876, for example, the Oregon Steamship Company was presented with a piece of art commemorating the tragedy. It included a figure of Neptune pointing to the sinking side-wheeler, its deck thronging with panicked passengers; to one side stood a male figure representing Grief, and to the other a female figure representing Supplication.[23] A year later, prolific historian Frances Fuller Victor, whose husband Henry died in the waters of that November night, published a chapbook of poems called *The New Penelope*—Penelope being the long-suffering wife of Odysseus—which included references to the tragedy. In "By the Sea," she lamented her profound loss in high Victorian meter:

Who treads the loathsome sand-beach,
　　With wet, disordered hair;
With garments tangled with sea-weed,
　　And cheeks more pale than fair?

O blue-eyed, white-browed maiden,
　　He will keep love's tryst no more;

His ship sailed safely into port—
　　But on the heavenward shore.

Elsewhere in the collection, she wrote, "But in that fleet sailed all 't was dear to me."[24]

Neither Mason's nor Fuller's articulations are surprising, given the elaborate mourning culture and iconography of the era. But what is perhaps more illuminating were the ways in which *Pacific*'s wrecking was enfolded into larger narratives of regional, and even global, history. Only eleven days after the sinking, for example, the *Colonist*'s editors made a case for the exceptional nature of the disaster. "Taking the number of persons lost and the smallness of the community from which they were drawn," they wrote, "the wreck of the *Pacific* is certainly one of the most terrible calamities the world has ever known."[25] Twenty years on, the magisterial *Lewis & Dryden's Marine History of the Pacific Northwest* had even more to say: "Long will be remembered the year 1875, when Death, clad in all his hideousness, rode the wave; and, while the relentless sea has supplied Northwestern history with many pitiful tales of disaster, this fatal year has never been equalled in the number of lives and amount of property sacrificed. . . . The bare mention of her name brings 'a pallor into the cheek and a mist before the eye' of those whose loved ones went forth on the ship fated never to reach her destination."[26] Later, the compendium would refer again to the wreck of *Pacific*, alongside other marine disasters, noting that "the very mention of their names causes a shudder of horror to those whose friends lie coffined within their rotten timbers somewhere in the depths of the ocean."[27]

In fact, this single massive tome would bring together the specifics of hundreds of individual instances of maritime misfortune with a master narrative that linked wrecks such as *Pacific* into the longer history of the Pacific Northwest, and indeed of empire and empires writ large. For, the book's editor E. W. Wright argued, "the vanguard of civilization for centuries has been led by the mariners, and their achievements from the days of Columbus mark the beginning of history in every new country which has become a portion of the known world."[28] This was a teleology—an inevitable unfolding of history—in which explorers, sailors, and others literally built the modern world. "Looking backward into the dim and shadowy past," Wright continued, "we find that . . . the men who navigated the waters of the earth were the pioneers of civilization. Centuries before steam and electricity began the work of building modern cities with magical rapidity, the mariner's compass was guiding brave navigators to every corner of this globe, enabling them to lay the foundations of a civilization which has since brought all nations on the face of the earth almost within speaking distance of each other." The passage ended, "This spirit of maritime conquest, finding no other worlds to conquer, eventually . . . brought to the notice of the world" the northwestern coast of North America, with its industry and potential.[29] Here, modernity is literally born in the Pacific Northwest. "Less than a decade has elapsed," the volume exclaimed, "since the first regular steamship left the Orient for the Northwest, yet the present year witnesses a dozen magnificent liners plying between China and Japan, and the Columbia River, Puget Sound, and British Columbia. Another line has established a fine trade with the Antipodes, while a third is finding a market for Northwestern products in far-away Africa."[30] The integration of the Northwest Coast into the world economy was the apotheosis of a trajectory that began in that "dim and shadowy past" and reached into the capitalist future.

That disasters such as that of *Pacific* featured prominently in *Lewis & Dryden's Marine History* only affirmed this story by emphasizing the sacrifice of their crews and passengers in service of the greater good and the greater story of colonialism. This is where the poetry of Victor and Mason, the elegies printed in regional newspapers, and the black-framed and grieving letters that must have flown from Victoria to far-flung places across the British Empire intersected with larger narratives of success such as that of the *Marine History* of 1895. A generation after *Pacific*, and only two years after Frederick Jackson Turner famously articulated American progress at the Chicago World's Fair, a single, very large book could crystallize a narrative that had been building since the days of John Rodgers Jewitt and John Jacob Astor: that death in fact undergirded imperial success and helped make it meaningful.

Sometimes, that narrative could be made manifest. Back in 1875, for example, a piece of debris had come ashore on the beach at the foot of Beacon Hill in Victoria. Sometime on the night of November 5, a mill owner named Sewell Moody, whose bustling little settlement of Moodyville squatted on the north shore of Burrard Inlet across from what is now Vancouver, realized his time was up. As *Pacific* came apart

Sewell P. Moody's final message: "all lost." *Vancouver Maritime Museum, photo by author*

around him, he grabbed a white-painted stanchion from the crumbling deck, took a pencil from his pocket, and wrote an inscription on it. Above his signature, which would be identified as authentic by his surviving family, were the words *all lost*. In that simple phrase, Moody offered not only a message from beyond the grave—one mirrored word for word in George Mason's ode—but also a meditation on the limitations of empire. All *could* be lost, even if that loss could at the same time create deeply felt settler claims to an entire region.[31]

Almost more than any other kind of wreck, derelicts and ships that simply disappeared haunted the nascent Graveyard of the Pacific. Five years before the sinking of *Pacific*, in 1870, the American bark *Maria J. Smith*, laden with Port Townsend lumber, lost control of its cargo in a heavy southeast gale and, after some of its sails were torn away, came ashore on a reef near the mouth of Barkley Sound on Vancouver Island. Its captain, crew, and passengers were taken to Victoria, and the wreck, its cargo, and its remaining sails were sold. The new owner managed to have the ship refloated, but as it was on its way to Washington Territory's Port Madison for repairs behind a tug, it had to be cut free in another one of the Northwest's trademark January storms. It blew out to sea, carrying its captain and crew, who were eventually taken off the ship. From that point, *Maria J. Smith* became a derelict that, according to *Lewis & Dryden's Marine History*, "for a long time promised to rival the famous *Flying Dutchman* in its wanderings," referring to the legendary ghost ship that had served as portent of doom since at least the eighteenth century. After two months of appearing, disappearing, and reappearing off the coast, it eventually wrecked for a final time on an island hundreds of miles to the north, where it soon went to pieces. A wreck like this one, lost to the whims of the currents and winds, confounded the orderly ideals of coastal shipping.[32]

A similar thing happened in February 1902, when the waterlogged schooner *Laura Pike* was abandoned off Cape Blanco near the Oregon-California border. For the next few weeks, the *Colonist* of Victoria would provide regular reports keeping track of the ship's peregrinations up and down the coast, to what was clearly a fascinated audience. Noting that *Laura Pike*, a "menace" to river-bound shipping, had been sighted adrift off the mouth of the Columbia, the *Colonist* also reported that plans were afoot to blow it up. That never happened, however, and it was soon seen off Vancouver Island's Carmanah Point. As the derelict crept northward, stories built up around it, to the extent that *Colonist* editors had to point out that "she has no corpses lashed to her rigging . . . nor was there any foundation for the sensational stories which, regardless of the sorrow they occasioned, were published by an evening paper." Making about thirty-five miles a day, the schooner also showed "the trend of current on this coast more plainly than any long-drawn-out discussion between shipmakers," suggesting that at the same time that derelicts like *Laura Pike* got away from maritime logic, they could also serve as teachers regarding the nature of the Northwest Coast. In early March, the drifting vessel was sighted by *Czarina*, whose crew tried to burn it to the waterline with kerosene, but the sea-dampened wood simply would not burn. By March 15, attempts to locate *Laura Pike* off the coast of Vancouver Island were unsuccessful, and with that, the doomed schooner disappears from the historical record. *Laura Pike*, like the other derelicts that drifted through print and rumor in places like Victoria, was the shadow of success in regional maritime culture.[33]

Worse yet, and even more haunting, were the derelicts whose crews had disappeared. Here, the ships were not so much *Flying Dutchman* as *Mary Celeste*, the legendary Atlantic ship whose crew and passengers had disappeared without a trace in 1872. Eleven days after *Laura Pike* was last seen, news came that *Amethyst*, another schooner, had been found wrecked, again in Vancouver Island's Barkley Sound. On board, there was no sign of its crew, and the article affirmed that the men were presumed lost.[34] While *Amethyst* was ultimately righted and repaired a few weeks later, it must have carried with it stories of its lost complement—one wonders how its future crews would have made sense of the disappearance of their predecessors.[35]

By far the most disturbing wrecks of all—the ones that would have sent the greatest shivers down the spines of *Colonist* readers and other locals, and the ones that most highlighted the limitations of modernity's marine technologies—were the ships that simply disappeared over the horizon with their crews and passengers. In December 1860, for example, the ship *John Marshall* was reported lost with all on board, having likely been wrecked a few weeks earlier. "The crews would have had ample time," the *Colonist* lamented, "to have reported themselves had they been alive."[36] Such losses were common in the annals of Pacific Northwest shipping. Thirty years after the disappearance of *John Marshall*, a period in which numerous other ships had simply disappeared, the schooner *Douglas Dearborn* and its eleven-man crew out of Seattle vanished, leaving "no clue as to their fate."[37] In 1901, meanwhile, the Esquimalt-based HMS *Condor* disappeared in a horrendous southeast gale off Cape Flattery en route to Hawaii, taking with it its complement of 140 men and leaving debris along the coast of Vancouver Island.[38] And in the spring of 1913, two vessels out of Astoria—*Eldorado* and *Americana*—went missing with a total of twenty-one men. One Oregon newspaper reported that their fates "probably will remain a mystery since no word has been received from them" and that "shipping men have abandoned hope of their reaching port."[39] Such events were the ne plus ultra of maritime disaster, in that they were unfinished stories, without resolution, without closure.

Perhaps the most elaborately documented disappearance of a Northwest Coast ship took place in the fall of 1894, when *Ivanhoe*, carrying Black Diamond coal from the foothills of Washington's Cascade Mountains, simply vanished, along with its sole passenger F. G. Grant, editor of the *Seattle Post-Intelligencer*.[40] The crew of another vessel, the lumber schooner *Fanny Dutard*, had noticed a ship in distress off the

Washington coast on the afternoon of September 30, but the ship suddenly disappeared.[41] The president of the Black Diamond Coal Company, meanwhile, still held out hope. "From time to time," the *Daily Morning Astorian* reported him as saying, "wreckage has been picked up along the coast north of San Francisco and reported as being part of the Ivanhoe. Afterward I have had it carefully examined, and I have found that not a bit of it came from our vessel. . . . I have enough confidence in her safety to believe she is now somewhere in the ocean, making slow headway for this port, and will arrive safely before long."[42] Captain Peterson of *Fanny Dutard*, meanwhile, was not so sure. His account appeared in another Oregon paper: "We could see that something was wrong with her, for her list was in the wrong direction, I was not concerned much about her, for I expected we would run much nearer together soon, and, having been up most of the night before, I went below about 1 o'clock and turned in. Twenty minutes later . . . my first mate Harry Staunton came below, and, calling me, said that the ship had disappeared . . . as if by magic."[43] Revenue cutters cruised the Washington coast in search of *Ivanhoe*, while any wreckage found on shore—life buoys, pieces of dinghies, and so on—was examined to see whether it might be from the collier, and captains throughout the region kept their eyes peeled for castaways, even "offering inducements to the natives for information."[44] Finally, evidence was found that *Ivanhoe* was indeed lost. In late December, the wife of the Willapa Bay lighthouse keeper discovered a board bearing the ship's name in gilt letters partially buried in the sand at North Cove.[45] Hope had died. "Over twenty shipmasters in Tacoma and Seattle have been interviewed regarding the missing ship *Ivanhoe*'s chances of reaching port," reported an Oregon newspaper. "No one expressed any hope that she will ever be seen again."[46] And *Ivanhoe* never was.

Ships that simply disappeared made up, as *Lewis & Dryden's Marine History* described the year after *Ivanhoe* went missing, "the long list of mysteries which made so many dark pages in marine records in the Northwest."[47] Such stories are, along with the grand spectacle of major losses such as *Pacific*, the most extreme elements of the folklore of the Graveyard of the Pacific, in that they are, again, unfinished stories. "The stories of those that perished far from shore have beginnings but no endings," wrote Pacific Northwest maritime historian Gordon R. Newell in 1955. "Briefly their pyramids of canvas rose off Flattery, then dropped below the horizon," he continued, "or were blotted from sight by in-sweeping storms, and they were seen no more. They left no trace. The best that can be hoped for such ships is that their crews died quickly. And they probably did."[48]

─────────

Sometimes, the Graveyard of the Pacific was simply that: a place of burial for the region's lost seagoers. In this sense, it was no metaphor. It could be found in places like just north of La Push, the main settlement of the Quileute people, where six sailors had been interred in 1893, the nameboard of their ship, *Leonor*, used as a grave marker along with a life preserver.[49] Ten years later, when the Norwegian bark *Prince Arthur*, bound for a British Columbia port from Valparaiso, wrecked on the Washington coast, only two of the vessel's crew were saved; the other eighteen were buried in a mass grave. A monument was erected at the site in 1904 and still stands today, the branches of surrounding trees festooned reverently with flotsam hung there by hikers who visit the lonely place, which is now part of Olympic National Park.[50] Then, a year after the obelisk commemorating the dead of *Prince Arthur* was raised, a ship's rockets were seen near the Vancouver Island settlement of Ucluelet during a big storm, shot into the air from the deck of the struggling *Pass of Melfort*. By the time anyone could reach the site, the British steel-masted bark had gone down with all twenty-five of its crew. As bodies came to land in the pounding surf, they were buried in the local Indigenous cemetery. Meanwhile, sailors' chests, furniture, blankets, pieces of the ship's boats, and most poignantly a woman's coat trimmed with red and black cord were all that remained of *Pass of Melfort*.

There was a kind of intimacy in the deaths associated with shipwrecks in the Graveyard. The settlers of Ilwaco, a tiny town just north of the Columbia, tended to those lost in a maritime misfortune when the British ship *Strathblane*, twenty days out from Honolulu in ballast, was driven ashore in a November fog at Willapa Bay. As it broke apart in the surf, the local lifesaving crew brought all but six, including Captain Cuthell, safely to dry land. The six drowned men, along with a seventh who died three days later "of terribly agony" due to internal injuries, were all buried in Ilwaco's cemetery, where a single headstone, over Cuthell's grave, carries the name *Strathblane*, and six crosses mark where the other men rest. Meanwhile, one of the survivors, James Murray, had stayed in Ilwaco and married a local woman. Encounters between the living and the dead that emerged from shipwreck could facilitate intimacies that both drew attention to colonial precarity and could facilitate the literal reproduction of settler society.[51]

———————

On the first evening of November 1915, a woman name Sarah Caldbeck wrote a letter to her family in Salem, Oregon, from aboard a ship traveling down the Columbia from Portland. "Dear Folks," it began, followed with "well I got started at last." She described leaving a foggy City of Roses that morning on the steamer *Santa Clara* after some breakfast, then the six-hour trip downriver to Astoria. Referring to the Columbia Bar, she wrote, "I hope we will be able to go on without waiting too long." She then described her shipboard experience:

> I have a room all to myself, with three berths in it. It is about six feet square. The berths are about two feet wide, one over the other, fastened to the wall. You have to go to the purser with a check. They tear off your ticket and he assigns you to a seat at a certain table and unless you take it 10 minutes after the call, you forfeit your place.

There is a sign up in each room with the rules of the vessel and one is that in case of delay in crossing the bar, or anything else, they are not responsible for meals, but you have to pay extra if you want any. Will write more later.

Mrs. Caldbeck did in fact write more later. She described the great river's estuary: "We are nearing the mouth of the Columbia now and there are scores of fishing boats putting out their nets for the night, and each one has two lights on a pole in the center of the boat. It is so cold I had to put on my blue jacket . . . to keep warm. I wish I had my muff, my hands are nearly frozen. We will cross the bar at 8 o'clock on high tide, the captain says. Will write more later." Finally, she ended her letter with another addition just after supper. "My, but it was fine scenery," she noted. "Will write when I get to Marshfield about the trip on the ocean. Goodbye, love to all, Mamma." Then, just before *Santa Clara* disembarked from the Astoria docks, Sarah—or Sadie, as her family called her—posted her letter home.[52]

A day later, Sadie Caldbeck was dead. While crossing the bar into Coos Bay—where Mrs. Caldbeck was planning to meet a relative—*Santa Clara* hit a shoal that had been created by recent heavy winds, right in the middle of the channel. The ship struck, lurched, turned in the rough waves of the bar, and was thrown against the spit on the north side of the bar. As night fell, boats were launched but quickly overturned, and Sadie was in one of them. Local papers described the scenes that followed. "Among the more than 75 survivors were relatives and friends who had kept an all night vigil on lonely Bastendorff beach," wrote one, "trying to fan the breath of life back into sand begrimed corpses." In another, the writers penned a scene of terrible pathos: "Crowded into a little Summer cottage at Bastendorff beach, 12 miles from aid and medical attention, four women and three little boys were being worked over during the night to bring back a spark of life, while the only light was two lanterns. Sailors who had come safely through the surf for half

The wrecking of *Santa Clara* at the mouth of Coos Bay in 1915 took the life of Sadie Caldbeck and eleven others and drew the attention of a public that included scavengers of the ship's cargo. *Coos History Museum*

a mile from the *Santa Clara* wreck were groping about in the dark for other victims of the disaster." In all, twelve died. They came from Hood River, Gold Hill, and Salem in Oregon; from Seattle and Sedro-Woolley in Washington; and from as far away as Butte, Montana.[53]

As some tended to the dead and to the survivors, others were engaged with saving *Santa Clara* and its cargo. Strangely, right after the wreck, the waters of the bar were relatively becalmed, so much so that it was expected that most cargo could be retrieved safely. But before long, the surging surf returned and the ship began breaking up. This failed to dissuade locals who had arrived at the site intent to plunder what remained and what had washed ashore. "A terrible orgy has been in progress since yesterday," lamented one paper, "when the cases of liquor began to pile up on the beach." Another published an article describing the looters as little more than criminals: "Great quantities of liquor floated ashore and drunken characters had things their own way. No one was in authority and looters looted without interference. One is reminded of the pirates that infest the coast of Patagonia." Liquor was drunk, cases of shoes were sold on the streets of Coos Bay along with other cargo, and not long after, someone set *Santa Clara* afire. The blaze could be seen for miles. A few days later, Sadie Caldbeck's letter reached her family in Salem, and the local newspaper printed it in its entirety.[54]

The Graveyard of the Pacific was more than metaphor. It was a place where real people died, where shoals, bars, winds, and rocks sank and smithereened barks and schooners and steamers alike. Messages from beyond the grave like Sarah Caldbeck's—or like Sewell Moody's note "all lost"—served as reminders of this, as did the countless newspaper columns devoted to maritime disaster and George Mason's long-winded ode. Even Tillamook Rock and the rough shores of Barkley Sound held stories that made up the thing settlers had come to call the Graveyard of the Pacific. These tales of trauma, of the quotidian precariousness of maritime life along the Oregon, Washington, and Vancouver Island coasts, were not just ones of terror or grief; they were also ways for settlers to connect themselves to place—not just through bodies in the ground or at the bottom of the sea but through accounts that moved minds and hearts. The making of a graveyard was also the making of settler society.

———

Nearly lost to regional historical consciousness, SS *Pacific* returned to public awareness in the fall of 2022, when for-profit salvage company Rockfish Inc. claimed to have found the side-wheeler's wreckage five hundred feet down off Cape Flattery. Of particular note were two eight-meter circular objects, discovered using sonar, that matched the size and shape of *Pacific*'s paddle wheels. The find received international attention, in no small part because of estimates that the wreck had carried some $11 million in Cassiar gold. Rockfish, which had been searching for

Pacific since 2016, received sole salvage rights to the ship's remains and, in partnership with the Northwest Shipwreck Alliance, plans further investigations and has a goal of creating a museum dedicated to *Pacific* and its disastrous end.

In an interview with the *Guardian*, Rockfish head Jeff Hummel noted the profound experience of finding the lost vessel. "You can't really travel through time, but finding a wreck, you can go back to a spot where all of the things come from a different time," he told the British newspaper. "You spend years studying the boat and passengers and then if you're lucky, you're the first to touch something that was last touched by them." The world of SS *Pacific* may seem far away now, and yet in terms of years, it is only two seventy-five-year-olds lying head to foot between us and Sewell Moody's foreshortened life. The rediscovery of the doomed side-wheeler has reawakened stories of settler loss and perhaps even a kind of melancholic nostalgia for the early decades of settler colonialism on the Northwest Coast. This is the lesson of shipwreck: the resurfacing of lost ships also resurfaces stories—the past is rarely fully past.[55]

As a newspaper clipping taped to the back
of this photograph describes, the "old wind ship"
Peter Iredale is visited by a "new wind ship":
an airplane used for aerial photography surveys.

Brubaker Aerial Surveys,
University of Oregon Special Collections

FOUR

The Green Fire of Emily G. Reed

Shipwreck Debris and the Construction of Coastal Culture

ON CHRISTMAS DAY, 1900, the *Morning Astorian* reported that Charles Payne, associate editor of the *Chinook Observer* in Long Beach, had received an unusual holiday gift. It was a "useful and picturesque" desk, made from wood taken from at least six local shipwrecks. It comprised parts of *Harvest Home*, which ran aground nearby in 1882 and became a popular tourist attraction; *Great Republic*, the giant passenger side-wheeler that hit a sandbar in the Columbia's estuary in 1879; *Strathblane* out of Honolulu, which took seven lives when it broke up in the Long Beach surf in 1891 (and whose dead are buried in the Ilwaco cemetery); *Glenmorag*, come ashore in 1896 north of the mouth of the Columbia with the loss of two crew members; American steam schooner *Point Loma*, also lost in 1896; and *Potrimpos*, a German barkentine that drifted into the Long Beach breakers that same year. The "historical desk" must have meant a great deal to Payne, who himself was a survivor of the destruction of *Strathblane*. From that desk, numerous stories about future shipwrecks would be written and edited, a recursive process in which the debris of shipwreck helped produce further public knowledge of dozens of other maritime misfortunes.[1]

The fact that someone had kept pieces of some of these wrecks for more than two decades suggests that the wood from ships could serve an almost reliquary function. It held and informed memories, carried and inspired stories; in short, the stuff of shipwreck helped shape culture in the Graveyard of the Pacific. Flotsam, jetsam, and other corporeal elements of lost ships were incorporated into everyday life and into the material and narrative vernaculars of the region, for both settlers and Indigenous people, giving physical sustenance and storied meaning to ways of living along the coast. Like Mr. Payne's wreck-desk in a newspaper office in a coastal town, these remains were key parts of the assemblage of coastal culture, from place-names and practices of "piracy" and salvage to the rise of shipwreck tourism in the late nineteenth and early twentieth centuries. At the heart of this culture was a growing nostalgia that would represent major changes in the meaning and experience of shipwreck in the Graveyard. As historian Jamin Wells has argued in his work on the eastern coast of North America, "disaster, simply stated, made the beach," and the Northwest Coast was no different.[2]

Halfway down the coast of Oregon, vast dunes, golden in summer sun and pale brown in winter dim, dominate the landscape, some reaching as high as half a thousand feet above sea level. Quicksand and bodies of water known as barrage lakes lie in the low places between the dunes, and today the place is a national recreation area, where hikers struggle up and down the shifting sand slopes and enthusiasts race across the grains in all-terrain vehicles and dune buggies. Just to the south, the de facto capital of the Oregon Dunes is the town of Florence, tucked away along the Siuslaw River, just inland from the open ocean. With its restaurants, art galleries, and antique shops, Florence is a favorite for travelers plying the many sights of the coast and sees a brisk tourist economy, especially in the summers. It is also a shipwreck town.

In November of 1875, a bark described in one history as a "veritable floating coffin" foundered about forty miles off the mouth of Oregon's Umpqua River. It had sailed from Port Discovery, Washington, and was carrying more than a quarter-million board feet of lumber. Caught in a heavy gale, it began leaking, forcing the crew to abandon the ship on the open sea. Later, as the vessel's boats approached shore after a long journey in which food and water ran short, they were swamped and tumbled in the violent breakers, with only one seaman, a Daniel Deary, surviving the ordeal. Deary was found by local Siuslaw people and taken into their care before being delivered to nearby settlers, where he shared the awful story of his vessel's demise. That ship's name was *Florence*. Five years after it sank, in 1880, a Siuslaw man found a large plank of driftwood on the beach not far from the Siuslaw River—but this was no ordinary piece of jetsam; it was the name-plank of the lost bark. Its finder brought the relic to a small settler outpost on the river, where it was first leaned against the side of the general store, then nailed above the door of an erstwhile hotel. Later, the hotel was designated a post office, and the town was formally christened Florence. A mix of tragedy and convenience had placed a new name on the land.[3]

A couple of hours north from Florence, up the winding 101, a small village nestles off the highway among the Sitka spruces at the mouth of a creek where elk still wander in the mornings and at dusk. Cannon Beach, a popular tourist destination and center of coastal art and writing, like Florence takes its name from a shipwreck. In this case it is USS *Shark*, an American military vessel that foundered at the mouth of the Columbia during the 1846 British-US territorial dispute that culminated in the establishment of the forty-ninth parallel.[4] Well before there was any non-Indigenous presence on the northern Oregon coast, debris from the disarticulated *Shark* drifted south. Decades later, it would reemerge near a tiny American settlement called Elk Creek, when in 1898, one of *Shark*'s cannons was found in the sands south of the village. By 1922, local residents had determined that the cannon was important enough to rename their community after it. Today, the cannon is held by a local museum, and a replica stands along Highway 101. In 2008, two more cannons were found nearby, also determined to be from *Shark*.

Cannon Beach, formerly known by settlers as Elk Creek, took a new name in the late nineteenth century, inspired by the cannonade of USS *Shark*, an 1847 wreck whose debris drifted far to the south. *Cannon Beach History Center & Museum*

Throughout the Graveyard of the Pacific, the names of shipwrecks mark the places where land meets water, serving to establish meaning on the land- and waterscapes and rendering those places legible to settler society. At the mouth of the Columbia, for example, maritime disasters littered the area not just with physical debris but with place-names. Peacock Spit, on the north side of the estuary, carries the moniker of a US Exploring Expedition sloop of war that came ashore there without loss of life in 1841. Beard's Hollow, just north of the Columbia, takes its name from the captain of *Vandalia*, whose body was discovered in the embayment after his vessel was lost on the bar in 1853. Just off Astoria, the part of Sand Island where *Great Republic* wrecked is still known by locals as Republic Spit. Further north, stalwarts who walk Vancouver Island's West Coast Trail pass Valencia Bluffs, Michigan Beach, and other points carrying references to shipwreck.

Naming is power, and these wreck-names in the Graveyard of the Pacific are acts of claiming, like calling the region the Oregon Country, Washington Territory, or British Columbia, but on a smaller scale. They are ways for settler society to project its presence into both the past and the future and, as such, are among the many technologies of colonialism on the coast. That they, like the countless towns and creeks and lakes and towns named for early homesteaders or venture capitalists, seem neutral is a result of the stories we tell ourselves about the inevitability of American and Canadian sovereignty over these spaces. While the Pacific Northwest and British Columbia are also replete with surviving Indigenous names, those toponyms sit alongside the everyday vernacular of names we rarely think of as colonial, and place-names related to shipwrecks are part of the mix. But beyond names on maps or stories of death and loss, shipwreck literally helped build settler society along the coast.

———————

Near the midpoint of the nineteenth century, the schooner *Willemantic* wrecked in Grays Harbor, and early settler and chronicler James Swan described in his memoirs how local residents took in the survivors of the mishap: "We received her crew, who were divided round among the settlers. Captain Vail, her owner, with the mate and crew, went down the beach with the different residents; Joe, the steward, came and stayed with me." The steward, Swan recounted, was Danish, and had spent some years living on Sumatra, where "he had learned to be an excellent cook, and was particularly fond of curry, which he could prepare to perfection." Happily for Swan and any dinner guests he might have had,

Joe had managed to rescue his stash of spices, which, his host reported, "enabled us to have many a savory mess: curried ducks or geese, venison, bear meat, oysters, or fish; and when these failed, he would get up a dish of curried beans; everything but our coffee or bread was sure to be seasoned with curry." Swan ended his account of Joe's culinary prowess by noting that "we managed to pass off the short days and long nights very pleasantly."[5] A ship with an Indigenous name from Connecticut, crewed by at least one Dane, and with linkages to what is now Indonesia, connected the nascent settler communities of coastal Washington Territory to far-flung locations.

A few decades later, in 1909, another schooner, *Soquel*, crashed into a skerry known to mariners as Seabird Rocks, in Huu-ay-aht Nuu-chah-nulth territory on the coast of Vancouver Island. Unlike *Willemantic*, the wreck of the Chilean *Soquel* was marked by tragedy: soon after the impact, one of the vessel's masts fell, instantly killing the captain's wife and their infant daughter. High and dry at low tide, the ship was nonetheless a total loss. But among its cargo were two very unusual things: wooden carvings from Rapa Nui (Easter Island), their feminine curves attesting to the woodworking skills of now-anonymous artisans from the easternmost Polynesian island. The figures were given in thanks to local rescuers and today rest in the collections of the University of British Columbia's Museum of Anthropology, where they serve as reminders of the ways in which vessels such as *Soquel*, whether successful or doomed, connected the Northwest Coast to distant lands in ways that were often unexpected. They were the Pacific world made manifest.[6]

More commonly, the fabrication of local coastal culture via shipwreck debris could start with the literal construction of settler homes. In addition to his enjoyment of Joe's curries, James Swan had also recorded his and his neighbors' more practical luck thanks to the misfortune of others. "The wrecking party was absent a week," he penned, "and brought, on their return, a quantity of boards from the wrecks, which were much needed, as at that time there were no saw-mills in the Bay."[7] Similarly, in

1890, the Norwegian vessel *Straun*, on its way from Washington's Port Discovery to Melbourne with one million board feet of lumber aboard, became waterlogged off the Oregon coast and was abandoned by its captain and crew. Attempts were made to tow *Straun* into port, to no avail, and the ship eventually drifted ashore. Nearby settlers enthusiastically used the vessel's cargo to build new houses.[8] Such windfalls continued well into the twentieth century; when *Trinidad*, a schooner refitted for steam power, went down just off Willapa Bay in 1937, the *Seattle Daily Times* described the scene that followed: "At dawn, automobiles from miles around were being driven along the dunes, and scores of people hurriedly collected the piles of lumber which were being washed ashore from the ship's deckload. By noon the roads were alive with automobiles and trailers loaded with lumber, and almost every nearby yard had a growing pile of boards and timbers. One man who had bought a truckload of lumber but two days ago stood on the site of a new house and shook his head sadly as his neighbors passed and repassed with their automobiles loaded with free timbers."[9] Many houses built this way no doubt still stand in coastal communities; some are even landmarks. In Ocean Park, Washington, for example, there is a house built largely out of doors salvaged from a wrecked ship, while nearby, a house known as "The Wreckage," constructed out of rough-hewn logs, tongue-and-groove lumber, and cement from various local maritime accidents, is listed on the National Register of Historic Places.

The staples of everyday settler life and livelihood often came from wrecked ships. When the Hudson's Bay Company barkentine *Woodpecker* crashed into Clatsop Spit in 1861, local residents were able to collect eight hundred pounds of flour, enough to last for several months, while one settler managed to save a cow that had been aboard.[10] Local historian Lucile McDonald, meanwhile, reported how an elderly woman living at Ocean Park in the early twentieth century recalled fine silk apparel retrieved from the wreck of the American bark *Industry*, a disaster that cost seventeen lives.[11] And in 1895, when the steamer *Bawnmore* wrecked south of the village of Bandon on the southern Oregon coast, bulls released from its cargo bred with local dairy cows, producing what was known locally as "the Bawnmore breed."[12] A few years earlier, in 1889, the loss of the ship *Abercorn* north of Grays Harbor had brought an especially important gift to local residents: a load of iron railroad rails. It took another two years to successfully salvage all the rails, which then were used locally to extend rail service from Grays Harbor to nearby coastal towns.[13] Decades later, in 1941, the Russian steamship *Vazlav Vorovsky*, on its way outbound from Portland, broke up on Peacock Spit and, according to one account, "scattered more shortening on Long Beach than its citizens could consume in ten years. Quantities of butter in tubs also came in. A soap company in Portland paid a dollar a box for the lard and the back porches of Long Beach residents were stacked with it."[14] A similar bounty came ashore that same year when the American steamship *Mauna Ala*, en route from Seattle to Honolulu, fell afoul of a wartime coastal blackout and lost its way, eventually coming to rest and wreck on the fabled Clatsop Spit. Its seasonal cargo—Christmas trees, oranges and other fruit, tins of candy, and thousands of frozen turkeys—decorated the beach, drawing hundreds of scavengers, who made short work of the holiday bonanza.[15]

Such maritime manna was an everyday part of life in the Graveyard of the Pacific, as in coastal communities elsewhere. As Brad Duncan and Martin Gibbs have shown in their study of a South Australian community's relationship with shipwreck, incidents such as these, "of greater and lesser catastrophe and consequence, crafted the social and physical nature of coastal communities." Moreover, they argue, the actions and understandings of those who collected debris "created a cultural landscape extending far beyond the individual wreck sites. This landscape evolved over time and across generations, even as each vessel transformed physically from ship, to derelict, to archaeological site and eventually to place."[16]

More than simply a sort of livelihood, shipwrecks in the Graveyard of the Pacific created a kind of culture. When the cattle-carrying *Bawnmore* wrecked in Oregon in 1895, the *Daily Morning Astorian* quoted the captain's wife describing the ensuing melee: "Men, women, and children then began to swarm in upon us from all directions. They came afoot, on horseback, in teams and four-horse wagons. There were some who did not molest us, but the majority of them came to carry away whatever they could lay their hands upon."[17] Such experiences were common. When *Lammerlaw* sank in Willapa Bay in 1881, two men from nearby Oysterville found the ship's furnishings floating in the bay, including a sideboard full of linen and silver and a rosewood wine service rack. According to historian McDonald, one of the men paid a medical bill with the loot while the rosewood rack was split up for kindling. McDonald also reports that two years later, the grounding of *Queen of the Pacific* at the Columbia Bar saw three hundred tons of merchandise thrown overboard to lighten the vessel in hopes of freeing it from the sand. Barrels of liquor, various sorts of machinery, pianos, and even Stetson hats were the basis of a "party" next to the wreck. As for the Stetsons, they could be seen on settler heads in local towns for years after.[18]

Indeed, McDonald's accounts of coastal life, drawn from interviews with residents of Washington's Long Beach Peninsula in the mid-twentieth century, illustrate a distinct culture of acquisitive beachcombing associated with marine disaster. "There were simple rules to the art of beachcombing," she writes. One of her informants, Gil Tinker, told McDonald that "everybody who owned land on the beach considered anything coming in on it was his . . . on the other hand, we'd go out to wrecks in the night and the first fellow there always wanted to keep the others off." Here, settler senses of ownership echoed, in some ways at least, long-standing Indigenous approaches to flotsam, jetsam, and other kinds of debris. For example, when the barkentine *Grace Roberts* ran aground near Oysterville in a heavy December fog in 1887, as soon as the crew were rescued, the beachcombers descended upon the vessel. The resulting fracas, as settlers vied with each other for access to the cargo, was described in McDonald's account as "a battle with fists, clubs, and canes. One settler had some teeth knocked out before it was over." Those who took from wrecked ships even had a nickname: they were called "sea gulls," the "local definition of which," McDonald reported, "is 'persons who can't leave unguarded property unmolested.'"[19]

McDonald's interlocutor Tinker described such scenes and their protocols in great detail. "In early days," he is recorded to have said, "we'd nick something we couldn't carry away at the time, with an identifying mark. We agreed that if a person infringed on our rights we'd gang up and beat him and he daresn't go on the beach in a storm. I got a broken finger once from teaching a newcomer a lesson. Then so many people moved here we couldn't observe the rules." In other words, access to stranded vessels distinguished one kind of settler from another, generationally dividing the local population into "old-timers" and "newcomers." Tinker also noted that his family had picked what likely amounted to tons of coal off local beaches after wrecks; other finds included oil-soaked blankets that, while almost impossible to clean, were important additions to the Tinker household, reminders of the relative lack of access to consumer goods in these still-remote areas of the coast.[20]

As for ships' captains and crews, to limit the predation of the sea gulls, they often kept men on board to prevent cargo from being taken. One incident in 1947 highlighted how tensions could run high over the fate of wrecked ships' cargo. When the Army transport *Arrow* grounded on Long Beach in 1947, it took only three hours for locals to be seen swimming out to the wreck and climbing the anchor chain. One local took a sink intended for his home, but a newly arrived coastguardsman warned him against it. Nevertheless, the next morning the man was back. One of the ship's crew was on watch, but other Oysterville citizens distracted the watchman long enough for the housebuilder to get the sink into his car—from which it was quickly stolen by another area resident. And no cargo item provoked more excitement or tension than alcohol. When a bootlegging gasboat called *Alpha* wrecked near Oysterville during the years of Prohibition, local residents circled men carrying contraband to prevent them from being shot by coastguardsmen from nearby Klipsan, while other locals with fake uniforms and papers managed to load two trucks with the cases of liquor.[21]

In the accounts collected by McDonald and other chroniclers of local history, there is clearly an element of fun and adventure threaded throughout. The activities of the sea gulls and other local beachcombers are presented as elements of local color and almost playful in nature, even when the accounts included violence. At the same time, such practices could offer a stark contrast between the very real dangers of the sea and erstwhile salvage parties on the beach. When the freighter *Iowa* approached the Columbia in a violent storm in January 1936, its captain mistakenly used the recent wreck of another ship called *Laurel* as a guiding marker, leading *Iowa* onto Peacock Spit with the loss of all thirty-four crewmen.[22] Spilling countless board feet of timber, thousands of cedar shingles, and hundreds of sacks of flour, among other cargo, the wreck, despite its grim toll, inspired a frenzy of beachcombing. Residents used everything from baby buggies to trucks to gather the spoils, and one local described the scene: "People closed their stores and went to the wreck. Trucks were at a premium. Men and women dragged what they could pick up, a piece at a time, or pushed wheelbarrows. It put a gold rush to shame. It was in January, the wind was blowing, you couldn't see fifty feet offshore, the tide was high, and everything that came in was covered with oil. You can identify lumber from the *Iowa* in houses to this day because of the oil discoloration." Meanwhile, among the wreckage strewn on the beach were bodies of *Iowa*'s crew members, their presence belying the very real and tragic costs of something that was also clearly a boon to local communities.[23]

If settlers incorporated shipwreck into everyday life according to local protocols, so too did Indigenous people, continuing older legal and cultural practices that had been in place for many centuries. Certainly, as Isaac Ingalls Stevens had discovered at the Chehalis River treaty negotiations in 1855, settlers noticed Indigenous sovereignties along the coast through the presence of goods from wrecks, even if they did not necessarily comprehend (or want to comprehend) the legal and cultural meanings of such things. George Luther Boone—grandson of Daniel Boone and an early homesteader at Yaquina on the central Oregon coast—made mention in his memoirs of a Chinese ship that came ashore nearby in 1849, laden with, among other things, fine silks. "Coast Indians wore shawls that would have sold for $100 a piece in San Francisco," he wrote, noting further that a Yaquina woman married to another settler used to do laundry for Boone's family, often while wearing a shawl that had come from the unnamed wreck.[24]

Ten years later and hundreds of miles to the north on Vancouver Island, another incident of maritime misfortune drew attention to the misunderstandings that had grown up between Indigenous and settler regimes of wrecking and salvage. Beached for repairs at Barkley Sound in 1859, the trading vessel *Swiss Boy* was quickly boarded by Huu-ay-aht and Tseshaht Nuu-chah-nulth people, who took everything of value and destroyed the ship's masts, rigging, and sails. The crew, meanwhile, had retreated to the forecastle, where they remained for several days before being rescued by a group of Makah mariners led by a man named Swell or Wha-latl. Soon after, naval officer James Prevost arrived in Barkley Sound and informed the Huu-ay-aht and Tseshaht that they had committed a crime in ransacking *Swiss Boy*, and in fact took several local men to Victoria to stand trial. The ensuing formalities resulted in no convictions due to lack of evidence, but as we have seen, similar events could all too easily result in colonial violence including judicial killings.[25]

It was not just that such happenings were manifestations of Indigenous legal orders that oversaw the disposition of maritime flotsam and jetsam, including whole ships. It was also true that the materials gathered from vessels could enter the nascent capitalist economy that was taking shape along the coast of Vancouver Island, if by Indigenous hands. When the ship *Becherdass-Ambiadass* wrecked at Pachena Point in July of 1879, the crew easily made shore and was taken to the lighthouse at Cape Beale for assistance. Meanwhile, Huu-ay-aht people were working the wreck and took the things they retrieved to a nearby trading post where they could become part of both potlatch traditions and the embryonic settler-centered trade on the island's west coast.[26]

Half a century later, another mishap in Makah territory highlighted the ongoing robustness of Indigenous law in the Graveyard of the Pacific, as well as the ways in which settler society had come to resign itself to (or perhaps more accurately, rely on) Makah and other sovereignties. In December of 1929, a steamship called *Skagway* ran onto rocks near Cape Flattery on its way to Tacoma, Washington. This was no ordinary wreck: the cargo was made up mostly of alcohol, lubricating oil, glycerin, tar paper, paint, and gasoline—and it had caught fire. Handled wrongly, *Skagway* could become an explosive disaster that would also no doubt foul the coastline around the cape. The crew, for their part, had been taken to Neah Bay by Makah boatsmen, but the coast guard noted that were any other ships to stand by for assistance, they themselves would be at risk should the weather come up. But the captain stayed stubbornly on board, to the extent that the coast guard made plans to take him off by force. Eventually, he would face a criminal inquiry in Seattle but be exonerated of incompetence, drunkenness, and misconduct. Meanwhile, *Skagway* was abandoned as a total wreck, and the *Seattle Daily Times* reported that the ship was "being relieved of all cargo that escaped the flames and stripped of all equipment by Neah Bay Indians, who went out to the doomed ship in canoes. The Indians went over the sides of the *Skagway*, a prize of the sea, and helped themselves to the cargo as has been their custom in abandoned wrecks." Nearly a century after the stranding of the "three Kichis" in their territory, and more than five decades after the 1855 treaty with the United States, the Makah continued to assert their control over marine resources including shipwrecks, and observers had come to expect this fact of coastal life.[27]

In this, the Makah, like other Indigenous peoples of the Graveyard of the Pacific, had much in common with coastal peoples around the world in their relations with shipwreck. Indeed, as historian Beverly Lemire has written, the scavenging of shipwrecks became an "informal pathway" for the creation of capitalist networks and meaning-making, in concert with the expansion of empires more generally. Whether in Southeast Asia, the southwestern coast of England, the northwestern coast of North America, or elsewhere, shipwreck spawned both new narratives and new ways of living. The materials taken from wrecks, Lemire notes, represented only a fraction of global trade, but when combined with the power of dramatic and pathos-laden stories of marine disaster, such objects—whether a wreck-desk, a ship's nameboard, or a Chinese shawl—could come to hold particularly powerful sets of meanings, including about those who collected them.[28] In the case of the peoples of the Graveyard, Indigenous and settler alike, they were often portrayed in newspapers and in local histories with no small amount of ambivalence: one beachcomber's "salvage" could easily be portrayed as "pillage" or "plunder" by observers. Indeed, historian Lucile McDonald noted that "white settlers, after viewing the bonanza each wreck represented, outdid the Indians in cupidity. It has been said that pioneer children went to bed with this prayer on their lips, 'God Bless Pa and Ma and bring a wreck in on our beach.'"[29] The hope of coastal communities for a shipwreck windfall highlighted the moral and ethical tensions between death and disaster on the one hand and need and ingenuity on the other.

———————

Charles Payne's shipwreck desk had been made in part out of an American bark called *Harvest Home*, which had wrecked on Long Beach, Washington, on its way from San Francisco to Port Townsend. The wreck had been caused by a defective chronometer and thick weather; indeed, it was only when the ship's watchman heard a rooster crowing that he realized they were anywhere near the coast. Driven high on the beach with only a light cargo, the vessel was in the worst possible situation for refloating. While no one died in the wreck—the crew members walked ashore without getting their feet wet—*Harvest Home* quickly became a beloved spectacle. The hulk, *Lewis & Dryden's Marine History* reported thirteen years later, still remained on the beach, "affording considerable interest to the thousands who summer on the beach," while one enterprising local made walking sticks out of parts of the ship to sell to tourists.[30]

Particularly on the Long Beach Peninsula, but in other parts of the coast as well, shipwreck tourism became a key element of local life beginning in the last years of the nineteenth century and, by the early twentieth century, had become a central part of the economy in seaside towns. For example, when the steel vessel *Potrimpos* ran ashore conveniently near to the Breakers Hotel, the small-gauge railroad that connected local communities ran special excursions so that both residents and tourists could view the ship where it sat high on the beach.[31] Meanwhile, another ship, *Glenmorag*, slowly decomposed in the elements within sight of *Potrimpos*. As the *Seattle Post-Intelligencer* noted in 1895, "Some skeptical seamen who have been beating up and down the coast for the last forty or fifty years venture the opinion that one or both of these vessels will furnish a summer attraction for the seaside visitors for many years."[32] Indeed, a few months earlier, a writer in the *Aberdeen Herald* had argued that shipwrecks could and should be a key attraction for residents of the cities of Puget Sound. "Why," the writer complained, "can't the railroad company give cut rates and season tickets to the beach? We understand that many would visit the beach from Tacoma, Seattle, and Olympia if they could have this privilege. It is estimated that there were fifteen hundred people in Westport last Sunday."[33] In other words, shipwreck could be good business.

By the early years of the twentieth century, in fact, shipwreck had become a pillar of the local tourist economy. When *Galena* came ashore in 1906 and jammed itself into the sand a half mile from deep water on Clatsop Spit, one Astoria newspaper reported that "people are swarming to the beach to see her and thousands will yet go down there," while a competitor noted that *Galena* "will doubtless attract many visitors from this city on next Sunday. The wreck . . . is easily accessible from west station and . . . can be reached within fifteen or twenty minutes walk from the stations indicated." And that was in the winter; by the following July, it was a noted feature of beachgoing leisure: the *Morning Astorian* offered the headline "Galena on Show. New Entertainment on Beach—the Galena Proves Drawing Card."[34] Three years later, the French bark *Alice* found itself stranded with its cargo of cement not far from *Galena* in January 1909, and schools let out early so that pupils might take in the sight of this newest addition to the Graveyard of the Pacific. Local train schedules were rejiggered to match steamer traffic so that more people might see *Alice*, which would slowly be dragged under the sand by its weighty cargo until only a mast stood above the crashing waves.[35] Similarly, when the three-masted lumber schooner *Charles E. Falk* wrecked during a gale at Copalis north of Grays Harbor in 1909, it proved, like *Harvest Home* and *Galena* and numerous other wrecks, to be a hit with visitors: an afternoon meeting of the Daughters of the American Revolution in nearby Moclips was postponed so that members might drive out to see the ship. "Twenty-one guests, warmly wrapped," the *Aberdeen Herald* reported, "took the trip seven miles down the beach, enjoying the ride on the sands with the surf of the Pacific rolling in on one hand and the verdure-clad bluffs rising on the other. To many the experience was a novelty, some seeing the Pacific for the first time."[36]

Shipwreck tourism also began to take shape in the early twentieth century in places that did not have the benefit of railways or roads. In early July of 1910, for example, a ship's captain named C. V. J. Millar and

A 1913 photo with *Glenesslin*, one of the most charismatic wrecks in the Graveyard of the Pacific and still a common sight on postcards and in museums along the Oregon coast. *Image courtesy of Columbia River Maritime Museum, Astoria, Oregon*

his wife returned from a ten-day canoeing trip along the southwestern coast of Vancouver Island, the site of so many lost ships. On the journey, the couple entered the so-called Valencia Cave, where they collected relics: brass items, pieces of paneling, doors. They saw the sunken hulls and boilers, anchors and chains, and more debris from a host of wrecks: *Janet Cowan, Vesta, Uncle Sam, Skagit, Michigan*. When the Millars returned to Victoria, the captain told a *Colonist* reporter that "It is not only a graveyard of ships . . . but it is also a graveyard of humans. There are scattered along the shore between Darling creek and the mouth of the Klanewah river some seventy or more graves, nearly all shallow mounds, where the bodies of victims of wrecks, most of them from the *Valencia*,

The Green Fire of Emily G. Reed **133**

still lie interred." Almost funereal in tone, especially given the recentness of the *Valencia* disaster only four years previously, Millar's account was a way of making sense out of the terrible tragedies and economic losses that had littered the island's shoreline with debris of all sorts. In truth, the trip was more pilgrimage than tourist outing. And yet, the account of the couple's journey appeared under the headline "HOLIDAYED IN OCEAN GRAVEYARD."[37]

Herein lies the tension at the heart of shipwreck tourism: one person's misfortune is another person's pleasure. Even if the Millars were, in their own minds, on a solemn journey to visit the graves of victims of maritime disasters, their trip was just as legible when framed for *Colonist* readers as a vacation. By the early twentieth century, shipwreck was becoming not so much a quotidian misfortune experienced by many settlers, but rather a vicarious spectacle in which the human costs of marine failure were often overshadowed by the desire for a picturesque past. And few wrecks were more picturesque than that of the British schooner *Glenesslin*, which wrecked at the base of Neahkahnie Mountain on the northern Oregon coast in 1913. Left almost entirely intact, its sails unfurled and the ship tilted at a jaunty angle, *Glenesslin* made for a particularly charismatic scene that has become an iconic image of the Graveyard of the Pacific. Indeed, it was iconic from the beginning, with locals having their pictures taken in front of the wreck. Meanwhile, a photo album of the mishap was made out of the vessel's very sailcloth; the album now resides in the Columbia River Maritime Museum, serving as a metonym for an entire doomed ship.[38]

Shipwreck tourism could also mask both the history of colonialism and the presence of the Indigenous peoples that had been so central to the story of maritime disaster on the coast. Fifty-two years after the wreck of *Glenesslin*, for example, a British Columbia historian named George Nicholson described Vancouver Island's Long Beach, to the north of the Millars' itinerary, in terms that captured this sense of nostalgia:

For the treasure-seeker, Long Beach is a happy hunting ground. It is for ever coming up with something new. The rusting plates, an anchor or chain, relics of ships which came to grief on these shores, are sometimes exposed after a big storm—only to be buried again by the next. . . . Hatch-covers, wooden gratings, broken boats and other pieces of wreckage; lifebelts, empty wine casks and wicker-covered demi-johns. A whale's vertebra, a sea lion's skull or the jawbone of a shark, along with similar curiosities, are eagerly sought and carried away by visitors, or to create an appropriate effect around the home of those people who live by the sea.

Visitors find no end of places to explore, among the old Indian burial grounds and abandoned villages. Also, the tumbled-down stockades and earthworks behind which the Clayoquots defended themselves against raiding tribes, principally the Makahs from Neah Bay. No Indians reside at Long Beach now.[39]

By 1965, the Graveyard of the Pacific was a long-established moniker for the Northwest Coast, but it had also become a way to talk about both shipwreck and Indigenous worlds as things of the past. On the northwestern coast of North America—including the area around Long Beach on Vancouver Island, where Nuu-chah-nulth people in fact continued to live in the 1960s, as they do today—accounts of the Graveyard of the Pacific became a way to distance the present from the past as shipwreck, like Indigenous presence, seemed to drift into a kind of nostalgic fog. Certainly, fewer wrecks were happening thanks to new technologies and the dominance of land-based travel, with the result that fewer people were dying. And yet, those who talked and wrote about the coast created the notion of a "past age" of funereal romance and settler victimhood that undergirded thinking about the region's history more generally.

Nostalgia can take us to strange places. Like, for example, Coos Bay. The southernmost city of any size on the Oregon coast, Coos Bay is located on an embayment of the same name. Like Aberdeen and Astoria and Port Alberni and the other cities of the Graveyard, it is a place that has always ridden the seesaw of extractive industry, in particular logging. This had a steep price for Coos Bay, which in the late twentieth century descended into economic precarity like so many other timber towns of the Pacific Northwest and British Columbia. The local economy is beginning to pick up somewhat, with brewpubs and a maritime museum serving as evidence of a new emphasis on tourism. Coos Bay is a place where the vagaries of Northwest Coast history are in many ways at their most acute, and it is here that shipwreck nostalgia took a particularly unusual turn.

One place to begin the story is with the wreck of *Santa Clara*, the ship on which the doomed Sadie Caldbeck embarked in 1915, and the local "pirates" who began scavenging the vessel's cargo even as bodies like that of Mrs. Caldbeck were still being recovered from the beach. Such scavengers inhabited a complicated place in the minds of local newspaper editors and other Coos Bay–area elites. One account of the aftermath of *Santa Clara* described that ambivalence:

> Until a brief few days ago a vestige of the romance of the middle ages clung about Coos Bay. We needed for our winter firesides no stirring tales of Barbarossa, for had we not his peers right on our shores? The dark deeds and wild prowess of the South Slough Pirate struck terror to the heart of childhood and inspired wonder in the minds of all. His deeds were related to the outsider as something worth the telling. He rode out to sea in a dugout, or swam, if necessary, and performed feats bordering on the supernatural. He appeared to combat human and divine law with equal spirit and success. Justice could not apprehend him; the sea never got him. While abhorring his lawlessness, we

told about it, nevertheless, with ill concealed pride in our possession of such a wonder.

These "pirates," located on the South Slough outside of town, had already achieved nigh-mythic—if also sarcasm-laden—notoriety. The article continued, contrasting the pirates with the more genteel city-dwellers of Coos Bay: "The mild eyed, peace loving, urbane Coos Bay citizen, enervated by generations of pink teas, learning and luxury, has . . . made the terror of South slough look like a current cartoon of 'the boy who wasn't raised to be a soldier.'" Referring specifically to the chaotic scene of salvage at the wreck of *Santa Clara*, the author of the article went on to describe how "to prevent such an outrage armed men were stationed about the wreck," but "in order to show their good will," authorities "distributed about five hundred dollars in presents to the savages who lined the shores, whereupon all fell to, boarded the vessel, and found the cargo soaked, with the exception of certain bottled goods on which many proceeded to put themselves in the same condition as the cargo." The article ended with a final volley of description: "The whole scene was bizzare and imposing. Never was Coos Bay's citizenry seen in such picturesque attire. The only way you could tell a Marshfield pirate from a South Slough pirate was by the superior strategy he showed in getting away with the flotsam. Even many ladies were in attendance, standing by with the courage of the Sabine women."[40] Clearly part of a local tradition like the "sea gulls" of Long Beach several hundred miles to the north, the "pirates" of the Coos Bay area—whether from the outlying town of Marshfield or the wilds of South Slough—occupied a space somewhere between polite society and all-out savagery.

While *Santa Clara*'s demise was one of the more spectacular instances of so-called piracy at Coos Bay, others had preceded it. When the lumber schooner *Advent* sank off Coos Bay's bar in 1913, the *Coos Bay World* reported that "the 'South Slough Pirates' did not get away with any valuables that might possibly be saved."[41] The *Advent*'s captain, meanwhile, was recorded lamenting that

> one of the regrettable features of the wreck were the robberies by the South Slough pirates. He says that they robbed the Advent of practically everything movable despite the guard that was placed there. They even stole articles from the ship that were piled up on the bluff, he says, and also took a life saving belt, belonging to the life saving crew. He says that this is a federal offense, first because the ship was never given up, and second, because the wreckage lies in the government reserve. He may ask for a federal investigation of the thefts and the prosecution of the offenders.[42]

Just a few days before the destruction of *Santa Clara*, another ship, *Claremont*, wrecked near the Coos Bay Bar. The *World* announced that a South Slough logger "was boasting that he secured seventeen pairs of silk stockings, all of a different hue. The supposition is that he must have secured part of the wardrobe of Miss Falkner whose three trunks are alleged to have been stolen from the boat," while South Slough residents were complaining that "the raids of the South Slough residents were nothing compared to what some parties from Marshfield and North Bend did." The article also noted that it was not only "savages" who pillaged wrecks, pointing out that "many well-known business men were busy with autos and teams taking goods off the wreck, taking anything they could find that was of value."[43]

Often, the pirates were portrayed with tongue placed firmly in cheek. One South Slough resident defended his and his compatriots' practices in the *World* in 1912, arguing that "this section has been much maligned in the past by its residents being referred to as the 'South Slough Pirates.' We are not pirates but a 'bunch of diamonds in the rough'" before offering a list of more than thirty eligible South Slough bachelors.[44] But the class tensions inherent in accounts of Coos Bay scavengers could at times spill over into more serious matters. During the First World War, for example, one editorial caricatured a lower-class dialect to critique

The Coos Bay Pirates with their "captives"—really a group of bank tellers—in the 1950s. The Pirates had their origins in the long history of settler scavenging of shipwrecks. *Coos History Museum*

South Slough men for their lax attitude toward enlisting: "It do look like Coos Bay fellers is a mite slow about recruitin' th' Coast Artillery to war strength. . . . Coos County is the th' home ov th' South Slough pirate, an' never in history wuz greater darin' displayed than by our men ov all classes in bravin' th' terrors of th' deep and savin' th' cargo of th' Santa Clara. Men ov Coos County hev fought through winter storms an' roll' waves fer years. . . . Come on boys, show yer spirit."[45] Ultimately, piracy could land men in jail. In 1925, for example, a *World* article claiming that the pirates were fading into memory nonetheless told the story of two locals who had been sentenced to thirty days for theft. "These two men," the account noted, "have been living in shacks on the shore of South slough eking out a precarious livelihood by occasional work and salvaging the flotsam and jetsam of the sea."[46] But in the early twentieth century, local salvage traditions did seem to be in decline. Indeed, by the 1930s, the pirates had received that ultimate imprimatur of local culture and heritage nostalgia: they had become a high school mascot. In November 1931, for example, the South Slough Pirates easily trounced their Empire High School opponents on the gridiron.[47]

In the decades after World War II, the pirates of Coos Bay retreated further into local mythology and further into strangeness. A local booster organization calling themselves the Coos Bay Pirates began appearing in Fourth of July parades and other festivities, its all-male membership dressed in stereotypical pirate gear. The group concocted numerous schemes to highlight Coos Bay's distinct heritage and to provide a sense of pride—and just plain fun—among the local populace. One involved "capturing" local "maidens" (actually bank tellers) for sale and/or ransom; another even stranger one involved taking (or at least pretending to take) blood samples from visiting dignitaries that included the likes of Robert F. Kennedy. This was a long way from the pirates' ramshackle roots in the hardscrabble years of *Santa Clara*, but there was also a through line between the two: both were ways of making sense of the area's maritime past—including that past's darker moments—and a means to give meaning to place and to lay claim to settler belonging, even as maritime deaths came fewer and further between.[48]

"The disaster never fully disappears," writes Steve Mentz of shipwreck, and in the Graveyard of the Pacific, there are many revenant ships.[49] These are the ones that reemerge from their graves, sometimes on multiple occasions. When *Solano* wrecked at Ocean Park on Washington's Long Beach Peninsula in 1907, no one died; in fact, the captain and crew lived aboard the beached ship for ten months after the incident, awaiting a flood tide that might refloat the vessel. But no such tide came, and the ship remained stuck on the beach as the sands slowly swallowed it. By the 1920s, *Solano* was mostly gone, but after a storm in 1933, the wreck became visible again. Local resident Gary Whitlow, who grew up in nearby Oysterville, recalled his childhood exploits and adventures with the wreck in the 1950s, when it was surrounded by tide pools filled with crabs: "I remember Dick and Don Robertson and me doing some fun and crazy things like hiking to the beach to fish. We could get up on the old shipwreck *Solano* and wait until the water came in enough for fishing. Then we would have to stay until the tide went out enough to get back off. Some days, we were stuck out there a long time. Mom never knew about those trips, and it was probably a good thing."[50] Then, in the 1960s, *Solano* once again sank into the sand. It hasn't been seen since.[51]

Shipwreck debris, in its emergence from sands and tides, kept stories of marine disaster alive long after the initial events. "When the spectacle passes on," anthropologist Anna Tsing has written, "what is left is rubble and mud, the residues of success and failure."[52] And certainly, a central element of the stories of shipwreck in the Graveyard of the Pacific, so closely bound to the material remains of vessels themselves, was an element of there-but-for-the-grace-of-God-go-we: a reminder of mortality and of the ongoing precariousness of settler life on the Northwest Coast. Despite the success of American and Canadian societies in this part of the world—the seemingly inevitable supremacy they had achieved by the early twentieth century—flotsam, jetsam, and wreckage recalled moments in which things might go wrong. That is, the material remains of ships reminded observers, chroniclers, and collectors that history might not run in only one direction: it might run not only toward manifest destiny but toward annihilation as well. At the same time, pieces of ships and components of their cargos literally helped build settler life along the coast.

The wreckage of *Emily G. Reed*, which ran aground on Valentine's Day 1908 in what is now Rockaway Beach, Oregon, is but one example of this phenomenon: something that seemed dead and destined for neglect could come alive again in practices of remembrance. Although twelve men died in the disaster, the hulk of the ship was soon buried by storms that tore across the fetch, and the ship seemed destined to become just one more largely forgotten example of maritime misfortune in the Graveyard. But as one local paper described it, *Emily G. Reed* then set about "playing peekaboo" for the next century, with sometimes up to one hundred feet of its hull appearing to rise out of the sand as tides and storms tore away the sand around it. It resurfaced several times in the 1950s, and local historian Don Best described his own adventurous encounter with the wreck:

> One time it came out more than it usually does. . . . It was like a big rib cage laying on the beach. I was about 8 years old. I dug on one side and I found out there was an air pocket underneath that rib cage. I went home and got my flashlight and slid on my belly under the ship. I thought at the time, "No one has seen this side of the ship since 1908." Somebody said, "Did your mother know that you did that?" And I said, "No, and she still doesn't know I did that."

Meanwhile, Best's grandfather had salvaged some copper sheeting and wood studded with copper nails from *Emily G. Reed* and developed an evocative shipwreck-inspired family ritual. Every Christmas, he would take a chunk of the ship and put it in the fireplace. His family would gather round and watch the green flames rise from the embers. "We thought it was magic," Best recalled. More than half a century after the fatal accident, *Emily G. Reed*'s remains continued to provide meaning, in this case to an Oregon family's holiday wonder. This was the truth of shipwreck in the Graveyard of the Pacific: that vessels rarely died entirely, but rather lived on in curried dinners and homes made of doors, in tourist railways and new cattle breeds, in powerful stories and remembered fires.[53]

Peter Iredale with a "bathing beauty" in 1959.
As the ship continued to fall apart over the course
of the twentieth century, it became
further and further ensconced in local culture.

Image no. 6364, Highway Dept. Records,
Oregon State Archives, Salem, Oregon

FIVE

Out of Time

Ghost Ships of the
Anthropocene

CALL SOMETHING A GRAVEYARD long enough, and you're bound to end up with ghosts.

In January of 1910, the *Seattle Times* printed a Sunday magazine feature article about phantom vessels plying the Northwest Coast. Drawing on sea-lore and commonly known sailor "superstitions," the article also noted that these ghost ships had been seen by "too many men whose integrity and sobriety are undeniable, to leave any room for skepticism." One ship in particular, lost only four years earlier, played a central role in such hauntings:

> During the last summer persistent reports were brought into Seattle by sailors on vessels passing frequently in and out of the Cape, of a phantom ship seen off the dangerous coast of Vancouver Island. They said it resembled the ill-fated *Valencia*, which went down in those waters a few short years ago with more than 100 souls, and that they could vaguely see human forms clinging to the masts and rigging. On some occasions the spectacle seemed immobile, and again the mystery was accentuated by the fact that the phantom moved steadily with the ship of those who watched, maintaining its relative position perfectly. Again, it leaped upon the rocks where the real ship met destruction.

Continuing with discussion of similar phantasms as far away as Alaska, South America, and the Red Sea, and with consideration of the physics of marine mirages, the article ended by again emphasizing "that reliable, sober men and women will take oath they have seen standing out in perfection of every detail, resting upright upon the ocean," ghostly vessels such as *Valencia*.[1]

This foggy apparition of the early twentieth century set the stage for future retellings of the *Valencia* tragedy. By the later part of the century, ghost-lore had accreted around the wreck's narrative just as rust and barnacles had around the dead ship itself. A 1972 edition of the *Colonist* cited the 1910 *Seattle Times* story about Valencia's phantom, noting that "surprisingly the *Valencia* horror occurred not once but several times—if one believes reports" and repeating the story of the cave in which a lifeboat manned by skeletons had been found long after the wreck.[2] A year later, the *Colonist* published an article titled "Phantom Derelicts of the West Coast" that included "the accursed SS *Valencia*," which had "inspired rumors of a phantom ship."[3] Yet another article published in 1976—by the same author—illustrated how *Valencia*'s ghost had become part of regional folklore.[4] Meanwhile, a second ghostly vessel was said to haunt Siletz Bay in northern Oregon, its anchor dripping seaweed as it disappears into the coastal fog. Stories of this particular wreck appear regularly in collections of the region's spooky tales, often including attempts to link the apparition to real historical shipwrecks.[5]

Such language is common in the literature of the Graveyard. Indeed, by millennium's end, the region more broadly had come to be haunted in the minds of some observers. Writer Anthony Dalton articulated it best in his history of the area's maritime disasters: "On cold, windy, wintry nights, when rain and snow bring visibility down to almost zero over the seas off the southwestern coast of Vancouver Island, one can almost hear the moans and groans and screechings of dying ships. Mixed with the unearthly sounds of tortured wood and metal are the low, mournful wailings of the ghosts of the long-dead passengers and crews who died on or close to the rocky shores. They were mostly men, but among them were a handful of women and a few children."[6] Such attributions of spectrality could also apply to the entirety of the ocean beyond the horizons of the Graveyard; journalist Terry Glavin wrote in 2000 that "the North Pacific is a haunted place, and seeing ghosts may be a necessary part of coming to terms with those disturbing forces we have come to see at work in the ocean."[7] Ghost stories, whether specific as in the case of *Valencia* or generalized like the Graveyard itself, had become a part of the region's history.[8]

This could be true for local Indigenous people as well. According to Carl Edgar Jr., a Ditidaht man who spent his childhood in the remote Vancouver Island settlement of Clo-oose, his grandparents, and especially his grandmother, worried about possible encounters with the ghosts of the shipwrecked dead: "My grandparents asked me if we experienced anything. 'Do you feel anything here along the coast?' she said. 'Lots of people died there,' she said. And I said, 'No, we don't experience anything,' but she said, 'If you do, there's probably somebody who died there,' she said. That's what we were told."[9] In a sense, then, the dead of *Valencia* and other wrecks could themselves colonize the coast, as Indigenous people learned to live with other people's ghosts.

Theorist of place Michel de Certeau has famously noted, "Haunted places are the only ones people can live in," and the northwestern coast of North America is no different.[10] Ghosts are things out of place and out of time: they are unmoored relics of a vanished world, but they are also implicated in the process of belonging. On the Northwest Coast, that sense of belonging is the result of historical processes that we call colonialism, and ghost stories are ways of claiming place. In her work on hauntings in the Hudson River Valley of New York, Judith Richardson has similarly argued that ghost stories are a means of working out, or at least making sense of, the ruptures of colonialism.[11] Certainly, this has been true of the Graveyard, where stories of the shipwrecked dead, and even of the ships themselves, take on tones both memorial and elegiac.

In the context of settler colonialism, the imagining of a ghostly land-scape—whether the haunted "Indian burial ground" trope or stories of phantom ships—is about both dispossession and (re)possession.[12] In the Graveyard of the Pacific, then, the haunted coast is an appropriated coast, manifest in tales of revenant vessels and the disembodied wails of the maritime dead that are ways of saying, "We died for this, and it is now ours."

But there is another kind of ghost along the littoral: one not from the past, but rather from the future.

———————

There is no question that the age of sail dominates the story of the Grave-yard of the Pacific. Accounts and images of maritime disasters like those of *Emily G. Reed*, *Glenesslin*, and *Alice*, with their waterlogged hulls and ragged canvases, are hard to beat in terms of coastal romance. And yet, steamships such as *Pacific*, *Valencia*, and *Santa Clara* also have their places in the Graveyard's tragic pantheon, in part because of their inher-ent pathos—so many lives lost, or lives lost so publicly, like Sadie Cald-beck's—but also because of the romance of a bygone era of side-wheelers and passenger liners. Together, they represent a world that has for the most part ceased to exist. In other words, they haunt.

And they haunt because they are no longer the norm. Today, the ships that ply the waters of the Oregon, Washington, and Vancouver Island coasts are mostly powered by diesel, a fuel that has come to dominate maritime transport since the Second World War. Compared with wind and coal and steam, diesel is heavy, viscous, and sticky, qualities that have had implications for the coast, its peoples, and its nonhuman inhabitants in the later twentieth century. Diesel also connects the Graveyard of the Pacific both to deep time and to far-off places. But the worlding of which the Graveyard's diesel seascape is part is difficult to see, let alone to comprehend. It stretches far beyond the coasts of British Columbia,

Washington, and Oregon and reaches far, far back in time, even beyond our species.[13]

The diesel age has also coincided with what blue humanities scholar Margaret Cohen has called "hydrophasia," a forgetting of the sea.[14] In this profound transformation, the ocean has become an empty space for most of us: something we gaze at from the beach—that "view from the shore" with which I began this book—but which we rarely encounter directly. Gone are the fur trade schooners, the barkentines carrying loads of lumber, and the liners ferrying passengers up and down the coast. In their times, people from many walks of life had direct experience of the sea. But in the decades since, overland transportation such as railroads and the triumphant ascendancy of the automobile meant that we had other ways to move than over the water. One now travels from, say, Salem to Coos Bay in far less time than the ill-starred *Santa Clara* ever could. With this change, the ocean beaches and rocky coastlines of Vancouver Island, Washington, and Oregon became two things for most people: places of leisure and sites of nostalgia for times long past.[15]

Except, of course, for those who continue to work on the sea. These people fall into three primary categories: the crews of massive container vessels and cruise ships that can be seen far offshore, the men and women who come to the rescue of seafarers when things go wrong, and those who earn a living through fishing. "If steam was the victory of the straight line over the zigzags demanded by the wind," contends photographer-essayist Allan Sekula, "then containerization was the victory of the rectangular solid," referring to the efficiency and consistency of metal boxes piled high atop freighters. Moreover, Sekula notes, there is a "cognitive blankness," reflected in the degree to which most of us never directly encounter the humans aboard such ships, that renders the sea "less comprehensible."[16] Plagued by difficult working conditions, the laborers on container ships, which make up some 90 percent of international trade transportation, are rarely seen or heard from on the shore.

Meanwhile, another group of marine professionals, those involved in rescue and lifesaving, continue to face great risk through their work on the water. While early lifesaving on the Graveyard's coast often fell to Indigenous people, formal settler institutions of marine rescue began to be established up and down the coast in the late nineteenth century.[17] This was, to say the least, dangerous work. The boats rowed exhaustingly out into the surf to reach imperiled ships, often by volunteers, became a fixture of coastal communities and regional memory, often featuring prominently in local histories.[18] With new maritime technologies that limited the number and nature of shipwrecks in the middle of the twentieth century, as well as the further expansion of government-sponsored systems of rescue such as the US Coast Guard, the loss of life in the Graveyard of the Pacific dropped considerably, further entrenching shipwreck in the world of nostalgia. And yet, lifesaving work remained especially risky for those involved. This was especially true on the Columbia Bar. In 1977, for example, a coast guard utility boat on a night exercise off Cape Disappointment capsized, trapping most of its crew in its rapidly flooding cabin. Three trainees died in the incident, while seven others survived. The sacrifice, real or potential, of lifesaving crews on the coast remains a key feature of the modern Graveyard of the Pacific.[19]

The most dangerous profession on the coast is, of course, fishing. Countless fishing vessels have been lost on the coast, many of them smaller boats that have garnered relatively little attention in the annals of the Graveyard despite their very human toll. Those who have survived such incidents and shared their stories offer insights into the embodied experience of earlier generations of shipwreck. For example, BC fisherman Lauren Holman described his 1994 encounter with deadly surf at Nitinat Narrows:

When I woke up I was on the bottom of the ocean, going around and around and around. All I could hear was gravel smacking the side of my head. I didn't know which way was up and which way was down. I didn't have a clue. . . . I'd come up into the foam—I had four or five feet of foam above my head so I didn't know where the wave was. I could hear them all around me, but I didn't know whether I was on shore or whether I was out in the middle of the wave. It was just bright white, and waves all around me.[20]

We might imagine the many lives lost in the breakers of the Graveyard ending much like this, with Holman's account offering a rare insight into the experience.

The end of the ages of sail and steam, and the concomitant rise of diesel, paralleled settler society's distancing from the ocean, leaving the open sea to only small numbers of workers: container ship crews, staff and passengers on distant cruise ships, lifesaving professionals, and fishers. In this, the Graveyard of the Pacific was not all that different from other stretches of water around the world, where terrestrial life carried on without much real engagement with the sea. But the vagaries of the weather and of geography would continue to create hazards for maritime traffic. In the late twentieth and early twenty-first centuries, the sea would remind coastal residents of its power, and new Grave-yard stories—many of them about oil spills—would be told by people throughout the region.

————

In 1989, just south of the Norwegian Memorial that commemorates the 1903 wreck of *Prince Arthur*, a woman walked the beach slowly, taking detailed notes in a journal. In late January fog, mist, and light rain, Diane Harvester had braved the tides on this rugged part of the Washington coastline, looking for signs of a small disaster. She noted sheens on the cobbles, writing that they needed "polish" work. Under sandy spots, she found viscous patties of a black substance that didn't belong in this place: oil. Harvester found strange "pompoms" above the tide line, intended to soak up the oil but having failed to do their job. She saw logs covered in the dark goo, and oil-drenched debris at the high-water mark. Before the encroaching tide forced her off the beach, she dug into what seemed like clean cobbles, only to find that four to six inches down, there was a layer of crude. Making one last entry in her log, Harvester noted that she would be back the next day to document the damage caused by a single wrecked vessel.[21]

Water and oil may not mix, but their histories are deeply entwined. From the beginning of the age of diesel and continuing to our present world of gigantic freighters, gargantuan container vessels, and enormous cruise ships, new fossil ecologies link the deep earthly past to the present, all in the name of a particular kind of future. Modern capitalism's dependence on hydrocarbons and their by-products, as well as on the sea as a territory of commercial transport, has created a world in which we are, each of us, entangled in the nature of oil. The history of oil spills in the Graveyard of the Pacific, many of them largely forgotten despite their recentness, illustrates the ways in which late capitalism, with its insatiable need for fossil fuels, has had obvious and at times near-catastrophic effects.

In early September 1956, for example, the Liberian-flagged and Greek-captained freighter *Seagate* was on its way to Vancouver to pick up a cargo of grain from Canada's interior. Caught in a dense fog without radar, the crew was taking soundings when the ship struck a reef and became stranded. So off course were they that the captain reported that the ship was caught on Race Rocks near Victoria, when they were in fact grounded on Sonora Reef off the Washington coast. Wherever they were, when *Seagate* hit the rocks, its side was torn open, and it began leaking oil. One newspaper account described the scene: "Thousands of birds have become casualties of the wreck of the freighter *Seagate* off the Washington coast near Point Grenville. A vast oil slick spread over the water when the *Seagate*'s fuel tanks ruptured as she ran onto the rocks of Sonora Reef. The slick drifted north along the coast, spreading a gummy film from Kalalock [*sic*] to LaPush. Yesterday, coastal residents reported thousands of birds, their bodies slick with oil, were dying on the beaches. University of Washington zoologists said nothing can be done to save birds once they are caught in the oil." Murres, guillemots, scaups: these bird species and others were caught up in the deadly petroleum sheen, dying by the thousands after a wreck in which the crew and their dog all survived, even as *Seagate* spilled mortality into the water.[22]

Eight years later in 1964, an unnamed barge loaded with gasoline refined on the shores of the Salish Sea and headed for Coos Bay became separated from its tug when its towline ran off the drum in a stormy night. Drifting freely, the barge grounded between Moclips and Pacific Beach on the Washington coast, just south of the Quinault Reservation. It took five days to pull it off the strand; in the meantime, more than a million gallons of petroleum had leaked into the water, fouling ten miles of beaches. Hundreds if not thousands of marine birds were killed, some 32,000 pounds' worth of razor clams died, and the local clamming season was shut down entirely. Ultimately, the barge's parent business, the United Transportation Company, paid only $8,000 in damages, an amount equal to just over $60,000 in today's numbers—small potatoes given the obvious environmental costs.[23]

Then, in early 1972, another failed towline led to an even larger catastrophe. This time it was attached to *General M. C. Meigs*, a naval vessel being towed from Olympia to San Francisco to join the reserve fleet there; when the line parted, the six-hundred-foot ship was forced onto the rocks just south of Cape Flattery and quickly broke into two massive pieces. As naval and civilian authorities debated how best to deal with the carcass, oil began covering nearby beaches, including the beloved Shi Shi Beach on the Makah Reservation. This time, a concerted cleanup led by the navy produced scenes that would be repeated in years to come: "Navy Cdr. Charles Rennacker calls his cleanup challenge a 'grim assignment.' And about 30 grim-looking men were working under his direction yesterday, stuffing greasy globs of sand into plastic bags and looking more like tar-blackened roofers than men of the sea." The *Seattle Times*, meanwhile, noted the amicable relations between the naval men and the local Makah Nation. "They want their beach cleaned up and that's what we're doing," reported Rennacker. Despite the enlisted men's labors, however, the area saw a massive die-off of purple sea urchins, while an unknown number of birds, sea otters, and other animals were killed.[24] And perhaps most alarmingly, oil from the wreck continued to appear for another five years.[25]

Two months after *General M. C. Meigs* broke apart against the offshore pinnacles south of Cape Flattery, another very large ship ran aground in Vancouver Island's Barkley Sound, having mistaken the sound's entrance for the Strait of Juan de Fuca. Burdened with more than three hundred automobiles built in Japan, *Vanlene* would ultimately spill 37,500 gallons of heavy bunker fuel into the many-islanded sound. Luckily, however, the weather intervened: fierce storm-winds pushed the spill away from shore, while heavy rain helped break down the oil. The relatively new technology of oil booms, meanwhile, helped corral the pollutant near its source. While not the largest spill on the coast by any means, the wreck of *Vanlene* inspired a fair amount of public discourse about government regulation and preparedness for the next big spill. One newspaper op-ed linked *Vanlene* to a much longer history: "The rugged, rocky coast of Vancouver Island and southern BC is called the Graveyard of the Pacific because of the large number of ships that have gone down there over the years. But with oil spills like the one this week in Barkly [*sic*] sound . . . it could become the graveyard for hundreds, even thousands, of mammals, birds, and tiny marine animals."[26] The discussion went all the way to the Canadian Parliament, where opposition leader Robert Stanfield confronted the Trudeau administration's policies on environmental regulation and asked when the nation could expect effective laws for preventing the next oil spill. Meanwhile, scavengers took everything they could from the wreck of *Vanlene*; one newspaper account described "hippies paddling leaking canoes, Indians in glass fibre speed boats, fishermen in their craft, pleasure crafts, and tugs towing barges" all availing themselves of the largesse. This diverse lot of salvagers—who might have been called "pirates" or "sea gulls" in another era—even took the tires from the cars on board despite authorities' warnings of the dangers.[27]

In these stories of shipwreck from the second half of the twentieth century, a pattern emerges: a growing willingness and capacity to respond to oil spills. These new priorities and infrastructures would be tested in 1988, when the oil barge *Nestucca*, in tow from a refinery on the Salish Sea to Aberdeen and Portland, broke its towline. Prevented from entering Grays Harbor by port authorities and having been torn open by its tug's propeller, *Nestucca* was already leaking when it was captured and towed far out to sea. Unfortunately, this meant that its errant cargo spread further north along the coast than it would have otherwise; soon places as far north as Carmanah and Long Beach on Vancouver Island began seeing globs of oil appearing on their shores. The most heavily oiled places lay between Grays Harbor and Cape Flattery; in these locations, oil was particularly thick on south-facing beaches, many of which were inaccessible by land. One *Seattle Post-Intelligencer* reporter described the scene: "There is something different about the beach music. There are no bird cries. There are fewer birds. The birds that remain . . . have mostly been sorted already into plastic bags. One for live birds, one for dead ones. Next to them are the other bags, also sorted. One for oil blobs, one for plastic trash, one for wood and other burnables." Another reporter, this time for the *Olympian* from the state's capital, detailed what had happened on the Quinault Reservation: "Oil oozed from the tidal pools tucked next to the sea stacks that jut skyward on the beach. Dime to quarter-sized pieces of algae and wood coated with oil dotted the beach, grim reminders of an unwanted visitor. . . . Dead birds were wedged in the debris left by high tide." Meanwhile, Quinault tribal members feared for the local bald eagles, some of which had been seen scavenging on the oil-soaked dead.[28]

To a much greater degree than with earlier spills, the demise of *Nestucca* inspired widespread governmental and citizen action. Hundreds of volunteers from across the Pacific Northwest and British Columbia, and even a few from farther afield, descended on the coast to join local residents, settler and Indigenous alike, in their efforts to save wildlife and clean up the beaches. Throughout the northern half of the Graveyard of the Pacific, individuals and agencies leaped into action as the first dead and dying birds began to wash ashore. Establishing bird treatment centers involved setting up complicated water delivery and treatment systems, organizing (and feeding and housing) the on-site human labor, and once under way, avoiding the sharp beaks of terrified patients. For some, cleaning oiled birds was a profound experience; Olympic National Park ranger Paul Crawford told a reporter that "once you have worked with an oiled bird, you would understand. It's a spiritual thing." For another volunteer, Constance Perenyi, the work found purchase in her life: "What I remember most is the smell. Even now one whiff of Dawn dishwashing detergent and I am no longer standing at the kitchen sink but in a . . . gymnasium filled with frightened animals. . . . Pumped by the gallon, this pungent blue liquid is vital to rescue efforts. It can also trigger memories." Perenyi continued her reflection by writing how "confronted by death, we worked hard to preserve life. We do what we can, and in the process are changed." Volunteers, many of them committed to their homeplace and at least some of them loyal environmentalists, would find themselves transformed by the experience and more deeply connected to the coast and its more-than-human inhabitants. The project of saving birds could also, however, provoke a bit of gallows humor, as illustrated by the list of puns volunteers had written on a sign:

DON'T BE LOUD, BE DEMURRE

IF YOU DON'T KNOW, WING IT

TRY NOT TO MAKE GREBEOUS ERRORS

STAY HAPPY—DON'T GET DOWN

IT WAS JUST MURRE-DER

COME AT 7:30 FOR THE OILY BIRD SPECIAL

MURRE-ACULOUS

MURRE OF THE SAME

THESE VOLUNTEERS LOOK POOPED

AND THEY BROUGHT HIM GOLD, FRANKINCENSE, AND MURRE

Collected by local newspaperman David C. Webster, these firsthand accounts of bird rescue speak to the affective bonds that settlers—locals and out-of-towners alike—were building with each other, with the more-than-human, and with the coast itself. Meanwhile, an estimated fifty thousand birds had died and only about one-third of the birds treated survived the experience.[29]

Local Indigenous communities, unsurprisingly, were among the most affected by the *Nestucca* spill, and among the most committed to its cleanup. One observer noted that Indigenous women from nations like the Quinault and the Makah were "more meticulous" than other volunteers and that Indigenous workers in general were more committed to the painstaking and exhausting work because of their knowledge of, and historical relationship with, local places. When the disaster was inexplicably declared "insignificant" by the British Columbia government, Indigenous leaders critiqued that decision in no uncertain terms. Richard Lucas from the Hesquiaht Nuu-chah-nulth, for example, proclaimed, "They didn't realize this was our home." Hesquiaht *hawiilth* Simon Lucas, meanwhile, decried the declaration of insignificance: "That's a scientist's word! Intelligent people are destroying this world. This whole dominant attitude has to go. . . . It will mean a change in lifestyle. Otherwise, I guarantee we will be doing this over and over again." As Chief Lucas gestured toward the petrochemical future, other Indigenous people provided historical context for the spill. Makah volunteer Bobby Rose, for example, remembered her grandfather talking about their nation experiencing numerous oil spills in the early twentieth century, while Nuu-chah-nulth people recalled cleaning up the beaches of Barkley Sound during the *Vanlene* disaster. Some Indigenous observers also had a critique of settler volunteers: Denise Dailey, a Makah fisheries biologist, noted pointedly that "non-native people focus on birds in an oil spill because they float up on shore. But that is tunnel vision. Education needs to broaden the vision of people in understanding the damage caused by an oil spill or other pollution and its effects on the culture of native tribal people." Bobby Rose agreed, telling David Webster that, "to us, as native people on our own land, everything is a cultural resource."[30]

Despite the profound differences in the depth of their historical relationship with place and despite having such differing stakes, both Indigenous people and settlers alike imagined a future in which shipwrecks and their environmental consequences would continue to threaten the Graveyard of the Pacific's ecologies and cultures. As David Webster himself wrote, "Anybody who has experienced an oil spill, even the relatively small but widespread Nestucca event, and has seen photographs of much greater disasters such as in Alaska or those in the Atlantic, knows it can happen along any coast. We've smelled one spill that we'll never forget; and we can, unfortunately, 'smell' the next one coming." In writing these words, Webster, like Chief Lucas in his "over and over again" statement, invoked a petrofuture that seems inevitable given our current economic and political reality. The apocalyptic narrative offered by the two men, grounded in having seen firsthand the embodied consequences of an oil spill—all those dead birds and those triggering smell-memories—projects our present into a future that has yet to happen. It also highlights the parallels in place-commitment on the part of Indigenous person and settler alike: Bobby Rose and Diane Harvester, Denise Dailey and Constance Perenyi. All of these people, like all of us who care about the coast, are haunted by the future.[31]

Nestucca was hardly the last oil spill in the Graveyard of the Pacific. Only three years later, in 1991, a Japanese fish-processing vessel called *Tenyo Maru* collided with the Chinese freighter *Tuo Hai* off Cape Flattery. *Tenyo Maru* sank immediately and, over the course of the next month, would release 361,000 gallons of fuel before a submersible was used to pump out the remainder. The spill killed more than 4,300 seabirds, including endangered marbled murrelets, while the mammals killed included endangered sea otters. Shi Shi Beach was hit again with blobs and patches of oil, and Cape Flattery saw a broad sheen pollute its surrounding waters. In 1994, the Maruha Corporation would pay $9 million for the accident.[32]

Tenyo Maru and *Vanlene, General M. C. Meigs* and even *Nestucca*: these are not household names on the coast, nor are they reflected in manifestations of place-making such as tourist postcards. Oil tankers and cargo freighters (but maybe not barges) have a brutal, industrial grandeur to them, to be sure, but they simply cannot compete with the high drama that is *Glenesslin* on the rocks, great sails billowing. These latter-day marine disasters, while greater in environmental impact than any lumber-laden bark of the nineteenth century, simply do not have the romantic and nostalgic—if also at times macabre—appeal of a good old wooden ship disappearing into the bar or of a steam-powered metonym of mobility and modernity perched precariously on a black-stone reef.

There is one exception. On the third day of February in 1999, a big storm was blowing on the southern Oregon coast, and a Philippine-flagged dry-cargo freighter was struggling. Owned by a Japanese company through a Panamanian subsidiary, 640-foot-long *New Carissa* and its crew of twenty-three were in trouble and sought entrance to Coos Bay, but authorities there denied the request because of dangerous conditions at the bar. So *New Carissa* dropped anchor and waited offshore. What the crew did not realize, though, was that the chain was too short, allowing the anchor to drag. No one noticed as *New Carissa* drifted closer and closer to the beach north of Coos Bay, and by the time anyone did notice, it was far too late: the massive ship ran aground in the early hours of February 4, and almost immediately, two of the ship's five fuel tanks began leaking. Coastguardsman Scott Knutson recalled the scene years later: "It was totally out of place. All that iron on all that sand was just kind of a sickening feeling."[33]

How to get the monster off the beach? The bad weather was carrying on, meaning that Coos Bay tugs couldn't get to the freighter even as *New Carissa* was driven farther into the sand. The freighter was beyond help, and on February 10, cracks began to appear in its hull thanks to the relentless, violent pounding of the surf. State authorities, who had been debating how best to prevent further disaster, decided the best option was to burn off the vessel's remaining fuel using napalm and explosives. The resulting explosion was watched by hundreds of local residents and lookie-loos from out of town. One newspaper described the scene: "A cheer went up from the thousands of people gathered at every high spot around town as flames and black smoke filled the sky above the stranded ship."[34] The resulting conflagration burned for a day and a half and was so intense that the wave-weakened ship finally broke in half on February 11.

Artist Henk Pander, who would famously paint the explosion, described the aftermath in decidedly aesthetic terms:

> And there it was, a few hundred yards to my right, lying on the beach, all enveloped in a hazy light, misty gray. The haze made it difficult to read its shape. Its bow, with its bulbous snout, was facing me. There was a huge rusty scrape diagonal across the bow. The red paint under the water line had pinks, rusty violets, blues, the light delicately bouncing off its face. Its superstructure looked complex and implacable; bundles of cables strung diagonally across the silvery sky. Enormous waves crashed against the seaward side of its rusty flank, and where the stern had been, an immense sheet of steel was bent and ripped. I started drawing immediately while the light was good.[35]

Henk Pander's 2000 painting of the burning of *New Carissa* captures the spectacle of a wrecked tanker being lit on fire using napalm. *Maribeth Collins Art Acquisition Fund, collection of the Hallie Ford Museum of Art, Willamette University, Salem, Oregon*

Meanwhile, local authorities and environmentalists continued to have very real concerns about further contamination, focusing in particular on the rich and delicate ecosystem of Coos Bay.

As the weather cleared, authorities made plans to remove the halved freighter off the beach. A tug finally arrived and towed the bow section away, followed by an oil skimmer, but the towline broke, and the bow grounded again further north, this time near the seaside town of Waldport. On March 8, it was refloated and hauled out to sea beyond the continental shelf, where a navy destroyer riddled it with live fire and a nuclear-powered submarine hit it with a torpedo. That last blow was the final one, and the bow quickly sank in waters that were ten thousand feet deep. There, any last vestiges of fuel would be rendered solid by the cold and intense pressure. The stern section of *New Carissa*, however, remained on the beach north of Coos Bay, slowly working its way several meters down into the sand as legal wrangling took place over whose responsibility the hulk was. That debate lasted for nearly eight years, and it was only in the summer of 2008 that Titan Salvage installed two jack-up barges, six three-hundred-ton hydraulic pullers, two cranes, and a *téléphérique* (a kind of cable car) to get workers from the beach to the wreck. Finally, by the end of the year, *New Carissa* was gone, its scrap sent inland to Eugene.[36]

In the nine years that the broken freighter's stern squatted on the beach, it became the subject of debates not just about legal responsibility but about both environmental impacts and effects on local tourism.[37] The fuel that had leaked from *New Carissa* immediately after its grounding amounted to around seventy thousand gallons, which fouled nearby beaches and killed more than three thousand birds of more than fifty species, including 262 endangered marbled murrelets, along with seals and shellfish. After the spectacular February 11 explosion burned off most of the remaining fuel, debates turned to the future of the stern section and continued for years. Some commentators, like Coos Bay city council president Jeff McKeown, argued that it should be allowed to remain. "Shipwrecks on the Oregon Coast are part of our history," he told a reporter. "There are a lot of ways you could better spend the money here." Others had different ideas. Assistant director of the Oregon Department of State Lands Steve Purchase, for his part, argued that "it's not over until the last square foot of dunes is recontoured and all the equipment is gone."[38] Meanwhile, an economist found that the aesthetic appeal of the derelict remains of *New Carissa* might have actually increased tourism, despite the fact that the beach and dunes near the wreck had been designated off-limits to the public.[39]

Historical narrative was at work here as well. One observer of the wreckage, poet Kari Wergeland, asked the readers of her chapbook to consider the long past of shipwreck on the coast:

This dying wreck, she knew quite well,
The sea does not play games.

Unforgiving to a grounded ship,
Think of the ghostly names:
The *Glenesslin*, the *Willapa*,
The *Peter Iredale*,
The *Oliver Olson*, the *Shark*,
And others—the same tale.

By invoking some of the most well-known and evocative historical wrecks in the region, Wergeland firmly placed *New Carissa* in the genealogy of the Graveyard of the Pacific. She also connected the demise of the freighter to other losses: "'First it was timber—then salmon— / and now this,' someone said."[40] In a town like Coos Bay, buffeted by booms and busts, a shipwreck could become a metaphor for the faltering extractive economic system. Indeed, it was even a meto*nym*; *New Carissa* was on its way to pick up wood chips, an end-stage timber product indicative of a dearth of big trees. That empty hold, worth millions, was late capitalism itself, in which nothing can be almost as valuable as something.

New Carissa, then, was representative of multiple strands of Graveyard history: the oil spills that affected the coast every few years, the frisson and aesthetics of maritime disaster, and even the region's economic history. But the wreck could also make history loop back on itself in surprising ways. Not long after the $22 million settlement paid by Japan's ironically named Green Atlas Shipping, the Confederated Tribes of Siletz Indians, whose ancestors had been forcibly removed from the coast in the late nineteenth century, announced that they had reclaimed land in their traditional territories as part of the deal. Formerly owned by timber companies, the four hundred acres would be divided between pristine marbled murrelet habitat, large-scale ecological restoration, and lumbering that would provide an economic base for the tribes. Tribal member Delores Pigsley declared to one observer, "We are proud to take this land back. We'll take care of the land as usual."[41] This was perhaps the greatest irony of the wreck of *New Carissa*: it sparked a reconnection between living Indigenous people and their ancestors' lands on the coast. Shipwreck continued to be a moment of rupture in the expected story, in this case of Indigenous dispossession and disappearance.

————

In the wake of the *Nestucca* disaster, a new organization was born: the Pacific States–British Columbia Oil Spill Task Force, which would take the lead in coordinating responses to such events in the future. Ironically, the day after the task force's first official meeting in March 1989, a huge single-hulled tanker hit rocks in Alaska's Prince William Sound and began immediately leaking massive amounts of crude oil. The *Exxon Valdez* horror, which ultimately saw nearly eleven million gallons of petrochemicals foul more than 1,300 miles of coastline, would overshadow all of the Graveyard's spills combined, both in scale and in media attention. It also, however, led to a broader public awareness of and demand for spill preparedness on the coast south of Alaska. Luckily, in the years since *Nestucca*, Oregon, Washington, and British Columbia, along with local tribes and First Nations, had begun to develop rapid-response systems for dealing quickly with spill incidents. The result is that today, a robust regional infrastructure is in place, ready to spring into action should another such event take place. The region has also seen a growing environmentalist and Indigenous-led movement drawing attention to the dangers of fossil fuel dependence; the departure point for *Nestucca* and the unnamed 1964 barge, the Cherry Point refinery on the Salish Sea, has seen protests intended to prevent expansion of the facility, with oil spill hazards—along with sea level rises associated with climate change—being the primary talking points.[42]

It is just as well that the region has been preparing for a history that hasn't yet happened, since lost ships sometimes return. Indeed, as *New Carissa* amply exemplified, some ships don't die easily; some, in fact, are more zombies than ghosts. In 2020, for example, the sunken freighter MV

Schiedyk began making headlines, more than five decades after its loss, when it suddenly began releasing oil into the waters in Nuu-chah-nulth territory on Vancouver Island. MV *Schiedyk* had been lost in 1968 when a rudder failure caused it to strike a reef in a narrow channel. "We saw the shoreline coming. We had lots of warning," the captain told the *Daily Colonist* at the time. "We knew what was going to happen if we didn't change our course, but the ship simply didn't turn."[43] While the crew of forty was safely rescued, the ship quickly sank. It leaked fuel for another few months before sinking farther into the channel. From that point, MV *Schiedyk* faded into statistics, just another victim of the Graveyard of the Pacific. *Hawiilth* Jerry Jack of the Mowachaht-Muchalaht First Nation, for example, had been surprised by the leak. "I lived here in '68," he told the Nuu-chah-nulth newspaper *Ha-Shilth-Sa* in 2021, "and I don't even recall my dad talking about a shipwreck that happened at Bligh Island."[44] But when a slick appeared in 2020, federal and provincial authorities and local First Nations leaped into action. Over the next seven months, slicks on the surface would be contained with booms and the oil taken to a treatment facility, while a private marine salvage company tapped the remaining fuel inside the wreck. Indigenous leadership was key to what was ultimately a successful operation. Chief Jack, who also served as incident commander for his nation, noted that "we set out directions for what the operation was going to do every day. My assessment is that everything went well. The Coast Guard couldn't do any more."[45] This was in stark contrast to what had happened with *Nestucca* more than three decades earlier, when Indigenous leaders were frustrated by the shortcomings of settler institutions' responses.

Reactions to oil spills, then, are about who is able to mobilize in the wake of an ecological disaster, which in turn has as much to do with social, legal, and political standing as it does with technology. In particular, the growing power of Indigenous tribes and nations to reclaim authority over their lands and waters, with or without explicit treaties enshrining that authority, has tracked closely with the broader growth of coastal infrastructures for dealing with oil spills. It stands to reason: simply put, Indigenous peoples have more at stake. But as Indigenous critics of spill responses have noted, consultation with and inclusion of Indigenous governments in response planning is not necessarily a given, and those responses are often understood as inadequate in meeting Indigenous communities' needs for protection of both environmental and cultural resources. Combined with the slow but accelerating violence of sea level rise and ever-more-intense storm systems, Indigenous tribes and nations in the Graveyard will continue to be on the front lines of environmental change and will no doubt take the lead in responding to those changes.[46] As it has throughout the history of the Graveyard of the Pacific, shipwreck invites us to consider power: who has had it, who has not, and how that power shifts over time.

––––––––

"The winds of the Anthropocene carry ghosts—the vestiges and signs of past ways of life still charged in the present," write anthropologist Anna Tsing and her colleagues in their 2017 collection *Arts of Living on a Damaged Planet*. "Ghosts," they continue, "are the traces of more than human histories through which ecologies are made and unmade." And, perhaps most importantly, they note, "anthropogenic landscapes are also haunted by imagined futures."[47] In the Graveyard of the Pacific, Indigenous and settler communities alike are contending with the impending transformations and travails of a new climatic regime, as well as the potential for more acute ecological disasters emerging from the petrochemical dependency that is producing that regime. The recent history of shipwreck on the coast, and in particular the history of oil spills, tells us a great deal about the relationship between past, present, and future. It highlights the ways in which the past is often not truly past, nor is the future entirely abstract. Both haunt our current historical moment.

Shipwreck, I've argued, is a particularly potent metaphor for the vagaries of colonialism and Indigenous survivance on the coast. Indeed, shipwreck is perhaps a metaphor for our era, for the Anthropocene. Theorist Bruno Latour, in his recent work examining the sorts of stories we need as we face climate catastrophe, turns to the imagery of shipwreck to explain the workings of both power and denial:

> To go back to the well-worn metaphor of the *Titanic*, the ruling classes understand that the shipwreck is certain; they reserve the lifeboats for themselves and ask the orchestra to go on playing lullabies so they can take advantage of the darkness to beat their retreat before the ship's increased listing alerts the other classes! For a clarifying episode that is not metaphoric in the least: Exxon-Mobil, in the early 1990s, knowing full well what it was doing, after publishing excellent scientific articles on the dangers of climate change, chose to invest massively in frenetic extraction of oil and at the same time in an equally frenetic campaign to proclaim the non-existence of the threat.[48]

Here, Latour calls out the cynicism of an industry that is at the center of the threat, and the ways in which that threat intersects with political, economic, and social capital. Who benefits, he asks, and who bears the burden? Latour then continues: "Looking down from the ship's rail, the lower classes, now fully awakened, see the lifeboats pulling farther and farther away. The orchestra continues to play 'Nearer, my God, to Thee,' but the music no longer suffices to drown out the cries of rage."[49] In invoking the very song that was sung by women tied into the rigging of *Valencia*—a full six years before *Titanic*, remember—Latour makes the case that understanding our present moment involves telling stories that go to the heart of the matter, providing powerful metaphorical meaning while also attending to questions of power and privilege.[50]

If the Earth is a vessel, it is on the rocks, and whatever we call it, ours is a haunted time. In the Graveyard of the Pacific, we are haunted by the ships, crews, and passengers already lost (and by the birds and otters and clams lost as well), and haunted also by the wrecks that have yet to happen. Our moment is a hinge between a past that has yet to finish with us and a future that may just finish us. If ghosts are "out of time" in one sense of the phrase, so might we be, in yet another.

———

Residents of and visitors to the Graveyard, meanwhile, continue their search for ghosts. In 2018, the long-running reality television show *Ghost Adventures* debuted a four-part special titled "Graveyard of the Pacific." In it, the series' four intrepid paranormal investigators visit Astoria and the surrounding area in search of signs of life after death and of malevolent spiritual forces. Interviewing local historians, Christian ministers, and psychics and using a suite of devices including electronic voice phenomenon recorders and something called a "spirit box," the quartet finds all sorts of evidence of the occult. In the basements of Astoria's so-called "underground," histories of violent shanghaiing, a fire in the 1920s, and occupancy by Chinese immigrants all serve as clues to the paranormal and, in particular, led to an encounter with an Aramaic-speaking demon that inhabits the dark and damp spaces beneath downtown. Setting up a "nerve center" in a fish-packing truck, the foursome travels the streets of Astoria in search of further spectral evidence. "We don't know what lurks beneath the surface of this water [or] inside the homes and buildings of Astoria," claims producer and ghost-hunter Zak Bagans's voice-over. "This is where our expertise, our knowledge is needed." Bagans and the others find what they were looking for at the Norblad Hostel, a recently refurbished hotel whose alleged history of child abduction, murder, and drug use confirms its mystique as a hot spot of evil in one of the "wickedest" cities in the world. Outside of town, the four men seek out spirits at Fort Stevens State Park, including the ghost of a "mean old lady" in the commander's house and some sort of angry entity in the maze of tunnels beneath the former gunnery. Meanwhile, eccentric local place-names like Creep and Crawl Lake and Coffenbury Road serve as further proof that *something* is going on around the mouth of the Columbia.

It is the Graveyard itself, though, that most inspires the team of adventurers. From the North Head Lighthouse at Cape Disappointment, they look out over the treacherous bar and imagine a land- and seascape of the occult. Speaking to a local historian, they hear the story of the 1853 wreck of *Vandalia*, the tragedy that informed the place-names Deadman's Hollow and Beard's Hollow. Not long after, the crew is on the beach with their equipment, seeking out evidence of the vessel's lost souls. (They don't find much: only a "mysterious" light far out in the ocean and cliff-cleft that had a vaguely human shape.) Much of the episode, though, focuses on the lighthouse itself, and on the keepers' house, telling the story of an early lighthouse keeper's wife who died in a fall from the encircling cliffs. Was it suicide? Murder? An accident? Ultimately, a faint voice caught on an EVP monitor gives them their desired answer, while Bagans is briefly possessed by the dead woman's husband's angry specter.

But it is the investigators' search for the ultimate reason for the density of hauntings and evil presences in and around the Graveyard, for its originary source, that brings the four of them into conversation with the larger, very real history of this place. As one of their psychics leads them to the lighthouse through the forest of salal and Sitka spruce, she informs them that she feels something deep, dark, and Native at the site, as though people had been punished there for some great wrong. A curator at the local maritime museum similarly notes that the estuary of the Columbia surely is home to spirits, because after all, Indigenous people had believed in them. And fueled by historical documents, including some from America's fabled Corps of Discovery, the four seekers find the hauntings' origins in the story of the epidemics that ravaged the local Chinook and Clatsop peoples. This, they argued, is the source of the evil they had encountered. In other words, colonialism made this place make sense.[51]

One hyperbolic television show does not reality make, of course. At the same time, the four episodes of *Ghost Adventures* involved not just local eccentrics but museum professionals, historians, hotel owners, and others invested in tourism and the creation of a sense of place, which in the twenty-first century are often the same thing. After all, these episodes first aired on the Travel Channel. And so, in Astoria and the Graveyard of the Pacific more generally, haunting has become a way to understand the connections between past and present, and between history and place. The challenge, though, is to see haunting working in both directions. The real ghosts of the Graveyard are the even larger ecological catastrophes that will someday visit the coast or that are already here. In searching for answers to local hauntings in the past rather than the future, the ghost adventurers were seeking the wrong sort of apparition. They were looking in the wrong direction.

A cleanup crew from Astoria walks
Clatsop Spit in 1988 with
Peter Iredale in the background.

SIX

Neahkahnie's Archive

Wrecklore and the Bedrock of the Past

NEAHKAHNIE LOOMS. Hulking more than sixteen hundred feet over the coast of northern Oregon, black-cliffed and festooned with rainforest, the mountain is the highest coastal point anywhere in the Graveyard of the Pacific. With a name that means something like Place of the Great Spirit in the Nehalem-Tillamook language, the eminence features prominently in local Indigenous cosmology. For American settlers, meanwhile, Neahkahnie Mountain has been both obstacle and attraction. It blocked littoral travel until the 1940s, when Highway 101 was finally built high around the seaward side, bridging chasms and creating a lookout where the wind is seemingly unceasing. Today, it bears trails on which intrepid hikers can explore the steep forested slopes and enjoy viewpoints offering glimpses out over the ocean. Partially incorporated into Oswald West State Park, Neahkahnie remains a powerful and imposing presence for all who travel this part of the coast.

At the base of Neahkahnie, where the pitiless surf slowly eats away at the black rock of the mountain, there are caves. Inaccessible except at low tide and then only briefly and dangerously, the caves are largely unknown and unseen by the public, even those standing several hundred feet above them on the highway lookout. It was in one of these caves, in the summer of 2022, that a team sponsored by *National Geographic* and made up of archaeologists, park rangers, and marine rescue technicians worked quickly where a local fisherman had seen timbers, well above the usual high tide line, that looked like they might have belonged to a ship of some sort. The brief caving expedition may have lasted only ninety minutes, the small window in which the sea retreated enough to make entry into the cave possible, but its members were engaged in a search more than three centuries in the making. In fact, as they labored to pull the timbers—crafted from a species of tree found only in Asia—from the dark place where they had rested for a very long time, the *National Geographic* team already knew the name of the ship to which the timbers had likely belonged.[1]

The degree of certainty with which the *National Geographic* explorers and their compatriots knew the name of their quarry was the result of a multiyear, interdisciplinary, international research initiative that had sought to corroborate a legend. Since the very first presence of non-Indigenous foreigners in the region, Indigenous stories had circulated among them of a shipwreck somewhere on this part of the coast, and with them accounts of beeswax, porcelain, and even buried treasure. Such stories had inspired more than two centuries of imagining, rumor-mongering, and digging, but it was only in 2017 that a team of researchers, made up of historians and archaeologists, was able to identify the ship in question. Drawing on analysis of ancient flotsam held in local museums and archival research in Spain, Mexico, and the Philippines, the "Oregon beeswax wreck," as the mysterious vessel had been known since the early nineteenth century, was identified as *Santo Cristo de Burgos*, a Spanish galleon that had disappeared on its way from Manila to Acapulco in 1693. Published in a 2018 special issue of the *Oregon Historical Quarterly* and widely disseminated in regional news networks and beyond, the identification of the ship inspired new interest in the long-standing mystery of its origins and fate.[2] And when the timbers discovered four years later were analyzed and found to be made of a type of wood found in the Philippines, that only sealed the deal. This time, media around the world paid attention.

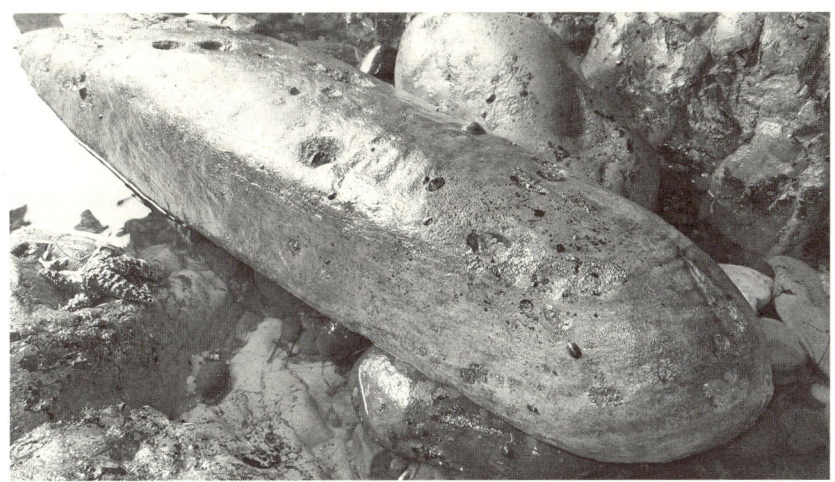

A fragment of the Spanish galleon *Santo Cristo de Burgos*, wrecked on the Oregon coast in 1693 and rediscovered in 2022. *Photo by Scott Williams*

Settler history is just as often made up of rumors as it is of verifiable facts, especially when it comes to the inevitable murkiness of a region's early colonial history. As Manu Karuka has argued in his work on narratives of the transcontinental railroad, the Chinese men who built it, and the Indigenous nations through whose territory it was built, rumor—whether of the colonizer or colonized—is bound up closely in the ways in which power is justified, exercised, and remembered or rendered invisible. This is all the more true when our queries have to do with Indigenous knowledge that has experienced the brunt of violent change. "The unanswerability of these questions," Karuka writes, "is itself a product of colonialism."[3] The possibility of a seventeenth-century fact, meanwhile, extended the colonial history of the Northwest Coast back by almost a full century, even if the history that came after was rife with conflicting information, wishful thinking, and outright fabulation. In the thirty-three decades since *Santo Cristo de Burgos* ran ashore near Neahkahnie Mountain, accounts of the beeswax wreck highlighted the unstable, mutable, and often capricious nature of settler histories, and yet, at the same, they drew attention to another truth: that the foundation of much of the history of the Graveyard of the Pacific is in fact Indigenous knowledge. Often misinterpreted, disregarded, or mythologized beyond easy recognition, Indigenous historical traditions—in this case the story of an ancient maritime misfortune—appear more consistent and stable than their settler analogues. As we sift through the layers of the colonial archive, moving backward in time, we find a stratigraphy of colonial desire built upon an Indigenous bedrock, eroded and yet enduring as Neahkahnie itself.

————

In the early decades of the seventeenth century, the Pacific was very much up for grabs in the eyes of various European empires. The Spanish, Dutch, French, English, and other imperial entities saw in the vast oceanic realm opportunities for new knowledge but also, more importantly, new wealth. The competition was fierce and often violent, including in 1632, when a privateer named William Pordobel, well-known for his one good eye, roamed the coastline of North America aboard his vessel *Inferno*. He had been a successful pirate, his coffers full of doubloons, jewelry, and other treasures. But fate would be cruel to Pordobel. The British Armada turned on him, and he made his last stand along the coast of Oregon. There, he sailed *Inferno* into a sea cave, but his hiding place was soon discovered, and the British authorities blew up the entrance to the cavern, with Pordobel and his crew sealed inside. In his desperation and maniacal greed, Pordobel killed all his crew and booby-trapped the cave before his own death. For centuries to come, *Inferno* would wait, silent and sailing in place.

Of course, none of this happened. But Richard Donner's adventure comedy *The Goonies*, released in 1985, presented the Oregon coast to the world on a cinematic scale through the story of One-Eyed Willy and *Inferno*. Filmed in Astoria and at several places on the outer coast, the movie was based on an original concept concocted by Steven Spielberg (which may not have been very original, as we shall see). It told the story of a group of kids from the "Goon Docks" of Astoria who, facing foreclosure on their families' homes and their entire neighborhood, luckily find a treasure map that points them toward One-Eyed Willy's gems and doubloons. Many hijinks ensue, but it is the final scene that sticks. In it, *Inferno*, crewed only by skeletons, is freed from its cavernous prison and sails off into the distance while the gang and their families watch, stunned, from the beach. The three-masted ship, straight out of every pirate movie ever made, had been liberated and was off to new adventures. Meanwhile, the plucky kids had managed to steal just enough treasure to stave off their neighborhood's destruction. A happy ending indeed.[4]

Shipwreck historian Cameron La Follette, who grew up in Oregon, recalled the place of *The Goonies* in her memory and imagination. "*The Goonies* was my sick movie, my 'Mom, I'm bored' movie, my Saturday afternoon movie, watched over grilled cheese and tomato soup," she told *Atavist Magazine* in 2020, in a story about the beeswax wreck. "Here's the thing I realized about *The Goonies*," La Follette continued. "It's a story where, in the end, wealth brings happiness. Jewels are salve for the world's problems—foreclosure, gentrification. The final scenes of the movie tell aspiring Goonies to take note: adventure itself is only good if it turns up something of value. Your spirit and cunning are, in isolation, frivolous things to be tucked away in an attic, just like Mikey's dad did with that dusty old map. Had they found nothing, Mikey and Chunk and Stef and Data merely would have worried their parents sick for a day."[5] Whatever its message (and whatever its filmic merits), *The Goonies* is now an indelible part of Pacific Northwest history, particularly for those who came of age in the final two decades of the twentieth century. The Astoria house where the kids hung out remains a tourist attraction despite its owners' attempts to keep curious fans away, and Goonies memorabilia appears in many local shops catering to visitors from Portland and beyond. But for all of its discombobulation of the actual history of the Oregon coast,

Donner's film has nothing on some of the other stories told about what would eventually be identified as *Santo Cristo de Burgos.*

————

In August of 1988, a man named Tony Mareno (sometimes known as Edward M. Fire) applied for a permit to dig on the beach at Nehalem, immediately to the south of Neahkahnie Mountain. This was not his first application; in fact, he had first sought permits to explore for treasure as early as the late 1960s. Over those years, he had developed elaborate theories about the nature and location of an alleged Neahkahnie trove associated with an early shipwreck. They involved biblical passages—most notably ones dealing with the Ark of the Covenant and the construction of Solomon's Temple—as well as references to constellations and to mysterious markings on stones that had been found in the area since the middle of the nineteenth century. He also claimed that the value of the treasure, gold and silver and more, might be upwards of two billion dollars. His use of a bulldozer and augur on the beach, however, concerned both state officials and local residents and led to the creation of a new Oregon State law around treasure hunting that would frustrate many of Mareno's efforts to find what we now know was *Santo Cristo de Burgos.*[6]

Tony Mareno, for all his eccentricities, was far from unique in his zeal for the mystery of the mountain. The 1980s saw another treasure seeker, a Bill Warren of Carlsbad, California, and owner of Golden Quests Inc., apply for a permit to dig for Spanish treasure on and near the beaches around Neahkahnie. His venture would involve a higher degree of technological practices, including remote sensing, careful excavation, and conservation of artifacts, but it was clear all the while that his was, ultimately, a commercial venture. As historians Cameron La Follette, Dennis Griffin, and Douglas Deur have illustrated in their account of Neahkahnie treasure seekers, Warren's relationship with both government employees and people who lived near the mountain was, in their words, "prickly." Indeed, as they show, Warren's activities inspired a new statute overseeing "treasure trove" discoveries. In return, Warren actively harassed state officials in both the Department of State Lands and the governor's office, accusing them of running a police state and receiving strongly worded warnings in response to his insults and threats. A rumor of treasure, it seemed, could be a powerful motivator for bad behavior.[7]

Other hopeful men had launched their own investigations into the phenomenon of the beeswax wreck in the late 1970s. Dean Grimes was one of them. Having founded the Tillamook Treasures company in 1970, by 1974 he and his colleagues were applying for permits to dig at Neahkahnie. Their claims centered on a collection of stones, found near the mountain, that bore arcane markings. Five years later, Grimes used these markings—which he admitted he had etched to make them clearer—along with other "evidence" to make the case to the Department of State Lands that Neahkahnie was home to treasure. Like those who would come after, Grimes connected the purported hoard to biblical passages. The twelve stones, he argued, had come from the Wailing Wall in Jerusalem. "The Bible says it's there, my camera says it's there," he told the *Tillamook Headlight Herald* in 1983. That same year, meanwhile, Grimes's partner Bud Kretsinger invoked Moses, King Solomon, and even the Queen of Sheba in his claims to the right to dig. The question of the carved stones, meanwhile, was always close to the center of Neahkahnie wrecklore. In 1971, a local treasure hunter named Orval Keller, who had been searching for almost two decades, applied to DSL for a permit claiming he had decoded the meanings of the carvings on the stones: an etching of a rabbit, for example, denoted gold.[8]

Perhaps the most outlandish story of the lost galleon had come a decade earlier, in 1961. That was the year that a man named Chris Mehlig from Cannon Beach claimed to have watched divers transfer treasure from a wreck to a submarine lying in wait offshore. Over four days and nights, Mehlig argued, the treasure of Neahkahnie had been absconded with by men who then paid taxes on $1.25 million worth of gold in cash at the Internal Revenue Service in Seattle. How Mehlig knew any of this is unclear, but while it is perhaps the most explicitly conspiratorial piece of *Santo Cristo de Burgos* wrecklore, it is still very much in keeping with other stories that had accreted around the lost vessel.[9]

In the late 1950s, more formal excavations had been taking place not far from Neahkahnie. At Netarts Spit, for example, some thirty miles to the south, trained archaeologists from the University of Oregon found bits of porcelain from the late Ming or early Qing dynasties and linked the fragments to similar ones—and to beeswax—found further north.[10] But other, more informal, sorts of forays continued as well: in 1958, treasure hunters from Seattle dug a 125-foot-deep pit next to Highway 101, a location they had chosen thanks to the trembling of a dowsing rod.[11] Whether informed by science or inspired by more occult practices, the wrecklore of *Santo Cristo de Burgos* had continued to fuel exploration and meticulous, if also destructive, research. Going still deeper into Neahkahnie's archive, we can see some of the origins of these mythologies, of these evocations of a half-forgotten past.

————————

In 1946, the Portland station KGW debuted a radio play that imagined the history of Neahkahnie's treasure. It began with a description of the mountain as a "place of romance and mystery," then continued with the questions that were at the heart of its fictional portrayal: "Is it true that impassive Neahkahnie Mountain holds a secret 266 years old? Does a fortune beyond the wildest dream lie buried somewhere in that mountainside? Gold doubloons . . . silver ingots . . . and even the bones of Spanish pirates? Mysterious marked beeswax and strangely-figured stones would have us believe so." The script continues with three actors voicing survivors of the 1679 destruction of a Spanish ship called *Guerrero*: Jacques, Don Emanuel, and Zemwa, an enslaved African who is portrayed in baldly racist terms. As the three lug their vessel's treasure up the mountain, Jacques reveals that he has a plan: after the men dig a deep hole and deposit in it their eighty thousand doubloons, Zemwa will be killed, leaving his spirit guarding the treasure from the depredations of local Indigenous people. And this is what happens; the radio play describes the result by indicating that "his black blood darkens the treasure-chest beneath him," while also noting that Don Emanuel was mortally wounded in the struggle. Carefully placing beeswax and figured stones to mark the location of their treasure, the pair prepares to depart—but then, suddenly, Don Emanuel stabs Jacques to death as well. In the end, none of the three shipwreck survivors would live to return to the site of their hoard.

The narration ends with an encapsulation of the enduring mystery that came of all this, and with a gesture toward the seemingly futile labor of treasure seekers: "Today the legend of Neahkahnie treasure lives on. The discovery of marked stones and figured beeswax on the mountainside has brought treasure-seekers from many miles around. Every method to determine the location of the fabulous pirate loot, from mathematical to spiritual, has been used, until the side of Neahkahnie Mountain is pockmarked with holes. In search of the Eldorado, one man dug for nine years . . . but the treasure, if such there is, has never been found on the stoical face of Neahkahnie Mountain." The 1946 radio play brings together all the elements of the story: piracy and treasure, the marked stones and beeswax, even murder. The mountain itself seems an active participant in the story, observing the men who dig in its slopes and keeping its own counsel.[12]

One of the people who might have listened to the KGW radio play, or who was at least inspired by the same wrecklore, was a man called Milo Merrill. As La Follette, Griffin, and Deur illustrate, Merrill had developed a theory that Spanish explorers had left some three hundred caches of gold and other treasure in sites around the Americas, to aid in eventual colonization. Merrill argued that more than twenty of those caches were buried somewhere on Neahkahnie and claimed to have cracked the Spanish code that would lead to a shocking and lucrative discovery. Relying on his interpretation of the marked stones and on what he understood as Spanish surveying practices, Merrill was certain he would eventually find his quarry. He did not. Meanwhile, for some erstwhile treasure seekers, the search could be dangerous and even fatal: in 1931, two Portland men, a father and son, died when the thirty-foot shaft they had dug on the side of Neahkahnie caved in on them.[13]

As men sought treasure on the mountain in the 1930s, a trio of women gave shape during the same decade to the Indigenous history of early shipwrecks. The linguist May Edel, for example, collected a story from Nehalem-Tillamook elder Clara Pearson early that decade:

These Indians were staying there at Nehalem. They went up river hunting Elk. One old person came down river. He saw at Kronan Place [Cronin Point] what kind of people he didn't know. Their clothes were dark with bright buttons. The Indian went over nevertheless to these people. He didn't land. They threw him beads and dentalium. They fell in his canoe. He went up river. He didn't land. He was afraid. He went back and told what he had seen, showed the beads. Then the next day they all went down. The wives of the Indians wanted to see the beads. The woman all landed. The white man gave out the beads to the women. They fed the Indians hardtack and molasses. Soon the white men wanted women. They had beeswax ashore. They kept on going, then they pack a large chest with money. They buried it deep in the ground. Some of the white people went. The rest stayed with the Indians. The white people learned how to talk Tillamook. The white people tried to teach the Indians white people's language. The Indians don't know. They cut iron and hammer it cold to make a knife. The white man took the iron and put it in the fire. He was going to teach them. This Indian grabbed the iron. He said, "He burned the iron." The white man poohed him. Finally the white man got tired. They wanted to go back. Evenings at sunset, these white men cried. They were lonely. And the white men said, "over there where the sun comes from there we come from." Then they said, "Let's go." They went to Seaside.[14]

While not identifying the wrecked ship as specifically Spanish, Pearson's account included many of the elements of the wrecklore that would drive men like Merrill and the others who came after him to spend years of their lives and large sums of their own money to pursue treasure on and around Neahkahnie Mountain.

Similarly, in 1933, an article in the *Washington Historical Quarterly* presented an account from Nehalem-Tillamook elder Ellen Center about what appears to be a different early shipwreck and the fate of its lone survivor. She had heard the story from her parents and presented it as "part of the history of their tribe." Paraphrased by historian J. Neilson Barry, the story went something like this: "A long, long time ago, a ship was wrecked off Nehalem Bay, and part of it broke off and drifted into the bay. On this was a white youth, unconscious. The friendly Indians succeeded in reviving him, and he subsequently married, had children and lived among the tribe. What seems to have particularly impressed the Indians was that when smallpox almost exterminated the tribe this sailor left his family and nursed the sick Indians, and so took the disease and lost his life."[15] Lastly, ethnologist Elizabeth Jacobs, working alongside her husband among the Nehalem-Tillamook, made note of the uses to which the people whose ancestral territory included Neahkahnie had put the beeswax they found on their beaches: the sealing of canoes, the waterproofing of cedar bark clothing, the concoction of salves to help with infections from tattooing, and possibly the creation of candles or lamps.[16] These stories—notably shared or collected by women—stand in contrast to the more eccentric imaginings of the male treasure hunters.

Some of the beeswax from *Santo Cristo de Burgos*, subject of much speculation over the last three centuries and then some. *Photo by Carmen Ripollés and Jesse Locker*

Instead of decoded stones and murdered slaves, constellations and the Queen of Sheba, we learn of social relations and trade with newcomers, everyday Indigenous life, and the incorporation of strange materials into quotidian uses. They are Indigenous accounts before all else, in which fantasies of treasure are muted or elided entirely. At the same time, however, the Nehalem-Tillamook stories shared in the 1930s are also part of the bedrock upon which the fanciful theories were built—theories on which men like Tony Mareno would later stake their claims and reputations.

The layers of settler fantasy go deep at Neahkahnie, though. In 1927, writer D. F. Howard published a historical novel about two Spanish survivors of a shipwreck on the Oregon coast. Both men fell in love with the daughters of local leaders, and one of the men, named Desoto, gave the name "Arigan" to the great river now known as Columbia. The rest of the story follows the men's return journey with their wives and, in Desoto's case, a son. They voyage through Mexico and Panama, at last arriving in Spain. Howard ends his novel with a poem that tells us a great deal both about the white imagination of early colonial history in the region and about the Indigenous knowledge that is its foundation:

> There's an Indian legend, handed
>> Down the past from sire to son,
> Of an unknown ship that stranded
>> On the coast of Oregon
> Long before the conq'ring pale men—
>> Fire and thunder at command—
> Ever heard of the Nehalem
>> Ever saw this western land.
> This is what the legend tells us,
>> With deductions reason casts,
> Of historic tales to guide us,
>> Of this mystery of the past. . . .
> Who the men and what their number,
>> Manned that pirate ship so bold?
> Old Neahkahnie's rocks shall crumble
>> Ere the mystic tale is told.[17]

In 1912, decades before the construction of a highway around Neah-kahnie's high cliffs, a tavern and hotel bearing the mountain's name was built. Owner Samuel G. Reed of Portland, seeking to draw tourists to what was at the time a very remote place, cast his lot with wrecklore. Broadcasting stories of the marked stones to market his business, he actively invited his guests to participate in the mystery of the buried treasure: he gave them shovels.[18]

In 1899, two men told different sorts of shipwreck stories.

In Portland, the Oregon Historical Society was holding its first ever meeting, and the featured speaker was a particularly unique individual. Born in 1839 to a Fort Vancouver teacher and the daughter of an important Clatsop chief, Silas Smith was also an attorney, having been admitted to the Oregon bar in 1876. Now, toward the end of his life, Smith had come to the historical society's annual meeting to share accounts of early wrecks on the Oregon coast. "Tradition among the Indian tribes at the mouth of the Columbia river and vicinity," he told the assembled audience, "tells us that long prior to that time their shores had been visited by at least three other vessels." He recounted the three ships: the treasure ship at Neahkahnie, the beeswax ship at Nehalem—which he identified as the galleon *San Jose* out of La Paz, Mexico—and a third near the mouth of the Columbia. Smith noted that the treasure ship didn't actually wreck, although the stories of buried treasure were, according to his people's historical tradition, true. At the same time, he said, "the natives have never pretended to know what was in that chest." Smith was more than aware of the interest settlers had developed in the treasure, noting that "it has developed a sort of literature peculiarly its own, and the end is not yet." Just as the founding meeting of a historical society featured an Indigenous knowledge keeper, the origins of wrecklore on the Oregon coast lay in Clatsop, Nehalem-Tillamook, and other Indigenous historical traditions.[19]

The same year that Silas Smith took the stage in Portland, another man was on the beach at Nehalem, just south of Neahkahnie. His name was Thomas Rogers, and while he lived in McMinnville over the Coast Range, he spent a great deal of time on the Pacific shore. In September 1899, he and a friend met a local named Pat Smith who was sawing walking canes out of heavy teakwood timbers taken from the remains of a ship. "The shifting sands," one account described, "had exposed the hull of an ancient wreck. This wreckage had supplied his cane-factory, and he had stored his woodshed with the precious raw material, against any possible scarcity that might be caused by relic hunters carrying off the wreck." Rogers and his friend each accepted a cane from Smith but declined to take away a timber, given that teak weighed nearly as much as iron. The account continued by linking the debris to deep history: "No wreck has occurred on that beach since the settlement of the Oregon coast, and there can be little doubt that this is the vessel from which came the beeswax which has been so plentifully found in that locality [and] the subject of many theories and surmises." "Mr. Rogers," the account went on to report, "says the Indians are as greatly excited over the find as are the whites. They have a tradition handed down from generation to generation, of a fight at sea between two monster 'canims' [canoes] and of one of them coming ashore on Nehalem beach. They believe this to be the same ship described by their forefathers, and are proud of the fact that proof of the story has been preserved and disclosed to the doubting white people."[20] Whatever the complex and conflicting stories of shipwrecks on the northern Oregon coast, Indigenous knowledge was at the center of the story.

Rogers was far from a dispassionate observer to the wrecklore of early coastal encounters; indeed, he was an important contributor to the "literature peculiarly of its own" to which Silas Smith had referred. The year before his trip to see Pat Smith, in 1898, Rogers had published a novel simply titled *Nehalem*. The fictional account of a shipwreck and its aftermath drew together many aspects of the legend of the treasure ship. In the work, a doctor named Thomas Moore, the "hermit of Nehalem," discovers a Spanish manuscript written by castaway Don Emanuel Zapata. Moore translates the manuscript, which includes an account of Zapata's life, his castaway experience after the wreck of his ship *Guerrero*, and his return home. Obviously the source material for the 1946 radio play, the plot of *Nehalem* also bears a strong resemblance to *The Goonies*; the novel features a large sea cave deep inside Neahkanie Mountain, and a Spanish doubloon plays an almost talismanic role in the story, not unlike in Richard Donner's 1985 film. Unlike the beloved adventure movie, however, Indigenous knowledge is at the root of the legend of *Guerrero*: a local Native guide leads the protagonist into the heart of the mountain.[21]

In historical lectures and works of fiction alike, Indigenous knowledge had migrated in the 1890s into what was becoming a canon of Oregon coast history and of the region more broadly. When E. W. Wright published *Lewis & Dryden's Marine History of the Pacific Northwest* in 1895, it included an entry about the beeswax wreck that centered on Indigenous historical narrative:

> In 1772, according to well-authenticated stories and traditions, one of Spain's Oriental fleet, while on a voyage from China, laden with beeswax and Chinese bric-a-brac, was blown to the northward and wrecked near the mouth of the Columbia. Most historical writers have given the location of this wreck as being on the north side of the Columbia, but there is a strong possibility that the scene of the wreck was near the mouth of the Nehalem River, at which place large quantities of beeswax have been and are still being found. Aside from the presence of the beeswax and other traces of the wreck, the Tillamook Indians have had the story handed down with considerable accuracy. Adam, a Tillamook chief, who died at Tillamook a few years ago, and who was a remarkably intelligent Indian, told the writer that his father, when a young man, had witnessed the wreck, and that all of the crew were drowned. As Adam was over one hundred years old at the time of his death, there is no reason to doubt that the Nehalem beeswax ship, of which so much has been written, was identical with the one wrecked in 1772.[22]

Although it transposed the wreck into the wrong century, the entry highlighted the fact that, at its core, this was an Indigenous story.

At the same time, however, it was a story that had found a place in the historical canon of the region. When historian Frances Fuller Victor included it in her travel narrative *Atlantis Arisen*, published in 1891, she linked the beeswax to an imagined Japanese vessel. "If the tourist is so fortunate as to secure an old Astorian for a guide, he may, if he chooses, call up manifold 'spirits from the vastly deep,'" she wrote. "One of the stories of wreck a century or so ago relates to our almond-eyed neighbors at the antipodes," Victor continued.

> The story-teller will most likely take from his pocket, where he must have placed it for this purpose, a thin cake of beeswax, well sanded over, which he avers was a portion of the cargo of a Japanese junk, cast ashore near the Columbia in some time out of mind. When we have wondered over this, to us, singular evidence of wrecking, he produces another, in the form of a waxen tube. At this we are more stultified than before, and then are told that this was a large wax candle, such as the Japanese priest, as well as the Roman, uses to burn before altars. The wick is entirely rotted out, leaving the candle a hollow cylinder of wax.

Victor's account of the beeswax wreck alluded to the different versions of the story that had been circulating in the late nineteenth century. "By this self-evident explanation," she ended, "we are convinced."[23]

———

Victor and Rogers both were mediums in a way; far from creating something entirely new in their accounts of marine caverns and Japanese vessels, they were both giving voice to stories that had already been migrating throughout the region. Early settlers to the Oregon coast all seem to have known the stories of these early wrecks, and their knowledge forms another layer down into Neahkahnie's archive. In July of 1883, for example, the *Daily Astorian* printed an article about the beeswax wreck by an unnamed resident of Seaside, highlighting Indigenous accounts:

> When I came here in 1843 I made all inquiries that anyone could concerning that wreck more on account of the great treasure that the Indians say was deposited there by those people. It was at the mouth of

the Nehalem River; there were thirty in number: that they had tails on their heads. They were white but not as white as we are. They were made slaves of by the Indians. When they came in from work they would sit with their backs to the wall to keep the children from bothering them. There was a blacksmith amongst them; they would go down the beach at sundown and cry, and tell the Indians that was where they lived. . . . This wreck was so many generations ago that the Indians have no idea when, but the beeswax is in there to this day.[24]

Meanwhile, George Gibbs, another early settler in Oregon and a key commentator on Indigenous-settler relations in the third quarter of the nineteenth century, wrote of the treasure ship anchored at Nehalem off Neahkahnie. "About twenty armed men, with cutlasses, came on shore," he wrote in the 1870s,

> bringing an iron chest, which they carried about two miles back in to the country, to a spot where an Indian trail crosses a brook on the south side of the promontory. The place was east of the trail and south of the brook. There they buried it between two rocks, letting down another on top, and cut an inscription of the rock. They then killed a man and went away. Some years ago, a party of Oregonians went to search for this box, under the impression that it was hidden treasure, but were unsuccessful, for, although the place is ascertained within a short distance, their Indian guides would not approach it. The incident of a man being killed on the spot is probably an Indian addition, drawn from their own usages.

Gibbs distinguished the treasure ship from the beeswax wreck. Of the latter misfortune, he described how the crew came ashore and lived among the Nehalem-Tillamook for a time, until their behavior toward local women "created an excitement," and eventually all the newcomers were killed. Of the beeswax, meanwhile, Gibbs noted that it "has often been mentioned by travelers, and pieces of it continue to be found after westerly storms. This vessel was probably a Japanese junk, several of which have from time to time been cast away on the coast." Gibbs also claimed that the Nehalem-Tillamook looked more "Asian" than their neighbors, suggesting a genetic link to shipwrecked Japanese voyagers.[25]

In these late nineteenth-century accounts, we can see confusion. Two ships? Three? Spanish? Japanese? Wrecked or merely anchored for a time? The crew adopted or killed? Many commenters on the history of early ships visiting the coast drew attention to this confusion. But no matter what the various versions of the story claimed, it was Indigenous knowledge that was at the core of that story. When settler and Indian agent James Swan published his account of his time in Washington Territory in the 1850s, for example, he recalled obtaining some of the mysterious flotsam: "I have had some of this wax given me by an old Indian doctor, who had picked it up on the beach. The crevices were still full of sand, and the action of salt water and sun had bleached it nearly white." He sent it to the California Academy of Natural Sciences.[26] Meanwhile, settler Hiram Smith, who built a homestead in Bay City south of Neahkahnie, found some of the marked stones that would feature so prominently in later, more fantastical components of local wrecklore.[27] And when John Hobson, one of the first Americans to settle in Oregon, visited Nehalem in 1848, he was led there by Coboway, an important Clatsop leader, and soon heard the story of both beeswax and treasure. "All they could tell us," he told the *Oregonian*, "was that long before they were born, the wax vessel was lost on the spit, and another anchored near the shore, and some people brought a chest up on Necanny [*sic*] Mountain and carried sacks of money and put them in the chest and killed a man, and put also in the chest. Afterward they marked a stone, or very large rock, rolled it on the chest, and went back to the ship and sailed away."[28] If the process of becoming local involved learning the stories of this place, then accounts of shipwrecks and treasure were at the very heart of the venture we call resettlement. In fact, they predated it.

Before American resettlement, there was the fur trade, and in that period—the first half of the nineteenth century—we can see the origins of the wrecklore that would drive men to dig pits in a mountain. When fur trader Alexander Henry visited the mouth of the Columbia in 1813, he described how an "old Clatsop chief" brought beaver meat and skins to trade, along with three trout and a few pounds of beeswax.[29] A few years earlier, John Ordway, a member of the United States' Corps of Discovery under the leadership of William Clark and Meriwether Lewis, had recounted how on a Sunday morning in March 1806, "several of the Clatsop Indians came to the Fort with Some Small fish and a little bears [sic] wax to trade to us."[30] Long before archaeologists or conspiracy theorists took up the wrecklore of Neahkahnie, the mysterious beeswax was already there, appearing in even the earliest newcomer accounts.

These accounts also often spoke to another sort of evidence for shipwreck: that found in Indigenous bodies. Alexander Henry gave one example, describing a man of about thirty years of age who had "extraordinary dark red hair and is much freckled—a supposed offspring of a ship that was wrecked within a few miles of the entrance of this river many years ago. Great quantities of beeswax continue to be dug out of the sand near this spot, and the Indians bring it to trade with us."[31] Meanwhile, fur trader Ross Cox, at Astoria in 1814, described the same man:

He was a perfect *lusus naturae*; and his history was rather curious. His skin was fair, his face partially freckled, and his hair quite red. He was about five feet ten inches high, was slender and remarkably well made; his head had not undergone the flattening process; and he was called Jack Ramsay, in consequence of that name having been punctured on his left arm. The Indians allege that his father was an English sailor, who had deserted from a trading vessel, and had lived many years among the tribe, one of whom he married; that when Jack was born he insisted on preserving the child's head in its natural state, and while young had punctured the arm in the above manner. Old Ramsay had died about twenty years before this period; he had several more children, but Jack was the only red-headed one among them.[32]

While not necessarily descended from *Santo Cristo de Burgos* specifically, the presence of Jack Ramsay—or Lamazee, as he was sometimes called—spoke to an early history in which shipwreck survivors, as they would be elsewhere, were incorporated into local Indigenous communities.

Another fur trader, Gabriel Franchère, described a second shipwreck descendant he encountered during his visit to the Columbia estuary in the 1810s: "We found here an old blind man, who gave us a cordial reception," Franchère wrote.

> Our guide said that he was a white man, and that his name was Soto. We learned from the mouth of the old man himself, that he was the son of a Spaniard who had been wrecked at the mouth of the river; that a part of the crew on this occasion got safe ashore, but were all massacred by the Clatsops, with the exception of four, who were spared and who married native women; that these four Spaniards, of whom his father was one, disgusted with the savage life, attempted to reach a settlement of their own nation toward the south, but had never been heard of since; and that when his father, with his companions, left the country, he himself was yet quite young.[33]

Here, the archive of Neahkahnie, and of the Oregon coast more generally, sets stories of treasure and beeswax within a matrix of kinship and family. One early Nehalem-Tillamook chief known to many fur traders, Kilchis, claimed descent from a Black blacksmith who survived a shipwreck, and accounts of the man often mention his height and curly hair.[34] Meanwhile, other local Indigenous people claimed descent from different wreck survivors, noting the red hair and freckles borne by some members of their communities and families, much like Jack Ramsay.[35] In this, Indigenous knowledge keepers were doing more than offering

Along with beeswax, *Santo Cristo de Burgos* carried a cargo that included porcelain. Local Indigenous peoples such as the Nehalem traded chinaware and sometimes made projectile points from it, which have been found in archaeology sites along the coast. *Tillamook County Pioneer Museum*

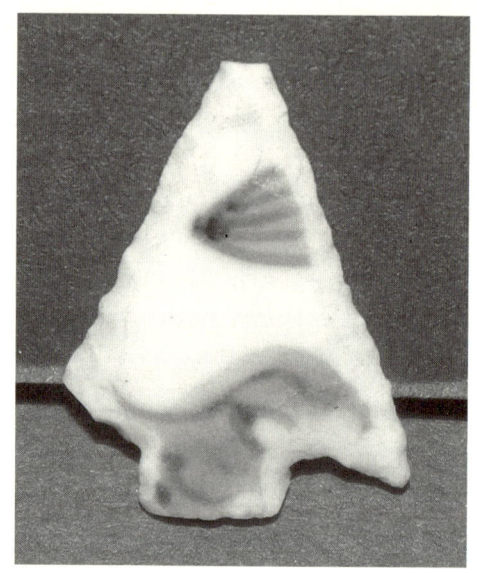

titillating accounts of marine disaster; instead, they were describing intimate, familial relations with shipwrecked newcomers and setting their stories within networks of kinship that had stretched along the coast long before any foreign ship ever approached the shore.

———————

January 26, 1700: the depth of winter, the heart of storytelling season. It's night on the Nehalem, families tucked cozily into longhouses curving around the lip of the estuary, protected from the open Pacific by a wide spit. As the people prepare to sleep, one man sits working on a new arrowhead, chipping away to find its shape in the raw material. But this is no typical projectile point; it is neither chert nor obsidian. It is porcelain, bright white and blue in the light of the fire. Taken from a strange giant canoe that had come to the Nehalem shore a few years earlier, wrecking itself in the sands, the porcelain glimmers in the flickering light as the hunter works carefully at its sharp edges.

Suddenly, the earth begins to shake violently. The longhouse rattles and sways, and the people—children, women, men, old people—cry out in fear. Out in the night, the sea withdraws from the shore; had anyone been out there in the darkness to witness it, they would have seen the surf pull far away, revealing deep places no human person should ever see. Then, the sea comes back in, in vast house-high white waves. The waves overrun the spit and barrel toward the homes of the Nehalem as, all along the coast, the tsunami rushes eastward: running up river valleys, crashing against cliffs, and tearing all asunder as the earthshaking subsides.[36]

Somewhere in the midst of this obliteration rest the hardwood bones of a ship, source of the porcelain the hunter had been making into an arrowhead and origin of the strange yellow pitch-like substance that the people have been experimenting with for the past few years. The violent surf tears apart whatever remains of the vessel. Some of its beams, caught in the maelstrom, are thrown high above the tide line, into a cave at the foot of the mountain where the Great Spirit lives.

———

Seven years earlier, in 1693, a ship approaches the coast, and it's not supposed to be there. It was intended for Acapulco, having left Manila several months before. But something has gone wrong: a storm, the loss of a rudder, a massive error in navigation—what, exactly, we will never know for certain. The crew surveys the shore, perhaps in falling rain: the long, low spit at Nehalem, the huge bulk of Neahkahnie. Or maybe all is shrouded in mist or fog, until the sound of breakers warns the men of their vessel's doom. Perhaps it jams itself into the sand on Nehalem Spit, or maybe it shatters against the rocks at the base of Neahkahnie Mountain. No matter the specifics, *Santo Cristo de Burgos*, in our reverse history, has finally arrived.

The galleon's crew, under the leadership of General Don Bernardo Iñiguez del Bayo y de Pradilla, a Basque noble who served as alcalde of

San Luis de Potosí in Mexico before joining the galleon trade, consists of more than 150 men. Most are Spanish, but many are likely Filipino or perhaps even Mexican *indios*. From artillerymen and blacksmiths to skilled seamen and even a few priests as passengers, the ship's community reflects the high-stakes and militarized nature of the galleon trade, which links Spain to Mexico and to the Philippines and Asia more broadly. *Santo Cristo de Burgos*'s cargo tells the story of these connections: cotton fabric from India, Chinese silks and paper fans, ivory votive sculptures, and of course beeswax and porcelain. We can imagine this cargo shifting and bumping as the galleon runs ashore, and we can imagine the people of Nehalem rushing out to see the spectacle of one of the "castles of the sea" come aground in their homeland. What happens next, though, is a mystery. Perhaps most of the crew drowned; perhaps some survived only to be killed by wary locals; perhaps some came to live with their new hosts and became Nehalem-Tillamook ancestors in their own right. Whatever the outcome, *Santo Cristo de Burgos* was beginning to suture together a new kind of Pacific world, if only by accident, and it remains the earliest known colonial presence on the coast.[37]

———

When the fragmentary remains of *Santo Cristo de Burgos* were finally found in the sea cave at the base of Neahkahnie Mountain in 2022—in a strange echo of both Rogers's novel *Nehalem* and *The Goonies*—a certain kind of mystery came to an end. Those centuries of stories about beeswax and porcelain, doubloons and murder, came to rest in the form of worn tropical hardwood beams that now lie in the collections of the Columbia River Maritime Museum in Astoria. The discovery represented the culmination not just of decades upon decades of wrecklore, legendry, and fantasy but also of years of dedicated research that had taken scholars not just into the archives of small museums and historical societies in Oregon but to Mexico, Spain, and the Philippines. The journeys of historians had, after a fashion, replicated the passage of the ship and its cargo.

As we have seen in the stories of the beeswax wreck, though, it is Indigenous tradition that holds the whole tale together. That knowledge is the sturdy weave of the past, through which settler rumors and theories and dowsing rods are imbricated. Whatever its at times seemingly fragmented nature—a fragmentation that should surprise no one, given the history of dispossession and forced relocation that removed the Nehalem-Tillamook from the lands and waters around Neahkahnie— there is also a surprising consistency to the accounts of early visitors to the coast: the appearance of great canoes crewed by strange animal-like men, the new things that they carried, the family connections made with survivors. Most importantly, though, the finding of *Santo Cristo de Burgos* vindicated oral tradition by giving material weight to ancient story. As Robert Kentta, former cultural resources manager and council member of the Confederated Tribes of Siletz Indians commented at the time, the discovery confirmed "that our ancestral people knew what they were talking about." In an interview in early 2024, Kentta said that when asked whether the discovery changed anything for him and his community, the answer was no. "It doesn't change anything," he said. "It confirms that the elders' stories ring true." Kentta also noted that for some young people at Siletz, especially those who have ancestry on the northern Oregon coast, the finding of the timbers is part of a "reawakening... it reinvigorates their interest in that part of their homelands."[38] As they have done elsewhere in the Graveyard of the Pacific, shipwrecks can serve stories of resurgence and deep connections between past and present.

Neahkahnie looms still, a place dense with fact and fantasy both. Such places tend to gather stories to themselves, and certainly the commanding presence of the place demands a kind of humility, even as it has inspired wild hubris and deep pits. It might be tempting to dismiss the men who dug obsessively on the spit and on the mountain as little more than cranks. As Cameron La Follette argues, though, there is another way to think about them. "Nobody who walks the borders of new ideas is going to be ordinary," she told *Atavist* in 2020. "They were responding in their own way to the enormous and powerful presence of Neahkahnie Mountain. And also responding to the ancient but vague tragedy."[39] It is true that the history of *Santo Cristo de Burgos* is necessarily vague, as is that of the other phantom ships of those early years, about which only fragments remain in Indigenous oral traditions. One ship is mistaken for a second or even third, stories are concatenated into each other, and all become fodder for settler rumor.

The twentieth-century French historian Fernand Braudel, whose work on the Mediterranean's long history has influenced those who write about place around the world, once offered a metaphor for thinking about the past at different scales. There are waves, tides, and the deep, he wrote. Waves are the small, often ephemeral events: a single life, a military battle, a particular season's blight on crops. The tides represent longer oscillations such as the rise and fall of empires. And beneath all of these is the deep: the powerful structures—in Braudel's case, the geology and geography of the Mediterranean—that give shape to the histories that happen above them.[40] In the Graveyard of the Pacific, we might think of individual shipwrecks as waves; indeed, there have been so many and they have been so quotidian, and so often poorly documented, that it makes sense to think of them as quickly passing into history. There are exceptions, of course—*Valencia*, *Tonquin*, and *Santo Cristo de Burgos* perhaps most notably—but the majority have been largely forgotten or are simply lost to the archive. The deep here, meanwhile, is the deep *here*: the geological scales of sea-level changes and great glaciations and the many millennia of Indigenous presence in territories that are currently known as Oregon, Washington, and Vancouver Island, home to so many nations for so very long, so long ago as to be time immemorial, otherwise known as forever. And the tides, we might consider, are the movements of empires themselves into these spaces: the Spanish and Russians, the British and the Americans, and Canada too. That these imperial and colonial presences are but recent incursions into Indigenous space is unquestionable; in the great scheme of things, even the wreck of *Santo Cristo de Burgos* happened only yesterday. It might just be possible, then, to imagine worlds without colonialism as it shapes our lives today, as Indigenous nations work to claim jurisdiction and sovereignty over terrestrial and marine spaces of the Northwest Coast. Such histories and stories invite us to ask, *Is the tide still coming in, or is it going out?*

The Wreck at the Edge of the World

IT IS HALLOWEEN MORNING. The day is crisp and blue over dark sands, golden beach grass, and deep green shore pines on Clatsop Spit at the southern side of the Columbia. Here, a rusting shipwreck the color of rotting cedar slumps in the tide: the bark *Peter Iredale*, cast ashore in thick rainy weather in 1906 and a tourist icon ever since. Above it, a small drone hovers, with my old friend Wes at its controls while his nine-year-old son, Guthrie, runs and rolls down the dunes. Wes is shooting pictures for the cover of this book, aerial photos of the ship's remains pounded by white surf. Meanwhile, my research associate Sarah and I are taking notes: the beat-up red truck racing past, the two young men whooping and rushing shirtless into the surf, the families with their dogs walking by in the wind. We share satsumas, and Wes and Guthrie tell us the ghost story they made up around a campfire the night before, about Short Straw McGraw, whose cursed apparition haunts anyone who lies or cheats in this place.

A year and a half later, I bring my husband, Noah, to Clatsop Spit. It's his first time on the Oregon coast. A small shipwreck conference has been organized at the Columbia River Maritime Museum in Astoria, and we have used that as an excuse to make the trip. When we arrive at the spit, I can convince myself that *Peter Iredale* is smaller than it was the last time I was here: there's really not much of it left. We debate the exact word for the color of the sand on this cold, blustery, and rainy February morning. A few hundred feet from the wreck, a dead sperm whale—young by its size—adds a pungent ammonia tang to the otherwise-fresh air, and several groups of people gather around it at just enough of a distance to avoid the worst of the smell. Noah comments on how the waves here, big and insistent, are so different from the mostly small ones we see along the Vancouver shores of the Salish Sea. In the morning, in Cannon Beach, we'll see a herd of elk walking the sands, and later that day, we'll have razor clams in Manzanita.

Wes, Guthrie, Sarah, Noah, and I were all on the edge: not just of a continent but of entire worlds. Sutured together by the movements of a machine, places with their own distinct stories come together in a larger narrative that we call globalization, or colonialism, or empire. Here in northwesternmost Oregon, vectors of trade, opportunity, and pain merge in the form of a rusting hulk that is ensconced in a region's nostalgic heart. Sutures, after all, first require a wound.

On the morning of October 25, 1906, the British bark *Peter Iredale*, a month out from Salina Cruz, was approaching the mouth of the Columbia. As the crew attended to their tasks, all seemed normal until the wind suddenly changed. Before its crew of seventeen could take action, the Liverpool-built sailing ship was blown eastward into the sands of Clatsop Spit. When it hit, it hit hard, but no one died or was even hurt in the accident, and the crew all reached dry land safely.[1] Little did those men know, however, that their vessel would become an enduring regional symbol of times long past.

Making regular voyages across the Pacific to places like Honolulu and Melbourne in the last years of the nineteenth century and the first years of the twentieth, *Peter Iredale* was a well-known visitor to Astoria, so much so that the local newspaper lauded both ship and crew. "One of the best crews that ever left this port," noted the *Morning Astorian* in 1893, "was shipped aboard the *Peter Iredale* yesterday."[2] The next day, the paper described the spectacle of the fully rigged sailing ship moving out toward the bar: "One of the prettiest sights of the year was seen on the river yesterday when the ship *Peter Iredale*, laden down to her Plimsoll, was towed out to sea by the Escort. The bright sunshine made her clean cut rig and trim spars glitter and flash, and she was saluted as she passed downstream by the dipping of flags on the *Parthenope* and the *City of York*."[3] This was despite the fact that *Peter Iredale* had experienced minor mishaps only a short time earlier, first when its anchor snapped off and wasn't found for two days, and second when tugs had to pull it off a sandbar within sight of downtown Astoria. Indeed, the vessel's pluckiness in the face of misfortune, in addition to its successes in transpacific trade, may have explained locals' fondness for it.[4]

This fondness led to constant press attention once the much-favored bark ended up on the beach. Every little shift in its position and alteration to its state merited daily coverage. "It was discovered yesterday that the vessel was taking water preceptibly [*sic*]," wrote one reporter, while the next day's paper noted that "the owners and agents of the wrecked bark *Peter Iredale* believe that the vessel is susceptible of being saved." As winter weather came in, it threw the ship into even greater jeopardy. "The breakers are fast driving the wrecked bark *Peter Iredale* farther in shore," reported the *Morning Astorian*, "and if bad weather comes, the vessel undoubtably will come to pieces." In the coming days, the pounding surf would push the vessel farther and farther up the shore, and another local paper claimed there was "every indication that her bones will bleach in the sand." And yet, some held out hope. "A scheme is now under consideration," wrote the *Astorian* in early November, "to sink her astern with sacked sand, explore her bottom for the now-conceded leak, repair it roughly, put mushroom anchors to seaward and gradually haul her into deep water and to the nearest drydock for repair and refitting." Only a few days later, it was reported that *Peter Iredale* was "now almost on her port beam-ends, her rail being but a few feet above the sands. The current storms are the cause of her shifting over and she will be in a forlorn shape very shortly, unless the protracted bad weather abates." Finally, in January, the paper heralded the ship's final transformation from ship to shipwreck: "Word was received here yesterday that the mainmast of the British bark *Peter Iredale* went by the board on Sunday last, and that the break amidships is now six feet wide. She is fast becoming a genuine wreck."[5]

In the end, no one was to blame for the destruction of *Peter Iredale*. The final report on the matter, completed a few weeks after the accident, noted that it was the vicissitudes of a westerly wind that caused the wreck, rather than any dereliction or malfeasance on the part of the captain or crew: "We consider that prompt action was taken by the master immediately when the wind shifted, to get his ship's head off shore, and by all accounts he was ably seconded by his officers and men. Having carefully considered the evidence, we do find that the master, and his first and second officers, are in no wise to blame for the stranding of the said vessel, and their certificates having accordingly been returned to them." After praising the lifeboat crew that had effected the crew's rescue and the officers and men of the local military installation for attending to the hungry, bedraggled sailors, the report also expressed "satisfaction with the quiet and orderly behavior of the crew when in Astoria." In the annals of the Graveyard of the Pacific, then, *Peter Iredale* was a relatively happy shipwreck.[6]

In the meantime, *Peter Iredale* had become the star attraction of northwesternmost Oregon. "The magnificent weather of Sunday," reported the *Morning Astorian*, "induced well on to a thousand visitors to make the trip, though some hundreds of them may have been from closely contiguous points." Local trains were scheduled to bring visitors to the wreck, and the *Morning Astorian* printed the schedules. When another ship, *Galena*, wrecked close by in early 1907, the paper noted that both ships "are still objects of great interest to everybody who can get down to see them, and last Sunday there were hundreds of people on the beach, many of them from Portland, viewing the helpless, yet handsome derelicts." The crew, meanwhile, was on board again, and threw belaying pins, tin cups and pans, and other now-useless gear overboard to happy souvenir seekers. In return, it was reported that the crew were "living high on the good things furnished by the kind women-folk of the country-side." In the weeks after its wrecking, *Peter Iredale* had begun its long love affair with the visiting public.[7]

In those same weeks, though, some came to the ship with more nefarious intentions. A few days after the beaching, the *Morning Astorian* reported that several local men had left for the wreck on the noon train. "Fortunately the vessel has been dismantled and all movables taken off and are now under guard, and the bark herself is hard and fast aground," read the short article, "so their quest of souvenirs will be disappointing. Her anchors are also submerged beyond the predatory reach of hands such as theirs." Notices from the Lloyd's agent, warning against trespassing, appeared regularly in the paper, and in early December a Dr. Judd of Warrenton was arrested for larceny while trying to take material off the vessel, and in the same raid, a local participant named Malcom Grider drowned when he fell into the surf. Judd was eventually found not guilty, and the *Morning Astorian* quipped that Judd's larceny trial "developed the relative rights of the owners and of souvenir-hunters in a manner not likely to be forgotten by many who were in court during its progress." Meanwhile, it was reported that the wreck had had a "crushing" effect on *Peter Iredale*'s captain, who soon returned to Liverpool.[8]

For all the attention it received, some observers actually found *Peter Iredale* wanting. In 1909, three years after the wreck, the *Morning Astorian*—the newspaper most intimately acquainted with the hulk—reported its disappointment with the circumstances of the accident:

> We are not at all anxious for the death of a single mariner, God knows but, if these vessels much come shore, why not do it with the old-time

snap and hurrah and risk? It must be disgusting to the very sailors themselves to go through a wreck so "flat, stale and unprofitable." How can they ever face their grand-children with these pointless, pithless tales of the high-seas and low-lying lands and of wrecks in which no man suffers, nor loses, nor jeopardizes anything? Why the kids will despise them. The reporters, quick and eager as they are to invest such tales with vim and verve, and a verity all their own, are not able to even fake a readable story, as there are not real facts enough upon which to predicate a few alluring lies and keep within sight of the actualities. It is getting so that a shipwreck-tale from out this field is as "punk" as the Legislative correspondence from Salem, and as common as a murder yarn from Portland.[9]

This would be something of a theme among some who wrote about *Peter Iredale* and other wrecks in the Graveyard. In the 1950s, local historian Gordon Newell offered a passage that claimed that if shipwrecks could be harrowing, they could also be prosaic or even mortifying: "It is true that great steamships died, carrying hundreds of helpless victims to awful death with them; that tall, lovely windships drove ashore in splintered ruin or went missing with all hands. But it is also true that other ships indulged in tranquil, charming shipwrecks that delighted their passengers and caused only minor inconvenience to their crews. Some ships even proved their human traits by getting themselves into ludicrous and undignified situations that embarrassed rather than endangered their crews."[10] Later, in the 1980s, yet another historian was flat-out unimpressed by the wreck, which by that point had disintegrated into a shadow of its former self. "The broaching of the *Peter Iredale* on a coast described with many a grim countenance as the 'Graveyard,'" wrote Don Marshall in 1984, "produced the most singularly unexciting shipwreck scenario in maritime history." While *Peter Iredale* may have been "majestic in her day," Marshall noted, the ship "gradually fell into a slumber disturbed only by the distant cawing of local gulls and the snap, snap, snapping of George Eastman's little black box, the 'Kodak.'"[11]

It is in his mention of the Kodak, however, that Marshall gave the story away: *Peter Iredale* was a beloved wreck, never mind the prosaic and ultimately uneventful "disaster" of the ship's coming ashore. Across the twentieth and well into the twenty-first century, *Peter Iredale* reached iconic status and was seen by locals and tourists alike as being worthy of saving. In the 1930s, for example, a gang of wreckers had tried to haul the hulk away but were run off by a local sheriff. Similarly, when the ship was targeted for scrapping in the 1960s, locals rallied around it and ultimately prevented any violation of the wreck's integrity.[12] It was clear that as both tourist attraction and icon of regional history, *Peter Iredale* was worth far more than the price of its metal skeleton. Indeed, given its location and accessibility, it is one of the most photographed shipwrecks in the world.

That said, *Peter Iredale* also has a secret.

———————

Seven years almost to the day before *Peter Iredale* ran aground on Clatsop Spit, in late October of 1899, its namesake and owner died in Liverpool, England. Peter Iredale—the man, not the ship—was co-owner of a shipbuilding and shipping firm in the city on the River Mersey. "He was a man of the old type," reported one obituary, "straight as an arrow, open hearted, and with ever a cheery word on his tongue. He had not an enemy but enjoyed the friendship of hosts of men." Another described him as "a Cumberland man, whose breezy manner and open hearted nature endeared him to all with whom he came into contact . . . keen in business, straight forward, practical and one whose word was as good as his bond in all his business transactions." The obituaries also mentioned more difficult times in Iredale's earlier life, mostly taking place on the coast of western Africa. "He was a man of great vigour and possessed an iron constitution," opined the *Liverpool Daily Post*. "He fought down fearlessly, even scornfully, attacks of all kinds, recovering from Yellow

Jack coast fevers, and other troubles, until he became almost inured from disease. While many others perished on that fatal coast, he triumphed over every disease, by which he was assaulted." The *Mercury*, meanwhile, noted that "during his sojourn on the West Coast he went through many serious attacks of illness, and the result was that he became proof against the worst that these tropical diseases could do." Peter Iredale was clearly someone who had earned his place in the higher echelons of Liverpudlian commerce.[13]

Peter Iredale seems, however, to have had a more complicated past, at which his obituaries would only hint. In a memoir published several decades later, a retired author and naval captain named Frank H. Shaw described a very different man to the one lauded in the *Post* and the *Mercury*:

> Peter Iredale . . . was a shameless opportunist, who ran his fleet on the thriftiest lines. He had made money in the slave-trade, running Black Ivory from the Guinea Coast to the Southern States; and had invested his gains in a considerable fleet of windjammers, all of them strictly utilitarian, and run much as he had run his Middle Passage contrabandists. He manned his vessels with romantic boys for the most part, supplementing them by the minimum allowable of fore-deck hands. He bought condemned Navy stores for feeding his flock. He was a flint-hearted miser, and seldom contacted his victims in person.[14]

That Iredale had worked on the coast of Africa in the 1850s and early 1860s was not in question; indeed, two notices of his death mentioned that he had been a supercargo and coast master there with the firm of Stuart & Douglas, and indeed both Peter Stuart and Peter Douglas attended his funeral. If Shaw was correct in his accusation that Iredale was involved in the trading of "Black Ivory"—African children, women, and men—then it would follow that the Liverpool merchant's later career, including the construction of the ship named after him, was fueled by human trafficking that was at that time technically illegal. If this is true, then our collective affection for *Peter Iredale* the wreck is in fact a kind of contaminated nostalgia.

To be certain, the evidence against Iredale is limited and even circumstantial to a degree, but if we expand our view to look at the ship's birthplace of Liverpool as a whole, the connections between industrial shipbuilding and chattel slavery become clearer. As numerous studies have shown, Liverpool as a modern city was built literally on the backs of enslaved people and their value during the eighteenth and nineteenth centuries. Many Liverpudlian merchants made their fortunes from plantation slavery in places such as Jamaica, and the city's remarkable economic and political growth was fueled by what Christina Sharpe has called "the asterisked histories of slavery, of property, of thingification, and their afterlives."[15] Like Bristol, Liverpool's coastal location linked it to both Africa and the Americas; like Manchester, its industrial revolution required unfreedom. It was out of this particular, stained world that the vessel *Peter Iredale* was born, built, and launched.[16]

This means that the northern Oregon coast, and perhaps the Graveyard of the Pacific more generally, is tied into yet another worlding: the Black Atlantic, where the forced migration of African people transformed not just their lives but the very nature of the ocean and the societies that lined its shores, from Virginia to Jamaica to Brazil and beyond. This also means that Black history is present on the beach at Clatsop Spit, if only somewhat indirectly. It is perhaps more direct, however, when we recall that lawmakers in the territory and later state of Oregon repeatedly attempted to prevent Black people from living there.[17] These histories of anti-Black racism, exploitation, and exclusion are part of *Peter Iredale*'s story. When it ran aground in 1906, it was already entangled in global histories of slavery and industrialization, and thus, so are we with every photo we snap or word we write.

———

Off the coast of Oregon, Washington, and British Columbia, vast tectonic plates collide deep beneath the seas, one sliding under the other. Every now and then—as in the winter of 1700—the line of collision ruptures, and the entire region is shaken by enormous earthquakes, which in turn generate tsunamis that overwhelm the littoral and cross the ocean, linking together the Pacific world through violent inundation. Although unknown to colonial science until the 1980s, the Cascadia Subduction Zone, or at least its effects, were always well known in Indigenous societies, many of which incorporated the recurring disasters into their cultural practices and cosmology. Stories of battles between Thunderbird and Whale, for example, were told in some communities to explain the frightening phenomenon, and Indigenous historical narratives, including material published by ethnographers and others, are full of references to the CSZ's catastrophic truth. In recent years, settler society has become more aware of the risk posed by the region's geological structures, with the result that the peoples of the Graveyard of the Pacific are both on the edge and on edge, waiting for the next disaster.[18]

There are other kinds of collisions here as well: those between diverse peoples from different continents, resulting in what scholar Lisa Lowe calls "intimacies" that developed in the late eighteenth and early nineteenth centuries—intimacies bound up in unfreedom and genocide.[19] While this collision between continents began more than half a millennium ago, its repercussions echo down the ages, and coming to terms with the complexities of the past teaches us how to live with the complexities of our shared now. In the Graveyard of the Pacific, the abrupt and violent changes associated with colonialism came fast and hard, not over centuries but rather compressed into mere decades. Perhaps for that reason, we can still see their traces on the landscape—timbers in a cave, iron rusting away on a beach, relics in museums—more clearly than is the case in other places. The tidal and tempestuous afterlives of these ships are the echoes of past eras, but just like lost times, they are never fully *in* the past. They do remain *of* the past, in that they constantly remind us that the larger narratives of which they are part—of colonialism, for example, or of Indigenous persistence—are far from over. They are revenant remains, telling stories, the final results of which are yet to be seen.

ACKNOWLEDGMENTS

THIS BOOK EMERGED FROM A FAILURE.

In 2018, I was several years into a book project about my hometown of Auburn, Washington. The book was to be called *SlaughterTown*, after the small city's original settler name of Slaughter, and would look at the ways that historical traumas leave marks on the everyday landscape. I was interested in four events that dramatically impacted the people and peoples living in the place that became Auburn. The first was the "Puget Sound Indian War" of 1855–1856, known among local Indigenous communities as the First Treaty War. The second was the transformation of local rivers, most notably the disastrous redirection of the White River around 1900. The third historical trauma was the incarceration of around one-third of the town's people in 1942 because of their Japanese ancestry. The fourth and final trauma, through which I lived as a teenager, was at that time the United States' largest serial killer case, that of the so-called Green River Killer, who was from Auburn and killed at least forty-nine women and girls beginning in 1982. Combined with accounts of my own family's experiences with intergenerational violence, the four stories would show how events like these—manifestations of settler colonialism, patriarchy, and white supremacy—leave traces in the landscape, with the earth itself an active archive of trauma.

In the summer of 2018, however, I was defeated by that archive.

Specifically, I failed to figure out a way to metabolize nearly seven thousand transcript pages of interviews with Gary Ridgway, the Green River Killer, who was finally identified and captured in 2001. I will likely never write—and to a large extent, never even talk—about what exactly I saw in those files. I will say that the experience deeply affected my mental health. I got inside his head, but he got inside mine, and I was forced to confront difficult memories through engaging with accounts of violence toward women and young people that would make most readers' hair stand on end. The intensity of the experience was made all the more palpable by its intimacy with the grounds of my own upbringing: the bodies found near my mother's favorite fishing spot, the remains discovered across the road from the town cemetery, the bones in the underbrush all over the part of the world that I knew as home. To put it mildly, reading those transcripts was an awful—if still vicarious—experience. And so, by the fall of 2018, I had decided to shelve *SlaughterTown* indefinitely. I was left, shall we say, rudderless.

Then, in the autumn of that year, I attended the Cascadia Environmental History Collaborative's annual gathering, in which scholars from Washington, Oregon, Idaho, and British Columbia come together to discuss the field and each other's work. In 2018, we were hosted at a retreat center on the Long Beach Peninsula just north of the mouth of the Columbia River. There, as I listened in on and contributed to conversations about everything from Pacific Northwest nuclearism to the eco-politics of harbor development, I found myself at something of a loss. Then, during our first meal together, I noticed a poster of the "Graveyard of the Pacific" on the dining hall wall. It suddenly hit me: I already knew many of these stories of shipwreck and indeed had been fascinated with them literally for decades. What if I wrote about the Graveyard, with its more than two thousand lost vessels?

Over the next two days, I workshopped the idea with colleagues, and all agreed that there was a project here, and one that was particularly "me." Soon after, a survey of existing literature on the intersections between maritime history and my usual fields of Indigenous and settler colonial histories suggested this was largely "uncharted" territory. I began working up a treatment for the project, and within a few months, I had obtained an advance contract for a book as well as a research grant from the Social Sciences & Humanities Research Council of the Canadian federal government. As this experience shows, our scholarly routes can sometimes take abrupt and unexpected turns, often as the result of serendipity, and *Wrecked* was launched in one such moment. My first thanks, then, go to Marsha Weisiger of the University of Oregon and Josh Reid and the late Linda Nash of the University of Washington for convening the Cascadia weekend every year, as well as the scholars, from graduate students to senior faculty, who attended in 2018. Without them, this ship would likely never have sailed.

After a decade working on Indigenous histories in London and Britain, *Wrecked* is me coming back to write about the northwestern coast of North America, and there are many who helped me navigate this return passage. Bill Deverell conducted and broadcast the first interview I did for this project, and Josh Reid and Boyd Cothran were fellow travelers in our three-person maritime history book club. Candace Wellman offered tips on local history sources, while Leslie Meyer and Micah Killjoy did genealogical and newspaper research. An academic writing group that helped me formulate *Wrecked* in its earliest stages included Colleen O'Neill, Chantal Norrgard, Boyd Cothran, Doug Miller, Andy Fisher, Cathleen Cahill, Farina King, and Kevin Whalen. More broadly, readers both within and outside the academy allowed me to test out drafts on them and included Hugh Leschot, Tarren Andrews, Karrie Zylstra Myton, Tom Peotto, Sunshine Stingl, Vange Holtz-Schramke, Sean Fraga, and Rebecca Goetz. Carrie Leonard also read and helped edit the epilogue. Scott Williams was an excellent resource and link to the underwater archaeology community; Feliks Banel kept me abreast of some big stories in Graveyard news, notably the rediscovery of *Pacific*. Alfred Burns and Deborah Brown provided something of a writing retreat at their home in St. Lucia; the fact that they happen to be my in-laws made it all the more welcome.

As is ever the case, archivists and librarians made this work possible. I especially want to thank Chelsea Shriver of UBC's Rare Books & Special Collections; Anne Jenner from the University of Washington's Special Collections; Eileen Price and Gwen Whiting at the Washington State Historical Society; Jonny Allen and Diane Wardle of the British Columbia Archives; the Oregon Historical Society's Scott Daniels; Jeff Smith, Matthew Palmgren, and Marcy Dunning at the Columbia River Maritime Museum; the staff of the Cannon Beach History Center; and Steve Greif of the Coos History Museum. I also have special gratitude for my conversations with Indigenous archivists, historians, and knowledge keepers, including Ashley Lewis, Rio Jaime, James Jaime, Carl Edgar Jr., Robert Kentta, Janine Ledford, and Maria Pascua.

My many conversations with history students over the past several years have also informed this project. At the graduate level, Stephen Hay, Mark Werner, Kaden Jelsing, Ella Bishop, Lily Hart, Michael Buse, Sean MacPherson, and Adina Reyes Williams helped me learn what was important about the work we all do together in ways that deeply shaped *Wrecked*. At the undergraduate level, students in my American West, Pacific, and maritime history courses confirmed for me that there was a story here that might appeal to a broad audience.

In May of 2024, I was honored to be able to host a manuscript workshop, funded by my department under the leadership of Bonnie Effros, that brought together several UBC colleagues and three out-of-towners. Together, we spent an entire day going through the manuscript. It was a remarkable experience, and the workshop's influence carries throughout this book. Steve Mentz, Josh Reid, and Bathsheba Demuth were the outside readers, and my UBC peers were John Christopoulos, Crystal Webster, Bonnie Effros, Desirée Valadares, Sara Ann Knutson, Kelly Midori McCormick, Tina Loo, Eagle Glassheim, and Alex Dick.

I also want to thank the team at the University of Washington Press.

I first worked with the UW Press on *Native Seattle*, in both its original 2007 publication and the release of its second edition in 2017. I eventually became a series editor there, facilitating the Indigenous Confluences series with Tseshaht Nuu-chah-nulth Indigenous studies scholar Charlotte Coté. The UW Press staffers are an amazing team, and I am thrilled to be working with them again. In particular, Larin McLaughlin and Mike Baccam deserve a ton of credit for shepherding the book along and providing insightful advice and warm support. UW Press also enlisted the expertise of two anonymous readers, who confirmed I was on the right track and offered important suggestions for final revisions. Josh Reid—who appears three times in these acknowledgments—is editor of the UW Press's Sick Series, in which *Wrecked* appears, and in this helped make this book what it is.

No one was more central to this project than my research associate Dr. Sarah Fox, who as a graduate student worked on this project for two years. Sarah was tasked with collecting and analyzing thousands of newspaper articles from online archives, and without this exceptionally rich material, *Wrecked* would be a very different book indeed. Just as important, the long conversations we had about the project—including during a two-week visit to archives and shipwreck sites in Portland, Astoria, and the Oregon coast—indelibly transformed the work. Whether traipsing around a mossy cemetery in search of the graves of the shipwrecked, excitedly sharing finds while in the archives, or gabbing for hours over beers, Sarah was there for most steps of the book's creation and knows it almost as well as I do. In short, it simply could not have been written without her participation, and I think of our work together as a true partnership.

Lastly, I want to thank my husband Noah, always my first reader and my grammar daddy. We spent a great deal of time fussing over semicolons and the proper color-words for sky and sand, and these long conversations made *Wrecked* a better and more accessible book. In holding down the fort while I was away on research trips, tagging along on one of those trips, and generally being a smart reader from outside the academic world, Noah made this work possible in the ways that spouses and partners so often do.

If I have forgotten anyone, my sincerest apologies.

Thank you all.

Preface

1 "As cultural icons," writes Langdon Cook, razor clams "predate floating bridges, the Space Needle, and cheap electricity." It's true. The razor clam (*Siliqua patula*) has long been a signature species of the Pacific Northwest, especially, notes Cook, among blue-collar settler families such as mine. Razor clam historian David Berger, meanwhile, offers a longer, enraptured account of the ways in which the "humble" mollusk "burrowed ever deeper into the Northwest psyche and self-definition" over the course of the twentieth century. See Langdon Cook, *Fat of the Land: Adventures of a 21st Century Forager* (Seattle: Skipstone, 2009), 17–28, and David Berger, *Razor Clams: Buried Treasure of the Pacific Northwest* (Seattle: University of Washington Press, 2017). Both books include razor clam recipes. As for my grandmother Martha Dean, her fritters were simple and unadorned: just clam meat, eggs, milk, flour, bread crumbs, and a little salt and pepper. Meanwhile, for a poetic treatment of clam digging, see Ann Spiers, *Back Cut* (Anacortes, WA: Blue Heron, 2021), 18–21, and for a description of a renowned chef's mother harvesting clams on the Oregon coast—a scene that mirrors my own very closely—see John Birdsall, *The Man Who Ate Too Much: The Life of James Beard* (New York: W. W. Norton, 2020), 14–15. And, finally, relevant to almost nothing, my best friend thinks my drag name should be Clam Patty.

2 R. E. Wells, *A Guide to Shipwreck Sites along the Washington Coast* (Victoria: Morriss, 1989), 81–82. Wells's book, with original drawings of forty-three wrecks in progress, is long out of print but remains one of the best entry points

for anyone interested in the history of marine disaster in this part of the world. For reporting on the cleanup of the site, visit "Catala Shipwreck at Damon Point State Park," accessed June 23, 2022, https://ecology.wa.gov/Spills -Cleanup/Spills/Spill-preparedness-response/Responding-to-spill-incidents /Spill-incidents/Catala-Shipwreck.

3   Jake the Alligator Man remains one of tidewater Washington's most famous residents, despite his ghoulish origins. According to the owners of Marsh's, he may have been created by sideshow impresario Homer Tate sometime in the mid-twentieth century and has been in residence at the museum since the 1960s. He once graced the cover of *Weekly World News,* and numerous spurious tall tales have collected around him. Today, he is the subject of bumper stickers and T-shirts that read "RESPECT THE LOCALS," and once a year, classic car owners come together in Long Beach from around the Northwest to honor him. What is most surprising (or perhaps not surprising at all) is that there has never to my knowledge been an effort to treat this person's partial remains as anything other than a deliberately mysterious joke.

4   Granted, there are other nautical graveyards, most notably the waters associated with the Pacific theater of the Second World War. But in terms of sheer volume of wrecks, the Northwest Coast wins the prize.

5   The extensive popular literature on shipwrecks along the Oregon, Washington, and British Columbia coasts includes James A. Gibbs, *Pacific Graveyard* (Portland: Binfords & Mort, 1950); James A. Gibbs, *Shipwrecks off Juan de Fuca* (Portland: Binford & Mort, 1968); R. Bruce Scott, *"Breakers Ahead!": A History of Shipwrecks on the Graveyard of the Pacific* (Sidney, BC: Review Publishing House, 1970); R. E. Wells, *A Guide to Shipwrecks: Cape Beale to Point Cox Including Barkley Sound* (Victoria: Morriss, 1984); James A. Gibbs, *Shipwrecks of the Pacific* (Portland: Binford & Mort, 1989); David H. Grover, *The Unforgiving Coast: Maritime Disasters of the Pacific Northwest* (Corvallis: Oregon State University Press, 2002); Theodore Schellhase, *Lost Treasure Ships of the Oregon Coast* (Atglen, PA: Schiffer, 2009); Anthony Dalton, *The Graveyard of the Pacific: Shipwreck Tales from the Depths of History* (Victoria: Heritage House, 2010); John MacFarlane, *Shipwreck! A Chronicle of Marine Accidents and Disasters in British Columbia* (n.p.: Nauticapedia, 2021); and Jennifer Kozik, ed., *Shipwrecks of the Pacific Northwest: Tragedies and Legacies of a Perilous Coast* (Guilford, CT: Globe Pequot, 2020).

6   W. S. Merwin, "The Shipwreck," in *Poems of the Sea*, ed. J. D. McClatchy (New York: Alfred A. Knopf, 2001), 163.

7   Throughout this book, I use *settler* to describe those who came willingly to the Northwest Coast and then stayed. It is a dynamic term; there are ongoing, vigorous, and critically important debates between and among several fields of scholarship and activism as to how racialized people and peoples (e.g., the descendants of enslaved people, Latinx people, or persons from Asia and of Asian heritage) relate to a term like *settler*, given the history of white supremacy in both the United States and Canada. These conversations involve thinking about the relationships between settler colonialism, anti-Blackness, and other manifestations of white supremacy, as well as the possibility of solidarity between communities, including within scholarly practice.

8   *Survivance*, a term coined by Ojibwe writer Gerald Vizenor, goes beyond mere survival to encompass resistance, creative adaptation, and even joy. For more on the term, see Vizenor, *Survivance: Narratives of Native Presence* (Lincoln: University of Nebraska Press, 2008).

9   Hester Blum, "The Prospect of Oceanic Studies," *PMLA* 125, no. 3 (2010): 670; Eve Tuck and K. Wayne Yang, "Decolonization Is Not a Metaphor," *Decolonization: Indigeneity, Education, & Society* 1, no. 1 (2012): 1–40.

Introduction

1   Minnie Patterson far overshadowed her husband for her role in shipwreck lifesaving. In addition to her assistance to the survivors of *Valencia*, she also played a key role in the rescue of the crew of *Coloma* later that same year, and today, the Maritime Discovery Centre in Port Alberni on Vancouver Island has a permanent exhibit on her. For examples of the coverage of her exploits, see "Work of Heroine Is Appreciated," *Victoria Daily Colonist*, December 9, 1906, 2; "Purse Is Prepared for Mrs. Patterson," *Victoria Daily Colonist*, December 19, 1906, 3; "Noble Work as Rescuer," *Washington Standard* (Olympia), December 14, 1906, 2; "'Grace Darling' of the Pacific Coast," *Victoria Daily Colonist*, June 6, 1911, 11 (Grace Darling was an English lighthouse keeper's daughter who also rescued shipwreck victims to widespread acclaim and fame).

2   My description of the wreck of *Valencia* is drawn from both primary and secondary sources. For firsthand testimonies of survivors, see Casualties and

Violation Case Files, 1887–1942, record group 41, box 63, National Archives & Records Administration, Seattle. Newspaper accounts in both American and Canadian newspapers are too many to cite here; see below for specific examples. Secondary treatments of the disaster include R. Bruce Scott, *"Breakers Ahead!": A History of Shipwrecks on the Graveyard of the Pacific* (Sidney, BC: Review Publishing House, 1970), 97–114; Fred Rogers, *Shipwrecks of British Columbia* (Vancouver: J. J. Douglas, 1973), 134–139; and David H. Grover, *The Unforgiving Coast: Maritime Disasters of the Pacific Northwest* (Corvallis: Oregon State University Press, 2002), 45–70. The most extensive secondary account is Michael C. Neitzel, *The* Valencia *Tragedy* (Surrey, BC: Heritage House, 1995), reprinted as *The Final Voyage of the* Valencia (Surrey, BC: Heritage House, 2020).

3   See, for example, C. R. Boxer, ed. and trans., *The Tragic History of the Sea* (Minneapolis: University of Minnesota, 2001); Jennifer H. Oliver, *Shipwreck in French Renaissance Writing: The Direful Spectacle* (Oxford: Oxford University Press, 2019); H. H. Huxley, "Storm and Shipwreck in Roman Literature," *Greece & Rome* 21, no. 63 (1952): 117–124; Jonathan Miles, *Medusa: The Shipwreck, the Scandal, the Masterpiece* (London: Jonathan Cape, 2007); David Cressy, *Shipwrecks and the Bounty of the Sea* (Oxford: Oxford University Press, 2022); William J. Palmer, "Dickens and Shipwreck," *Dickens Studies Annual*, no. 18 (1989), 39–92; A. E. Stallings, "Shipwreck Is Everywhere," *The Hudson Review* 70, no. 3 (2017): n.p.; and Carl Thompson, ed., *Shipwreck in Art and Literature: Images and Interpretations from Antiquity to the Present Day* (London: Routledge, 2013).

4   *Titanic* of course dominates all talk of shipwreck, becoming what the *Onion* satirically called "the world's largest metaphor." See Scott Dikkers, ed., *Our Dumb Century: The Onion Presents 100 Years of Headlines from America's Finest News Source* (New York: Three Rivers, 1999), 13.

5   Michael Titlestad, *Shipwreck Narratives: Out of Our Depth* (London: Palgrave Macmillan, 2021), 2.

6   Randall Sullivan, *Graveyard of the Pacific: Shipwreck and Survival on America's Deadliest Waterway* (New York: Atlantic Monthly Press, 2023), 23 and 237.

7   Sara Rich, *Shipwreck Hauntography: Underwater Ruins and the Uncanny* (Amsterdam: Amsterdam University Press, 2021), 77.

8   Steve Mentz, *Shipwreck Modernity: Ecologies of Globalization, 1550–1719* (Minneapolis: University of Minnesota Press, 2015), xxvi.

9   "A Heroine," *Seattle Star*, January 27, 1906, 4.

10 "Old Man Haunts Coast Looking for the Dead," *Spokane Press*, February 2, 1906, 1. *Valencia* was not the only Graveyard wreck that was observed in real and agonizingly slow time by large numbers of people. Four years after *Valencia* wrecked, the steamer *Czarina* foundered on the Coos Bay Bar. The *Coos Bay World* of January 13, 1910, described the scene: "The weakness and helplessness of man's puny efforts before the fearful forces of nature in action uncontrolled were never more vividly portrayed than in this tragic event. To the scores assembled on the beach, the scene was one of heart wringing torture. There in the gathering grey twilight of a January evening within easy reach but unable to render any assistance, they watched silent and helpless as the members of the crew one after another went down to death in the angry waves. The final act in this terrible sea tragedy was most awful and awesome. Six men including Capt. Duggan and Harold Millis, who had clung all night long to the single remaining mast, dropped off to their death in sight of the watchers on the shore. First two fell exhausted and then three of their companions, with hope of assistance abandoned, evidently took their last chance and stripping their clothes leaped into the sea."

11 *Seattle Star*, January 25, 1906.

12 "Wrecks That Victorians Remember," *Victoria Daily Colonist*, November 27, 1910, 1–2.

13 "Seattle Demands Thorough Inquiry," *Seattle Star*, February 14, 1906, 1.

14 "Attorney Frye As Inquisitor," *Seattle Star*, February 5, 1906, 1.

15 Philip French, "The Loss of the *Valencia*" (Seattle: Philip French, 1906), Washington State Historical Society.

16 For critical discussions of lighthouses in colonial contexts, see Veronica Strang, Tim Edensor, and Joanna Puckering, eds., *From the Lighthouse: Interdisciplinary Reflections on Light* (London: Routledge, 2018), and Eric Tagliacozzo, "The Lit Archipelago," *Technology and Culture* 46, no. 2 (2005): 306–328.

17 Steven Biel, *Down with the Old Canoe: A Cultural History of the* Titanic *Disaster* (New York: W. W. Norton, 1996), 8.

18 "DOES IT PAY?," *Seattle Star*, February 3, 1906, 1.

19 Allan Sekula, *Fish Story* (London: MACK, 1995), 107.

20 "The Fate of the *Valencia*," *Victoria Daily Colonist*, January 25, 1906, 4.

21 "What of the Future," *Seattle Star*, January 27, 1906, 1.

22 Anthropologist Patrick Wolfe's classic formulation that settler colonialism is

a historical and ongoing structure that requires the "elimination of the native" remains the most influential articulation of the settler colonial studies framework, although scholars such J. Kēhaulani Kauanui have argued convincingly that sustained Indigenous intellectual critique of settler colonialism has existed for centuries. Other scholars, meanwhile, have critiqued Wolfe's articulation for its overly unitary nature, arguing instead for a diverse suite of colonialisms that have taken place across time and space. For entry points into the conversation, see Patrick Wolfe, "Settler Colonialism and the Elimination of the Native," *Journal of Genocide Research* 8, no. 4 (2006), 387–409; J. Kēhaulani Kauanui, "'A Structure, Not an Event': Settler Colonialism and Enduring Indigeneity," *Lateral* 5, no. 1 (2016); and Nancy Shoemaker, "A Typology of Colonialism," *AHA Perspectives on History*, October 2015. For selected additional works on settler colonialism in the United States and Canada, see Kevin Bruyneel, *Settler Memory: The Disavowal of Indigeneity and the Politics of Race in the United States* (Chapel Hill: University of North Carolina Press, 2021); Lorenzo Veracini, *Settler Colonialism: A Theoretical Overview* (London: Palgrave Macmillan, 2010); Cole Harris, *A Bounded Land: Reflections on Settler Colonialism in Canada* (Vancouver: UBC Press, 2021); and Walter Hixson, *American Settler Colonialism: A History* (London: Palgrave Macmillan, 2013).

23 *Settlerist*, as opposed to *settler*, is to my knowledge a neologism. It is meant to distinguish between settler identities and the robust ideologies and structures that explicitly and aggressively undergird the colonial project. It is akin, I suppose, to the difference between *racial* and *racist*, the latter a more active, verb-y word that denotes direct action rather than merely a state of being.

24 Mark Rifkin, *Settler Common Sense: Queerness and Everyday Colonialism in the American Renaissance* (Minneapolis: University of Minnesota Press, 2014).

25 Jean M. O'Brien, *Firsting and Lasting: Writing Indians Out of Existence in New England* (Minneapolis: University of Minnesota Press, 2010).

26 For examples of Indigenous resurgence in the region, see Charles Wilkinson, *The People Are Dancing Again: The History of the Siletz Tribes of Western Oregon* (Seattle: University of Washington Press, 2010); Joshua L. Reid, *The Sea Is My Country: The Maritime World of the Makahs* (New Haven, CT: Yale University Press, 2016); Jonathan Daehnke, *Chinook Resilience: Heritage and Revitalization on the Lower Columbia River* (Seattle: University of Washington Press, 2017); Alexandra Harmon, *Reclaiming the Reservation: Histories of Indian Sovereignty Repressed and Renewed* (Seattle: University of Washington

Press, 2019); and Charlotte Coté, *A Drum in One Hand, a Sockeye in the Other: Stories of Indigenous Food Sovereignty from the Northwest Coast* (Seattle: University of Washington Press, 2022).

27 *White Bluffs Spokesman*, April 30, 1926, 3.

28 Personal communication with Heather Feeney, British Columbia Maritime Museum, May 13, 2022.

29 For examples, see "Shores of Ill Repute," *Victoria Colonist* Sunday Magazine, October 4, 1936, 1, 3; Frank Kelley, "Nesika Illahee (Our Land)," *Victoria Colonist* Sunday Magazine, April 17, 1951, 4.

30 See, for example, Jacques Marc, "Commemorating the *Valencia* Wreck of 1906," *Foghorn* 33, no. 2 (2006): 1, and the *Valencia* entry in the Parks Canada Directory of Federal Heritage Designations, accessed February 28, 2024, at https://www.pc.gc.ca/apps/DFHD/default_eng.aspx.

31 Christina Sharpe, *In the Wake: On Blackness and Being* (Durham, NC: Duke University Press, 2016), 9.

32 Eugene Arima and Alan Hoover, *The Whaling People of the West Coast of Vancouver Island and Cape Flattery* (Victoria: Royal BC Museum, 2011), 65–75, and E. Y. Arima, Denis St. Claire, Louis Clamhouse, Joshua Edgar, Charles Jones, and John Thomas, *Between Ports Alberni and Renfrew: Notes on West Coast Peoples* (Ottawa: Canadian Museum of Civilization, 1991), 103. Coastal Indigenous peoples had and have their own stories about maritime misfortune; early Washington Territory settler James Swan noted in his diaries that among the Makah, who are related by culture and kinship to the Nuu-chah-nulth Nations, the belief was that men who drowned at sea would return as owls with shells in their bills and rings in their ears. See James Gilchrist Swan, "Diaries, 1859–1866," University of Washington Special Collections, 129.

33 For the history of the Cape Beale Lighthouse in an Indigenous context, see Jesse Robertson, "Lightkeepers on Huu-ay-aht Shores: Reinserting Indigenous Labour and Knowledge into the History of Coastal Navigation," *BC Studies*, 222 (2024), 47–69.

34 "Victims of Wreck Reach Victoria," *Victoria Daily Colonist*, February 2, 1906, 7. See also "Old Man Haunts Coast Looking for the Dead," *Spokane Press*, February 2, 1906, 1.

35 R. Bruce Scott, *People of the Southwest Coast of Vancouver Island: A History of the Southwest Coast* (Victoria: Morriss, 1974), 58, and Scott, *"Breakers Ahead!,"* 111.

36 "Caves Which Held *Valencia* Wreckage," *Victoria Daily Colonist*, September 1, 1906, 3. See also "Valencia Skeletons," *Seattle Star*, September 1, 1906, 3, and "The *Queen City*," *Victoria Daily Colonist*, September 15, 1906, 6. The question of Indigenous testimony and whether it could be believed or even included in court cases, for example, has a long history. For discussion of the issue in Canada, see Arthur J. Ray, *Telling It to the Judge: Taking Native History to Court* (Toronto: McGill-Queen's University Press, 2012).

37 Lauren Harding, "Walking the Wild Coast: Territory, Tourism, and Belonging on the West Coast Trail" (PhD diss., University of British Columbia, 2020).

38 Parks Canada, *West Coast Trail Map*, 2019.

39 Marcus Rediker, *The Slave Ship: A Human History* (New York: Penguin, 2007), 4.

40 Frances Steel, *Oceania under Steam: Sea Transport and the Cultures of Colonialism, c. 1870–1914* (Manchester: Manchester University Press, 2011), 215.

41 Antoinette Burton, *The Trouble with Empire: Challenges to Modern British Imperialism* (Oxford: Oxford University Press, 2015), 3.

42 Gastón R. Gordillo, *Rubble: The Afterlife of Destruction* (Durham, NC: Duke University Press, 2014), 20.

43 Renisa Mawani, *Across Oceans of Law: The* Komagata Maru *and Jurisdiction in the Time of Empire* (Durham, NC: Duke University Press, 2018), 10.

44 Josiah Blackmore, *Manifest Perdition: Shipwreck Narrative and the Disruption of Empire* (Minneapolis: University of Minnesota Press, 2002), xxvi.

45 Amy Mitchell-Cook, *A Sea of Misadventures: Shipwreck and Survival in Early America* (Columbia: University of South Carolina Press, 2013), 3.

46 Originally, I had used the term *failed* in this conceptualization, but one of my Indigenous undergraduate students convinced me that *failing* was perhaps a better term. My thanks go to Amber McSwain for this insight, which shifted the entire framing of this book.

47 See Mentz, *Shipwreck Modernity*; Rich, *Shipwreck Hauntography*; and Killian Quigley, *Reading Underwater Wreckage: An Encrusting Ocean* (London: Bloomsbury Academic, 2024). In 1981, Pacific Northwest historian Kent D. Richards lamented the state of the region's history. "It has added no new fact to human knowledge—has produced no high illustration of any fact already known, has produced no warrior, or scholar in any branch of human knowledge, in fact not a single name that for any merit or acts of its possessor deserves to live in the memory of mankind." In the years since Richards's

rather depressing claim, much has changed. For successful works on settler colonialism in the region, see Laura Ishiguro, *Nothing to Write Home About: British Family Correspondence and the Settler Colonial Everyday in British Columbia* (Vancouver: UBC Press, 2019); Daniel Clayton, *Islands of Truth: The Imperial Fashioning of Vancouver Island* (Vancouver: UBC Press, 2000); Bruce Braun, *The Intemperate Rainforest: Nature, Culture, and Power on Canada's West Coast* (Minneapolis: University of Minnesota Press, 2002); Gray H. Whaley, *Oregon and the Collapse of Illahee: U.S. Empire and the Transformation of an Indigenous World, 1792–1859* (Chapel Hill: University of North Carolina Press, 2010); Paige Raibmon, "Unmaking Native Space: A Genealogy of Indian Policy, Settler Practice, and the Microtechniques of Dispossession," in *The Power of Promises: Rethinking Indian Treaties in the Pacific Northwest*, ed. Alexandra Harmon (Seattle: University of Washington Press, 2008); and Cole Harris, *The Resettlement of British Columbia: Essays on Colonialism and Geographical Change* (Vancouver: UBC Press, 1997). The reader will note the predominance of British Columbia–focused projects here; indeed, studies of British Columbia are far more engaged with critical approaches than scholarship about the American Pacific Northwest. For Richards's original accusation, see Kent D. Richards, "In Search of the Pacific Northwest: The Historiography of Oregon and Washington," *Pacific Historical Review* 50, no. 4 (1981): 426.

48   "Wrecks That Victorians Remember," *Victoria Colonist* Sunday Magazine, November 27, 1910, 2.

49   "Fear Wreck," *Seattle Star*, February 2, 1906, 1.

50   "Believe Missing Woman Committed Suicide," *Seattle Star*, October 21, 1907, 7.

51   *Seattle Star*, June 11, 1914, 1.

ONE   Everything That Comes Ashore Is Mine

1   Kurt Cobain—who needs little introduction as the lead singer-songwriter and guitarist for the 1990s global phenomenon that was Nirvana—grew up in this part of Washington, and his lyrics and music, while known the world over, emerge from and resonate closely with his Northwest origins, describing both lyrically and sonically a downtrodden and misunderstood landscape marked by poverty, longing, and decrepitude. As with the title of the 1996 album *From the Muddy Banks of the Wishkah*, he invokes a very particular sort of local geography: a tarp under a bridge, "disease-covered Puget Sound," "soft pretentious mountains," and birds that sing in D minor. Cobain's Northwest was

Generation X's run-down and sad Northwest, a far cry from the picturesque tourist icon of Mount Rainier or the lofty Boomer optimism of the Space Needle. His legacy still brings devotees to Aberdeen, and a decade after his 1994 death, the city added "Come As You Are," the title of one of Nirvana's biggest hits, to the roadside signs welcoming visitors to town. For further commentary on Cobain, Nirvana, and the Northwest landscape, see Kurt Cobain, *Journals* (New York: Riverhead Books, 2003); Charles R. Cross, *Heavier Than Heaven: A Biography of Kurt Cobain* (Paris: Hachette Books, 2019); and Mark Yarm, *Everybody Loves Our Town: An Oral History of Grunge* (New York: Crown, 2012).

2   For Grays Harbor history, see John C. Hughes and Ryan Teague Beckwith, *On the Harbor: From Black Friday to Nirvana* (Las Vegas: Stephens Press, 2010), and Aaron Goings, *The Port of Missing Men: Billy Gohl, Labor, and Brutal Times in the Pacific Northwest* (Seattle: University of Washington Press, 2020).

3   Robert Brockstedt Lane and Barbara Lane, "Treaty Rights Workshop: Chehalis River Treaty Council and the Treaty of Olympia" (Washington, DC: Institute for the Development of Indian Law, n.d.), n.p.

4   Manuel J. Andrade, *Quileute Texts* (New York: Columbia University Press, 1931), 206–211.

5   *Hiba' Kwashkwash/The Jay Squawks* newsletter, Quileute Nation, August 2010, n.p.

6   Andrade, *Quileute Texts*, 206–207.

7   Arthur Howeattle MS 1509, Diaries and Reminiscences, Oregon Historical Society, 6–7.

8   *Hiba' Kwashkwash*, n.p. Thanks to James Jaime of the Quileute Nation for sharing this source.

9   See Cary C. Collins, "The Water Is My Land: The Di·ya· Treaty Council of 1855," *Pacific Northwest Quarterly* 104, no. 1 (2012/2013): 21–39.

10 Judith Hudson Beattie and Helen Margaret Buss, eds., *Undelivered Letters to Hudson's Bay Company Men on the Northwest Coast of America, 1830–57* (Vancouver: UBC Press, 2003), 414.

11 For a discussion of oceanic histories across the world, see the forum in the *American Historical Review* 111, no. 3 (2006), featuring Kären Wigen, Peregrine Horden, Nicholas Purcell, Alison Games, and Matt K. Matsuda.

12 Matt K. Matsuda, *Pacific Worlds: A History of Seas, Peoples, and Cultures* (Cambridge: Cambridge University Press, 2012), 8.

13   For examples of First Salmon ceremonies and their cultural import around the North Pacific, see Judith Roche and Meg McHutchison, eds., *First Fish, First People: Salmon Tales of the North Pacific Rim* (Vancouver: UBC Press, 1998).

14   As just one example, take this description of beaching territories around Willapa Bay and Long Beach in what is now southwestern Washington: "When travelers from Chehalis find a whale it is taken back from them. If it is found at Oysterville, it belongs to the people of Sealand; when it is found north of Oysterville, it belongs to the Willapa. When the people of Sealand find a whale north of Oysterville, it is claimed by the Willapa. If the Willapa find one south of Oysterville, it is claimed by the people of Sealand." Taken from Franz Boas, *Chinook Texts* (Washington: Government Printing Office, 1894), 259–263. Whaling—whether by hunt or by harvest—is well documented throughout the Graveyard of the Pacific. For the Nuu-chah-nulth, see Eugene Arima and John Dewhirst, "Nootkans of Vancouver Island," *Smithsonian Handbook of North American Indians*, vol. 7, *Northwest Coast* (Washington, DC: Smithsonian Institution, 1990), 395, and Charlotte Coté, *Spirits of Our Whaling Ancestors: Revitalizing Makah and Nuu-chah-nulth Traditions* (Seattle: University of Washington Press, 2010). For the Makah, see Ann M. Renker and Erna Gunther, "Makah," *Smithsonian Handbook*, 423–424; Joshua L. Reid, *The Sea Is My Country: The Maritime World of the Makahs* (New Haven, CT: Yale University Press, 2015); and Robert Sullivan, *A Whale Hunt* (New York: Scribner, 2000). For the Quileute, see James V. Powell, "Quileute," *Smithsonian Handbook*, 431, and for the Quinault, see Yvonne Hajda, "Southwestern Coast Salish," *Smithsonian Handbook*, 507. For the Chinook and Clatsop, see Michael Silverstein, "Chinookans of the Lower Columbia, *Smithsonian Handbook*, 537. For the Tillamook-Nehalem, see William R. Seaburg and Jay Miller, "Tillamook," *Smithsonian Handbook*, 564, and for Coosan peoples, see Henry B. Zenk, "Siuslawans and Coosans," *Smithsonian Handbook*, 573.

15   Ryan Tucker Jones, "Running into Whales: The History of the North Pacific from Below the Waves," *American Historical Review* 118, no. 2: 349–377. For an example of scholarship that takes more-than-human (in this case cetacean) temporalities seriously, see Bathsheba Demuth, *Floating Coast: An Environmental History of the Bering Strait* (New York: W. W. Norton, 2019).

16   The ethnographic literature on potlatching is too extensive to list here, but for some Indigenous—and specifically Nuu-chah-nulth—perspectives on the tradition within larger cultural and environmental frames, see Umeek/E. Richard

Atleo, *Tsawalk: A Nuu-chah-nulth Worldview* (Vancouver: UBC Press, 2005); Coté, *Spirits of Our Whaling Ancestors*; and George C. Clutesi, *Potlatch* (Sidney, BC: Gray's Publishing, 1969). For a literary analysis of colonial attitudes toward potlatching, see Christopher Bracken, *The Potlatch Papers: A Colonial Case History* (Chicago: University of Chicago Press, 1997).

17   Arthur Howeattle MS 1509, Diaries and Reminiscences, Oregon Historical Society, 4.

18   Jay Powell and Vickie Jensen, *Quileute: An Introduction to the Indians of La Push* (Seattle: University of Washington Press, 1976), 15.

19   Harry Hobucket, "Quillayute Indian Traditions," *Pacific Northwest Quarterly* 25, no. 1 (1934): 53.

20   Jarold Ramsey, comp. and ed., *Coyote Was Going There: Indian Literature of the Oregon Country* (Seattle: University of Washington Press, 1977), 174–175, gathered from Boas, *Chinook Texts*, 278–279. For further discussion of the story, see Gray H. Whaley, *Oregon and the Collapse of Illahee* (Chapel Hill: University of North Carolina Press, 2010), 3–5.

21   Silas B. Smith, "Tales of Early Wrecks on the Oregon Coast, and How the Bees-Wax Got There: Address to the Oregon Historical Society, December 16, 1899," *Oregon Native Son*, no. 1 (1899–1900), 3.

22   Reid, *The Sea Is My Country*, 30.

23   Clarence L. Andrews, "Russian Plans for American Dominion," *Washington Historical Quarterly* 18, no. 2 (1927): 86.

24   For general discussion of the pelt trade, see Richard Ravalli, *Sea Otters: A History* (Lincoln: University of Nebraska Press, 2018). For connections around and beyond the northern Pacific Rim, see Ryan Tucker Jones, "Kelp Highways, Siberian Girls in Maui, and Nuclear Walruses: The North Pacific in a Sea of Islands," *Journal of Pacific History* 49, no. 4 (2014): 373–395 and (2013): 349–377.

25   See David Igler, "Hardly Pacific: Violence and Death on the Great Ocean," *Pacific Historical Review* 84, no. 1 (2015): 1–18, and Jones, "Kelp Highways," 373–395.

26   The account offered here is drawn from Tarakanov's account as published in Kenneth N. Owens, ed., and Alton S. Donnelly, trans., *The Wreck of the Sv. Nikolai* (Lincoln: Bison Books, 2001). The quotation is from page 44. I have chosen to avoid using the term *slavery* to describe the relations at the heart of this chapter for two reasons. First and foremost, the term is redolent of American-style chattel slavery, so different in valence and extent than systems

of unfreedom on the Northwest Coast, to the extent that it gives the wrong impression. Second, I have a sense that these foreigners were treated differently to some extent from Indigenous captives taken from elsewhere on the coast. I do want to acknowledge, though, that some Indigenous nations and historians use the term *slavery* in this context, and my position is not meant as a criticism of their framing of their own history.

27 Owens and Donnelly, *The Wreck of the Sv. Nikolai*, 65.

28 Owens and Donnelly, *The Wreck of the Sv. Nikolai*, 41.

29 George I. Quimby, "Japanese Wrecks, Iron Tools, and Prehistoric Indians of the Northwest Coast," *Arctic Anthropology* 22, no. 2 (1985): 10–11.

30 *The Letters of John McLoughlin from Fort Vancouver to the Governor and Committee*, first series, *1825–1838*, ed. E. E. Rich (Toronto: Champlain Society, 1941), 122.

31 Charles Wilkes, *Narrative of the United States Exploring Expedition, During the Years 1838, 1839, 1840, 1841, 1842* (Philadelphia: Lea and Blanchard, 1851), 4:315–316, and Samuel Parker, *Journal of an Exploring Tour beyond the Rocky Mountains* (Auburn, NY: C. Derby, 1846), 162–163.

32 Reid, *The Sea Is My Country*, 103–104.

33 See Horace Davis, *Record of Japanese Vessels Driven upon the North-West Coast of America and Its Outlying Islands* (Worcester, MA: Charles Hamilton, 1872), and Charles Wolcott Brooks, *Japanese Wrecks, Stranded and Picked up Adrift in the Pacific Ocean, Ethnologically Considered* (San Francisco: California Academy of Sciences, 1876).

34 *Kairei/Adrift at Sea*, dir. Masahisa Sadanaga (1983), http://www.archive.org.

35 Imbert Matthee, "Makah, Japanese Mark Historic Link," *Seattle Post-Intelligencer*, October 1, 1997, B-1.

36 "Musical at Meydenbauer Center Kicks Off Japan Week Festivities," *Seattle Times*, October 1, 1997, B3.

37 For the details of this publishing history, see Owens and Donnelly, *The Wreck of Sv. Nikolai*, 13–15.

38 Albert B. Reagan, "Some Traditions of the West Coast Indians" (1934), 87, quoted in Olympic Peninsula Intertribal Cultural Advisory Committee, *Native Peoples of the Olympic Peninsula: Who We Are*, ed. Jacilee Wray (Norman: University of Oklahoma Press, 2003), 137.

39 See the *Sviatoi Nikolai* kiosk texts in the Historical Marker Database, accessed December 26, 2022, http://www.hmdb.org.

40 Peggy Herring, *Anna, Like Thunder* (Victoria: Brindle & Glass, 2018), 54. Anna also appears in a locally published collection of women's history as "the first white woman to Washington." See Gary Peterson and Glynda Peterson Schaad, *Women to Reckon With: Untamed Women of the Olympic Wilderness* (Forks, WA: Poseidon Peak, 2007), 14–17.

41 Report of Indian agent Michael T. Simmons, Washington Superintendency, 1858, 232.

42 Neah Bay Agency Report, Washington Superintendency, 1862, 409–410.

43 Quinaielt Agency Report, Washington Superintendency, 1874, 335.

44 Neah Bay Agency Report, Washington Superintendency, 1879, 2.

45 Adeline Willoughby, "Wreck of the 'Sir Jamsetjee Family' near Point Elizabeth, Quinaielt, December 2nd, 1887," University of Washington Special Collections.

46 *Daily Astorian*, September 2, 1888, 3; *Aberdeen Herald*, January 15, 1891, 5; and "This Indian a Lifesaver," *Tulsa Weekly Democrat*, May 13, 1909, 5.

47 See Douglas Deur, "The Making of Seaside's 'Indian Place': Contested and Enduring Native Spaces on the Nineteenth Century Oregon Coast," *Oregon Historical Quarterly* 117, no. 4 (2016): 536–573.

48 See Jon D. Daehnke, *Chinook Resilience: Heritage and Cultural Revitalization on the Lower Columbia River* (Seattle: University of Washington Press, 2017).

49 See Lane and Lane, "Treaty Rights Workshop."

50 See Jacqueline M. Storm, ed., *Land of the Quinault* (Taholah: Quinault Indian Nation, 1991).

51 See Powell, "Quileute," *Smithsonian Handbook*.

52 See Reid, *The Sea Is My Country*.

TWO Troublous Days

1 For the early history of the society, see Amanda Laugesen, "George F. Himes, F. G. Young, and the Early Years of the Oregon Historical Society," *Oregon Historical Quarterly* 101, no. 1 (2000): 18–39.

2 Proceedings of the Oregon Historical Society, December 15, 1900, appendix A (1901), 22.

3 See Douglas Deur, "The Making of Seaside's 'Indian Place': Contested and Enduring Native Spaces on the Nineteenth Century Oregon Coast," *Oregon Historical Quarterly* 117, no. 4 (2016): 536–573.

4   McLoughlin to the Governor, Deputy Governor, and Committee, August 25, 1829, in *The Letters of John McLoughlin from Fort Vancouver to the Governor and Committee*, first series, *1825–1838*, ed. E. E. Rich (London: Champlain Society, 1941), 732. For discussion of the wider deployment of violence by fur trade companies in the period, see Jonathan R. Dean, "The Hudson's Bay Company and Its Use of Force, 1828–1829," *Oregon Historical Quarterly* 98, no. 3 (1997): 262–295.

5   Gabriel Franchère, *Narrative of a Voyage to the Northwest Coast of America in the Years 1811, 1812, 1813, and 1814, or the First American Settlement on the Pacific* (New York: Redfield, 1854), 112–113.

6   F. W. Howay, "Captain Cornelius Sowle on the Pacific Ocean," *Washington Historical Quarterly* 24, no. 4 (1933): 243.

7   Washington Irving, *Astoria* (New York: G. P. Putnam's Sons, 1836), 159.

8   The song's full lyrics are reproduced in Edmond S. Meany Jr., "The Later Life of John R. Jewitt," *British Columbia Historical Quarterly* 4, no. 3 (1940): 147–148.

9   For a reproduction of the playbill for this performance of *The Armourer's Escape*, see Hilary Stewart, *The Adventures and Sufferings of John R. Jewitt, Captive of Maquinna, Annotated and Illustrated by Hilary Stewart* (Vancouver: Douglas & McIntyre, 1987), 182. The original is held by the Historical Society of Pennsylvania.

10 Linda Tuhiwai Smith, *Decolonizing Methodologies: Research and Indigenous Peoples* (New York: Zed Books, 1999), 149.

11 For a detailed account of the event based on published sources available by the early 1970s, including precipitating incidents of violence against the Mowachaht that led to the killings, see Jean Brathwaite and W. J. Folan, "The Taking of the Ship *Boston*: An Ethnohistoric Study of Nootkan-European Conflict," *Syesis*, no. 5 (1972): 259–266. For a more recent summary and analysis, see Keith Carlson, "Clash at Clayoquot: Manifestations of Colonial and Indigenous Power in Pre-settler Colonial Canada," *Western Historical Quarterly* 48, no. 2 (2017): 159–188. Unlike Jewitt, McKay—who may have been illiterate—appears to have been unable to translate his experience for the broader public and disappears from the historical record after his rescue.

12 Robert F. Jones, ed., *Annals of Astoria: The Headquarters Log of the Pacific Fur Company on the Columbia River, 1811–1813* (New York: Fordham University Press, 1999), 191–195. In fact, word of Tonquin's demise had already reached

Astoria, but the traders were loath to believe their Chinook neighbors or publicly acknowledge that they were now in a position of vulnerability vis-à-vis those neighbors.

13 Joshua L. Reid, *The Sea Is My Country: The Maritime World of the Makahs* (New Haven, CT: Yale University Press, 2015), 56–57.

14 "Reviews," *Analectic Magazine*, no. 9 (1817), 141.

15 Meany, "The Later Life of John R. Jewitt," 143.

16 For two examples, see Samuel Patterson, *Narrative of the Adventures and Sufferings of Samuel Patterson: Experienced in the Pacific Ocean, and Many Other Parts of the World, with an Account of the Feegee, and Sandwich Islands* (Wilbraham, MA: Press in Palmer, 1817), and Solomon Bell, *Tales of Travel West of the Mississippi* (Boston: Gray and Bowen, 1830).

17 Stewart, *The Adventures and Sufferings of John R. Jewitt*, 182–184.

18 Daniel W. Clayton, *Islands of Truth: The Imperial Fashioning of Vancouver Island* (Vancouver: UBC Press, 2000), 142.

19 "Destruction of the Tonquin," *Atheneum; or, Spirit of the English Magazines*, October 1, 1831, 2, and Ross Cox, *Adventures on the Columbia River, Including the Narrative of a Residence of Six Years on the Western Side of the Rocky Mountains among Various Tribes of Indians Hitherto Unknown: Together with a Journey across the American Continent* (New York: J. & J. Harper, 1832), 63–67. See also Edmund Fanning, *Voyages to the South Seas, Indian and Pacific Oceans, China Sea, North-West Coast, Feejee Islands, South Shetlands, &c. &c. with an Account of the New Discoveries Made in the Southern Hemisphere, Between the Years 1830–1837* (New York: William H. Vermilye, 1838), 137–149.

20 Edgar Allen Poe, "Review of *Astoria*," in *The Works of the Late Edgar Allen Poe* (1856), 4:420–447.

21 For discussion, see Thomas Philbrick, *James Fenimore Cooper and the Development of American Sea Fiction* (Cambridge, MA: Harvard University Press, 1961), 135–145.

22 For discussion of captivity narratives, see Lawrence A. Peskin, *Captives and Countrymen: Barbary Slavery and the American Public, 1785–1816* (Baltimore: Johns Hopkins University Press, 2009); Pauline Turner Strong, *Captive Selves, Captivating Others: The Politics and Poetics of Colonial American Captivity Narratives* (London: Routledge, 1999); and Robbie Richardson, *The Savage and Modern Self: North American Indians in Eighteenth-Century British Literature and Culture* (Toronto: University of Toronto Press, 2018).

23 Robin Miskolcze, *Women and Children First: Nineteenth-Century Sea Narratives and American Identity* (Lincoln: University of Nebraska Press, 2008), 2.

24 Jason Berger, *Antebellum at Sea: Maritime Fantasies in Nineteenth-Century America* (Minneapolis: University of Minnesota Press, 2012), 13; Hester Blum, *The View from the Masthead: Maritime Imagination and Antebellum Sea Narratives* (Chapel Hill: University North Carolina Press, 2008); Caleb Scofield Doan, "Pacific Crosswinds: Antebellum American Fiction and the Transpacific World" (PhD diss., Louisiana State University, 2020); and Amy Mitchell-Cook, *A Sea of Misadventures: Shipwreck and Survival in Early America* (Columbia: University of South Carolina Press, 2013).

25 John R. Gillis, *The Human Shore: Seacoasts in History* (Chicago: University of Chicago Press, 2012), 140; "Reviews," *Analectic Magazine*, no. 5 (1815), 496.

26 H. G. Chipman, "Historical Sketch: The Fate of the Tonquin," *Saturday Evening Post*, September 15, 1849, 4.

27 "Narrative of a Voyage from London to Columbia River, and an Account of the First Settlers There," *Literary Gazette*, September 22, 1821, 605.

28 See Boyd Cothran, *Remembering the Modoc War: Redemptive Violence and the Making of American Innocence* (Chapel Hill: University of North Carolina Press, 2014), and Emilie Cameron, *Far-Off Metal River: Inuit Lands, Settler Stories, and the Making of the Contemporary Arctic* (Vancouver: UBC Press, 2015).

29 Peter Stark, *Astoria: John Jacob Astor and Thomas Jefferson's Lost Pacific Empire* (New York: Ecco, 2014), 24.

30 Franchère, *Narrative of a Voyage*, 186; John Scouler, "Dr. John Scouler's Journal of a Voyage to N. W. America," *Quarterly of the Oregon Historical Society* 6, no. 2 (1905): 194.

31 Cox, *Adventures on the Columbia River*, 55.

32 Irving, *Astoria*, 61; Samuel Parker, *Journal of an Exploring Tour beyond the Rocky Mountains* (Auburn, NY: C. Derby, 1846), 162.

33 F. W. Howay, "A Ballad of the Northwest Fur Trade," *New England Quarterly*, no. 1 (1928), 78–79.

34 F. W. Howay, W. N. Sage, and H. F. Angus, *British Columbia and the United States: The North Pacific Slope from Fur Trade to Aviation* (New York: Russell & Russell, 1942), 12.

35 "Reviews," *Analectic Magazine*, no. 5 (1815), 494.

36 Tracy Banivanua-Mar, *Violence and Colonial Dialogue: The Australian-Pacific Indentured Labor Trade* (Honolulu: University of Hawai'i Press, 2007), 36.

37 F. W. Howay, "Ballad of the Bold Northwestman: An Incident in the Life of Captain John Kendrick," *Washington Historical Quarterly* 20, no. 2 (1929): 117.

38 Hiram M. Chittenden, *The American Fur Trade in the Far West* (New York: Francis P. Harper, 1902), 849. Not long after his account of the fur trade was published, Chittenden would lead the construction of a set of locks in Seattle that linked Puget Sound to Lake Washington. Ultimately named after him, the locks profoundly changed local watersheds by, among other things, eradicating the Black River, a centrally important place of residence and sustenance for the local Duwamish people. For the story of the locks and their legacy, see Coll Thrush, "City of the Changers: Indigenous People and the Transformation of Seattle's Watersheds," *Pacific Historical Review* 75, no. 1 (2006): 89–117.

39 Kenton Storey, *Settler Anxiety at the Outposts of Empire: Colonial Relations, Humanitarian Discourses, and the Imperial Press* (Vancouver: UBC Press, 2016), 13.

40 Storey, *Settler Anxiety*, 41–42.

41 Quoted in Storey, *Settler Anxiety*, 57.

42 Barry M. Gough, *Gunboat Frontier: British Maritime Authority and Northwest Coast Indians, 1846–1890* (Vancouver: UBC Press, 1984), 109. See also Chris Arnett, *The Terror of the Coast: Land Alienation and Colonial War on Vancouver Island and the Gulf Islands, 1849–1863* (Vancouver: Talonbooks, 1999).

43 Heidi Kiiwetinepinesiik Stark, "Criminal Empire: The Making of the Savage in a Lawless Land," *Theory & Event* 19, no. 4 (2016): n.p.

44 Gough, *Gunboat Frontier*, 109.

45 Laura Ishiguro, *Nothing to Write Home About: British Family Correspondence and the Settler Colonial Everyday in British Columbia* (Vancouver: UBC Press, 2019).

46 Quoted in Storey, *Settler Anxiety*, 113.

47 For the development reel of a forthcoming documentary that will chronicle the *Kingfisher* incident and its aftermath, see "Illustrated Legacies Development Reel 24.03.22," YouTube, accessed October 5, 2024, https://www.youtube.com/watch?v=YZZt6cYtFCc.

48 Eugene Arima and Alan Hoover, *The Whaling People of the West Coast of Vancouver Island and Cape Flattery* (Victoria: Royal BC Museum, 2011), 179–181, and Gilbert Malcolm Sproat, *Scenes and Studies of Savage Life* (London: Smith, Elder and Co., 1868), 196. For what appears to be Denman's account of

the attacks, see "Reporting Proceedings Respecting the Murder of the Crew of the *Kingfisher*," H. Janssen Fonds L4587, British Columbia Maritime Museum.

49 "The Naval Fight with the Indians," *Victoria Daily Colonist*, October 12, 1864, 2.

50 For one account of the trial, see "Bench Books for Criminal Cases Heard by Judge Joseph Needham, 1867–1869," Vancouver Island Supreme Court of Civil Justice, GR-2030 vol. 2, microfilm B09802, BC Archives, 171–227.

51 D. W. Higgins, *The Passing of a Race and More Tales of Western Life* (Toronto: William Briggs, 1905), 183, 185.

52 August-Joseph Brabant, *Vancouver Island and Its Missions, 1874–1900: Reminiscences of the Rev. A. J. Brabant* (Montreal: Messenger of the Sacred Heart Press, 1900), 22–23.

53 "Clayoquot Sound Indians," *Victoria British Colonist*, May 23, 1875, 3.

54 E. W. Wright, ed., *Lewis & Dryden's Marine History of the Pacific Northwest* (Portland: Lewis & Dryden Printing, 1895), 27n19, 62, 229, 272–273, 279–280, 314, 333, 340–341, 359, 381–382.

55 Interview with Carl Edgar Jr., February 15, 2024.

56 R. E. Wells, *There's a Landing Today: Stories about the Lives of West Coast Residents of Vancouver Island between Port Renfrew and Cape Beale* (Victoria: Sono Nis, 1988), 20.

57 "Saw Victoria at Its Birth," *Victoria Daily Colonist*, January 21, 1912, 7; F. W. Howay, "Indian Attacks upon Maritime Traders of the North-West Coast, 1785–1805," *Canadian Historical Review* 6, no. 4 (1925): 304.

58 For examples, see "The West Coast of Vancouver Island," *Victoria Daily Colonist*, October 8, 1922, 22; "Old Trading Post," *Victoria Daily Colonist*, August 3, 1924, 32; "Maquina's [sic] Massacre of Boston's Crew Recalled," *Victoria Daily Colonist*, June 26, 1927, 15; "John Rodgers Jewitt Slave of the Nootkas," *Victoria Daily Colonist*, July 5, 1953, 4; "Massacre on the Boston," *Victoria Daily Colonist* Sunday Magazine, January 7, 1979, 2.

59 "Jewitt's Captivity with Indians Makes Exciting Adventure Story," *Victoria Daily Colonist*, December 15, 1968.

60 For examples, see "The 'Tonquin' Massacre: Slaughter of Crew on Account of an Indignity Done a Chief by the Captain," *Victoria British Colonist*, September 29, 1886, 8; "Correcting History: Captain Walbran's Recent Discoveries Concerning the Memorable 'Tonquin' Massacre," *Victoria Daily Colonist*,

August 6, 1896, 3; "Disappearance of the Tonquin," *Victoria Daily Colonist*, August 13, 1896, 6; Cyrus Townsend Brady, "The Cruise of the 'Tonquin': A Forgotten Tragedy in Early American History," *Harper's Monthly Magazine*, no. 108 (December 1, 1903), 463–469; Edmond S. Meany, *Vancouver's Discovery of Puget Sound: Portraits and Biographies of the Men Honored in the Naming of Geographic Features of Northwest America* (New York: Macmillan, 1907), 49; and F. W. Howay, "The Loss of the Tonquin," *Washington Historical Quarterly* 13, no. 2 (1922): 83–92.

61 Charles Moser, *Reminiscences of the West Coast of Vancouver Island* (Victoria: Acme, 1926), vii.

62 "The War That Both Sides Lost," *Victoria Daily Colonist*, May 19, 1935, 6.

63 "Franchot Tone Stars in 'This Woman Is Mine,'" *Victoria Daily Colonist*, December 7, 1941, 20. For a review of the film, see "'This Woman Is Mine,' a Tepid Tale of Adventure and Fur Trading, with Franchot Tone, at the Rivoli," *New York Times*, October 13, 1941. "Instead of full-blooded fiction," the reviewer "T.S." wrote, director Frank Lloyd "has filmed an ordinary and trivial romantic episode in which the characters are too ridiculous to be interesting in themselves. A good ducking in salt spray would have done them, and the picture, a lot of good." For the children's page, see "The Massacre of the Tonquin," *Victoria Daily Colonist*, June 20, 1943, 7.

64 Thomas M. Aumack, *Rivers of Rain: Being a Fictional Accounting of the Adventures and Misadventures of John Rodgers Jewitt, Captive of the Indians at Friendly Cove on Nootka Island in Northwest America* (Portland: Binfords & Mort, 1948).

65 "Expedition Seeks Long-Lost Ship," *Victoria Daily Colonist*, July 12, 1962, 33.

66 Gilbert Malcolm Sproat, *Scenes and Studies of Savage Life* (London: Smith, Elder, 1868), 11.

67 Paul Kane, Wanderings of an Artist among the Indians of North America (London: Spottiswoode, 1859), 237: "He [Yelakub] accompanied me to my room, where I made a sketch of him, and had from him a recital of much of his private history. Yellow-cum's father was the pilot of the unfortunate 'Tonquin,' the vessel sent out by John Jacob Astor to trade with the Indians north of Vancouver's Island, mentioned in Washington Irving's 'Astoria.' He was the only survivor who escaped from the vessel previous to her being blown up, the rest of the unfortunate crew having been butchered on board, or blown up with the ship. It was impossible to obtain a clear narrative of this melancholy event,

as no white man lived to tell the tale." For the Fort Langley example, see B. A. McKelvie, *Tales of Conflict* (Montreal: Southam Press, 1950), 5.

68 Stewart, *The Adventures and Sufferings of John R. Jewitt*, 7–8; Brian Tate, "Maquinna and Jewitt Families Reunite," *Ha-Shilth-Sa*, August 14, 2003, 1, 11.

69 Randy Boswell, "A Veteran Diver from the Vancouver Island Community of Tofino Discovered and Raised a 200-Year-Old Anchor that He's Convinced Came from the Tonquin, a Legendary U.S. Ship," *CanWest News*, September 24, 2003, 1.

70 Christine Lowther, "The Tonquin Promises to Anchor the Economy," *Vancouver Sun*, December 20, 2003, F17, and Chris Lowther, "Anchor a Way," *Beaver* 84, no. 1 (2004): 4–5.

71 Keven Drews, "Historic Trade Ship Tonquin to Be Built Again," *Alberni Valley Times*, July 4, 2005, 1.

72 In her article "A Debt to the Dead? Ethics, Photography, History and the Study of Freakery," historian Jane Nicholas discusses the moral and ethical quandaries involved in showing photographs of people, and especially children, in states of abjection. While such images can serve as a kind of witnessing, they can also reify and rehearse the power dynamics of the gaze that informed the creation of the photo in the first place. Writing of two siblings with a rare skin condition, Nicholas argues that as a scholar, she is implicated in those politics of looking, although she ultimately decides to include the photo of the children in her article. See Nicholas, "A Debt to the Dead?" *Histoire Sociale/Social History* 47, no. 93 (2014): 139–155. In the case of the young Ahousaht girl renamed "Maggie Sutlej," a photo of the child is held by the British Columbia Archives, but I have chosen not to include it in this book. I was not able to establish a formal relationship with the Ahousaht First Nation to determine their wishes before submitting the manuscript, and because the photo is one of captivity and abjection, I ultimately decided to forgo using it in *Wrecked*. Of course, interested readers can find it on their own.

73 Katie DeRosa, "Ahousaht First Nation, Sikh Agency Connect to Right Wrong of British Past," *Victoria Times-Colonist*, October 26, 2018, http://www.timescolonist.com, and Denise Titian, "Who Was Maggie Sutlej? Humanitarian Aid Group Reaches Out to Ahousaht 150 Years after Wartime Abduction of Child," *Ha-Shilth-Sa*, October 11, 2018, https://hashilthsa.com.

74 "Hesquiaht and B.C. Come Together to Begin Healing an Old Wound," Hesquiaht First Nation and Government of British Columbia joint press

release, November 17, 2012, https://news.gov.bc.ca/releases/2012ARR 0031-001806.

75 "Editorial: Port Alberni's Hesquiaht First Nations Healing Wounds after 143 Years," *Victoria Times-Colonist*, November 23, 2012, http://www.timescolonist .com.

76 Wawmeesh G. Hamilton, "Hesquiaht First Nation Forgives Province for Century Old Hanging," *Alberni Valley News*, November 18, 2012, http://www .albernivalleynews.com.

77 Armina Ligaya, "'Closure to the Pain': B.C. Government Expresses Regret over First Nations Hangings," *National Post*, November 18, 2012, https:// nationalpost.com.

78 Eric Plummer, "Exoneration from Ottawa Resurfaces a Historic Injustice for a Hesquiaht Chief," *Ha-Shilth-Sa*, April 4, 2018, https://hashilthsa.com.

79 Franz Boas, *Chinook Texts* (Washington: Government Printing Office, 1894), 5.

80 Deur, "The Making of Seaside's 'Indian Place.'"

THREE All Lost

1   E. W. Wright, ed., *Lewis & Dryden's Marine History of the Pacific Northwest* (Portland: Lewis & Dryden Printing, 1895), 289; "The Wreck of the *Lupatia*," MSS 1, box 35, folder 1119–1124, Boise State University Special Collections; and *Annual Report of the Light-House Board to the Secretary of the Treasury for the Fiscal Year Ending June 30, 1881* (Washington, DC: Government Printing Office, 1881), 124. In a 2015 contribution to the website Backpacker, writer Cody Bond described a night spent within sight of Terrible Tilly, during which he and his fiancée imagined they heard a dog howling in the darkness. Cody Bond, "The Last Night of the Lupatia," Backpacker, October 21, 2015, https://www.backpacker.com/survival/the-last-night-of-the-Lupatia. The Graveyard of the Pacific, as we shall see, is haunted in many ways.

2   For more details regarding the storm, along with reproductions of news articles from May 1880, see Liisa Penner, *Salmon Fever: River's End, Tragedies of the Lower Columbia River in the 1870s, 1880s, and 1890s* (Portland: Frank Amato, 2006), 33–44.

3   "The Lost Lumber Ship," *Seattle Post-Intelligencer*, December 15, 1894, 1; "Six Days Overdue," *Seattle Post-Intelligencer*, December 17, 1894, 1; "Almost Surely Lost," *Seattle Post-Intelligencer*, December 18, 1894, 1; "Ten Vessels Missing,"

Seattle Post-Intelligencer, December 20, 1894, 1; "Bark Columbia Safe," *Seattle Post-Intelligencer*, December 31, 1894, 2; "Ship J. B. Brown Reaches Port," *Seattle Post-Intelligencer*, January 1, 1895, 1; "The Lost Sealers," *Seattle Post-Intelligencer*, May 8, 1895, 1; Wright, *Lewis & Dryden's Marine History*, 415–417.

4   Fred Lockley, description of the *General Warren* wreck, July 3, 1930, Oregon Historical Society Archives, and James G. Swan, *The Northwest Coast; or Three Years' Residence in Washington Territory* (New York: Harper & Brothers, 1857), 259.

5   Jennifer Kozik, "*Desdemona*: Namesake from the Oregon Territory, 1857," in *Shipwrecks of the Pacific Northwest: Tragedies and Legacies of a Perilous Coast*, ed. Jennifer Kozik (Guilford, CT: Globe Pequot, 2020), 48.

6   "Fourteen Lives Lost," *Dalles Daily Chronicle*, October 21, 1896, 1, and "The Wrecked Arago," *Daily Capital Journal*, October 22, 1896, 1.

7   "The Loss of the Reed," *Daily Morning Astorian*, February 16, 1908, 2.

8   "58 Perish When Steamer Sinks," *Athena Press*, September 25, 1914, 1; "Newport," *Lincoln County Leader*, September 25, 1914, 1, 3; and "The Pitiless Ocean," *Daily Capital Journal*, September 28, 1914, 5.

9   John M. Shively, "John M. Shively's Memoir," *Oregon Historical Quarterly* 81, no. 1 (1980): 4–29, and 81, no. 2 (1980): 190.

10 *Vancouver Independent*, April 24, 1879, 5; *Seattle Daily Intelligencer*, May 13, 1879, 3. For a detailed account of the wreck of *Great Republic*, see Wright, *Lewis & Dryden's Marine History*, 265–266.

11 *Daily Astorian*, May 8, 1881, 3.

12 *Puget Sound Weekly Argus*, January 27, 1882, 5, and "Wreck of the Harvest Home," *Washington Standard*, January 27, 1882, 2.

13 August-Joseph Brabant, *Vancouver Island and Its Missions, 1874–1900: Reminiscences of the Rev. A. J. Brabant* (Montreal: Messenger of the Sacred Heart Press, 1900), 30.

14 In this, the Graveyard of the Pacific served a function similar to other death-scapes in the nineteenth century. Of particular note are British graves in overseas colonies, the six thousand dead along the Oregon Trail, and the narratives of Civil War battlefields that undergirded white supremacy, articulated through the mourning of a war "between brothers." See Andrew Prescott Keating, "Empire of the Dead: British Burial Abroad and the Formation of National Identity" (PhD diss., University of California–Berkeley, 2011); Sarah Keyes, *American Burial Ground: A New History of the Overland Trail* (Philadelphia:

University of Pennsylvania Press, 2023); and Kirk Savage, *Standing Soldiers, Kneeling Slaves: Race, War, and Monument in Nineteenth-Century America*, 2nd ed. (Princeton: Princeton University Press, 2018).

15   *Victoria British Colonist*, November 9, 1875, quoted in Wright, *Lewis & Dryden's Marine History*, 225.

16   "Jeff Howell," *Puget Sound Dispatch*, December 2, 1875, 3.

17   "The Topic of the Week," *Washington Standard*, November 13, 1875, 2; Wright, *Lewis & Dryden's Marine History*, 225. For the life of one *Pacific* victim, see Greg Stott, "A Great Old Tramp: Letters from a Canadian Sojourner in British Columbia, 1873–1875," *Ormsby Review*, September 26, 2018, https://ormsby review.com/2018/09/26/123-ill-bid-you-klahowya [link is no longer active].

18   Wright, *Lewis & Dryden's Marine History*, 225.

19   Wright, *Lewis & Dryden's Marine History*, 227.

20   "Death on the Wave," *Victoria British Colonist*, November 24, 1875, 2, and "Captain Howell," *Victoria British Colonist*, November 26, 1875, 2.

21   For examples, see "Mr. Hastings," *Victoria British Colonist*, November 23, 1875, 3; "Discovery with Respect to Mrs. Helmuth's Body," *Victoria British Colonist*, November 26, 1875, 3; "What Captain of the *Arkwright* Saw," *Victoria British Colonist*, December 5, 1875, 3; and Wright, *Lewis & Dryden's Marine History*, 223.

22   George Mason, *Ode on the Loss of the Steamship 'Pacific,' Nov. 4, 1875* (Nanaimo, BC: George Norris, 1875). See also James P. Delgado, "Loss of the Steamship *Pacific*, November 4th, 1875: Poetry and Commentary," *Canadian Literature*, no. 218 (2013): n.p.

23   *Victoria British Colonist*, February 12, 1876, 3.

24   Frances Fuller Victor, *The New Penelope: Stories and Poems* (San Francisco: A. L. Bancroft, 1877). In Victor's earlier work, she had used maritime metaphors to describe American colonization of the western part of North America. "Upon Oregon, California, and Utah there followed Nevada, Colorado, Idaho, Montana," she wrote in the *Overland Monthly*, "each the result of one of those great and sudden impulses which move the 'human sea;' not in that 'low wash of waves,' by which ordinary emigration is symbolized in one of our typical American poems, but in great tidal waves of astonishing power." She could not possibly have imagined that such oceanic metaphors would become a tragic reality in her own life. See "Manifest Destiny in the West," *Overland Monthly* 3, no. 2 (1869): 158.

25 "The Veil Lifted," *Victoria British Colonist*, November 16, 1875, 2.

26 Wright, *Lewis & Dryden's Marine History*, 223.

27 Wright, *Lewis & Dryden's Marine History*, 70.

28 Wright, *Lewis & Dryden's Marine History*, v.

29 Wright, *Lewis & Dryden's Marine History*, 1.

30 Wright, *Lewis & Dryden's Marine History*, 421.

31 "The Pacific," *Weekly Argus*, November 20, 1875, 2. The piece of wood is now on display at the Vancouver Maritime Museum.

32 Wright, *Lewis & Dryden's Marine History*, 180, and Maria J. Smith file at Vancouver Maritime Museum.

33 *Victoria Daily Colonist*, February 22, 1902, 8; *Victoria Daily Colonist*, March 1, 1902, 8; "That Derelict," *Victoria Daily Colonist*, March 5, 1902, 2; *Victoria Daily Colonist*, March 6, 1902, 8; *Victoria Daily Colonist*, March 7, 1902, 8; and *Victoria Daily Colonist*, March 15, 1902, 3.

34 *Victoria Daily Colonist*, March 26, 1902, 1.

35 *Victoria Daily Colonist*, May 3, 1902, 3.

36 "The Ship John Marshall Really Lost," *Victoria British Colonist*, December 18, 1860, 2.

37 *Daily Morning Astorian*, January 8, 1890, 3.

38 James A. Gibbs, *Shipwrecks of the Pacific Coast* (Portland: Binfords & Mort, 1957), 35–41.

39 *East Oregonian*, September 23, 1913, 1.

40 *Dalles Daily Chronicle*, October 29, 1894, 2.

41 "Disappeared in the Waves: The Fanny Dutard Sights a Vessel in Distress, which Afterwards Sinks—Thought to Be the Ivanhoe," *Daily Morning Astorian*, November 3, 1894, 1.

42 *Daily Morning Astorian*, November 3, 1894, 1.

43 *Dalles Daily Chronicle*, November 3, 1894, 1.

44 *Lincoln County Leader*, December 13, 1894, 1; *Seattle Post-Intelligencer*, November 28, 1894, 1; *Seattle Post-Intelligencer*, October 24, 1894, 3.

45 *Daily Morning Astorian*, December 21, 1894, 1.

46 *Hood River Glacier*, November 3, 1894, 1.

47 Wright, *Lewis & Dryden's Marine History*, 339.

48 Gordon R. Newell, *SOS North Pacific: Tales of Shipwrecks off the Washington, British Columbia, and Alaska Coasts* (Portland: Binfords & Mort, 1955), 96.

49 "The Wreck of the Leonor," *Seattle Post-Intelligencer*, November 6, 1893, 4.

50 "Eighteen Were Drowned," *Pullman Herald*, January 10, 1903, 7.

51 Wright, *Lewis & Dryden's Marine History*, 394; "On a Perilous Coast," *Seattle Post-Intelligencer*, November 4, 1891, 1; "Drifting in the Fog," *Seattle Post-Intelligencer*, November 5, 1891, 1; "Sufferings at Sea," *Seattle Post-Intelligencer*, November 8, 1891, 2; "From Mother Lodge," *Seattle Post-Intelligencer*, June 10, 1897, 5.

52 "Received Letter as from the Dead," *Daily Capital Journal*, November 10, 1915, 3. Thanks to Leslie Anne Meyer for conducting genealogical research to back up newspaper accounts.

53 "The *Santa Clara* Is Wrecked," *Daily Capital Journal*, November 3, 1915, 1; "Bodies Recovered Are All Identified," *Daily Capital Journal*, November 4, 1915, 3; "Nine Die as Steamer Santa Clara Goes Aground on Coos Bay Shoal," *Weston Leader*, November 5, 1815, 1; and "Gold Hill Boy Lost in Wreck," *Ashland Tidings*, November 8, 1915, 1.

54 "*Santa Clara* Wreck Pounding to Pieces," *Daily Capital Journal*, November 6, 1915, 6; "Arrests Are Expected," *East Oregonian*, November 9, 1915, 6; and "Looters Burn the Wreck of the *Santa Clara*," *East Oregonian*, November 12, 1915, 2.

55 Leyland Cecco, "Has the SS *Pacific*'s Gold-Laden Wreck Been Found 150 Years after It Sank?," *Guardian*, December 15, 2022, http://www.guardian.co.uk , and David Carrigg, "No Takers for Long-Lost Gold in Sunken Ship That Departed Victoria in 1875," *Vancouver Sun*, January 1, 2024.

FOUR   The Green Fire of *Emily G. Reed*

1 *Morning Astorian*, December 25, 1900, 3.

2 Jamin Wells, *Shipwrecked: Coastal Disasters and the Making of the American Beach* (Chapel Hill: University of North Carolina Press, 2020), 2.

3 E. W. Wright, ed., *Lewis & Dryden's Marine History of the Pacific Northwest* (Portland: Lewis & Dryden Printing, 1895), 228–229; "Wreck of Bark Florence," *Weekly Argus* (Port Townsend), December 4, 1875, 2; Lionel Youst, *She's Tricky Like Coyote: Annie Miner Peterson, an Oregon Coast Indian Woman* (Norman: University of Oklahoma Press, 1997), 103–104.

4 Don Marshall, *Oregon Shipwrecks* (Portland: Binford & Mort, 1984), 82–84; Neil M. Howison to George Abernathy, September 15, 1846, MSS 929, OHS; and letter from James Douglas to James M. Yale, May 21, 1848, Columbia River Maritime Museum.

5   James G. Swan, *The Northwest Coast; or Three Years' Residence in Washington Territory* (New York: Harper & Brothers, 1857), 43–44.

6   "Wrecked on Seabird Rocks," *Victoria Daily Colonist*, January 24, 1909, 10; "Rescue of Soquel Crew," *Victoria Daily Colonist*, January 26, 1909, 10; "Incidents of Soquel Wreck," *Victoria Daily Colonist*, January 27, 1909, 10. The carvings are in the collection of the University of British Columbia's Museum of Anthropology.

7   Swan, *The Northwest Coast*, 54.

8   Wright, *Lewis & Dryden's Marine History*, 382–383.

9   *Seattle Daily Times*, May 8, 1937, 1, 14.

10 Wright, *Lewis & Dryden's Marine History*, 104.

11 Lucile McDonald, *Coast Country: A History of Southwest Washington* (Portland: Binford & Mort, 1966), 127.

12 Gail Oberst, "Shipwreck Discovery," *Oregon Coast*, January/February 2008, 26.

13 "Rescuing the Abercorn's Rails," *Seattle Post-Intelligencer*, June 18, 1891, 4, and "The Abercorn's Cargo," *Aberdeen Herald*, June 25, 1891, 8.

14 McDonald, *Coast Country*, 133.

15 Robert Johnson, "Mauna Ala: Yule Ship," in *Shipwrecks of the Pacific Northwest: Tragedies and Legacies of a Perilous Coast*, ed. Jennifer Kozik (Guilford, CT: Globe Pequot, 2020), 120–135.

16 Brad Duncan and Martin Gibbs, *Please God Send Me a Wreck: Responses to Shipwreck in a 19th-Century Australian Community* (New York: Springer, 2015), 1, 2.

17 "Held at Bay," *Daily Morning Astorian*, September 22, 1895, 3.

18 McDonald, *Coast Country*, 126–128.

19 McDonald, *Coast Country*, 128–130.

20 McDonald, *Coast Country*, 134–135.

21 McDonald, *Coast Country*, 130, 133–134.

22 For the story of *Iowa*, see Jim Sharpe, "*Iowa*: Hurricane-Force Winds and Tragedy on Peacock Spit, 1936," in Kozik, *Shipwrecks of the Pacific Northwest*, 95–106.

23 McDonald, *Coast Country*, 132–133.

24 Eva Emery Dye, "Boone Family Reminiscences as Told to Mrs. Dye," *Oregon Historical Quarterly* 42, no. 3 (1941): 220–229.

25 Gough, *Gunboat Frontier*, 111–112. For a particularly unflattering portrayal of the events, see Wright, *Lewis & Dryden's Marine History*, 90.

26 R. Bruce Scott, *"Breakers Ahead!": A History of Shipwrecks on the Graveyard of the Pacific* (Sidney, BC: Review Publishing House, 1970), 37–39.

27 "Ship Afire on Rocks Near Flattery," *Seattle Daily Times*, December 16, 1929, 1, 5; "Captain Awaits Fate," *Seattle Daily Times,* December 20, 1929, 15; "Captain Acted to Save Lives," *Seattle Daily Times*, December 21, 1929, 1, 3.

28 Beverly Lemire, *Global Trade and the Transformation of Consumer Cultures: The Material World Remade, ca. 1500–1820* (Cambridge: Cambridge University Press, 2018), 171.

29 McDonald, *Coast Country*, 122.

30 Wright, *Lewis & Dryden's Marine History*, 301–302; McDonald, *Coast Country*, 127–128.

31 McDonald, *Coast Country*, 131–132.

32 "The Glenmorag and Potrimpos," *Seattle Post-Intelligencer*, December 26, 1895, 8.

33 *Aberdeen Herald*, August 1, 1895, 1.

34 "Galena Comes Ashore," *Daily Capital Journal* (Salem), November 16, 1906, 6; *Daily Astorian*, November 16, 1906, 4; "To the Wrecks," *Morning Astorian*, November 17, 1906, 5; and *Morning Astorian*, July 2, 1907, 2.

35 Sydney Stevens, *North Beach Peninsula's IR&N* (Charleston, SC: Arcadia, 2009), 44.

36 "Driven Ashore," *Aberdeen Herald*, April 5, 1909, 1.

37 "Holidayed in Ocean Graveyard," *Victoria Daily Colonist*, July 6, 1910, 8.

38 For the longer biography of the ship and the wrangling over the cause of its loss, see Jennifer Kozik, "*Glenesslin*: Iconic Sailing Ship vs. Neahkahnie Mountain, 1913," in Kozik, *Shipwrecks of the Pacific Northwest*, 79–94.

39 George Nicholson, *Vancouver Island's West Coast, 1792–1962* (Victoria: Morriss, 1965), 248–249.

40 "Pirates and Pirates," *Coos Bay World*, November 12, 1915, n.p.

41 "Simpson Lumber Company Schooner Total Wreck Off Point at Coos Head," *Coos Bay World*, February 19, 1913, n.p.

42 *Coos Bay World*, February 25, 1913, n.p.

43 "Claremont Turns," *Coos Bay World*, November 8, 1915, 1.

44 "South Inlet Wants In Too," *Coos Bay World*, January 19, 1912, n.p.

45 "Remarks of the Waterfront Observer," *Coos Bay World*, March 30, 1917, n.p.

46 "Slough Raiders Sent to Prison," *Coos Bay World*, June 17, 1925, n.p.

47 "Football Teams Play," *Coos Bay World*, November 13, 1931, n.p.

48 Phil Matson, "Pirate Days," *Coos Bay World*, April 30, 2012.

49 Steve Mentz, *Shipwreck Modernity: Ecologies of Globalization, 1550–1719* (Minneapolis: University of Minnesota Press, 2015), 22.

50 Sydney Stevens, *Ghost Stories of the Long Beach Peninsula* (Charleston, SC: History Press, 2014), 56.

51 Stevens, *Ghost Stories of the Long Beach Peninsula*, 51–57.

52 Anna Lowenhaupt Tsing, *Friction: An Ethnography of Global Connection* (Princeton, NJ: Princeton University Press, 2004), 74.

53 Lori Tobias, "Waves Exhume a Skeleton," *Oregonian*, December 30, 2010, C1–C2. See also "Shifting Sands Reveal Lost Treasure," *Daily Astorian*, January 7, 2011.

FIVE Out of Time

1 "Have You Seen the Phantom Ship?," *Seattle Times* Sunday Magazine, January 30, 1910, 1.

2 T. W. Paterson, "Mysteries of the Deep," *Victoria Colonist* Sunday Magazine, July 30, 1972, 12, 13.

3 T. W. Paterson, "Phantom Derelicts of the West Coast," *Victoria Colonist* Sunday Magazine, June 17, 1973, 10, 11.

4 T. W. Paterson, "Rescuers Watched Helplessly As 117 Died on Valencia," *Victoria Colonist* Sunday Magazine, January 4, 1976, 14, 15.

5 For two recent examples, see Janice Oberding, *The Big Book of Oregon Ghost Stories* (Essex, CT: Globe Pequot, 2022), and Bess Lovejoy, *Northwest Know-How: Haunts* (Seattle: Sasquatch Books, 2022).

6 Anthony Dalton, *The Graveyard of the Pacific: Shipwreck Tales from the Depths of History* (Victoria: Heritage House, 2010), 11.

7 Terry Glavin, *The Last Great Sea: A Voyage through the Human and Natural History of the North Pacific Ocean* (Vancouver: Douglas & McIntyre, 2000), 12.

8 See, for example, Shannon Sinn, *The Haunting of Vancouver Island: Supernatural Encounters with the Other Side* (Victoria: Touchwood Editions, 2017), which includes an account of *Valencia* and its spooky aftermath.

9 Interview with Carl Edgar Jr., February 15, 2024.

10 Michel de Certeau, *The Practice of Everyday Life*, trans. Steven Rendall (Berkeley: University of California Press, 1984), 108.

11 See Judith Richardson, *Possessions: The History and Uses of Hauntings in the Hudson Valley* (Cambridge, MA: Harvard University Press, 2009).

12 For the cultural functions of Indigenous ghosts, see Emilie Cameron, "Indigenous Spectrality and the Politics of Postcolonial Ghost Stories," *Cultural Geographies* 15, no. 3 (2008): 384; Natalie J. K. Baloy, "Spectacle, Spectrality, and the Everyday: Settler Colonialism, Aboriginal Alterity, and Inclusion in Vancouver" (PhD diss., University of British Columbia, 2014); Renée L. Bergland, *The National Uncanny: Indian Ghosts and American Subjects* (Hanover, MA: University Press of New England, 1999); and Coll Thrush and Colleen E. Boyd, eds., *Phantom Past, Indigenous Presence: Native Ghosts in North American Culture and History* (Lincoln: University of Nebraska Press, 2011).

13 The larger petroscape of which the coast is now firmly a part might be considered what Timothy Morton calls a "hyperobject," something we cannot directly experience on the scale of human spatial or temporal understandings. We might encounter a hyperobject's local manifestations, but as Morton makes clear, those manifestations are not the thing itself. In other words, the rainbow sheen left by an oil spill is not the global petrochemical system but merely a local instantiation of it. And notably, like diesel, Morton's hyperobjects are viscous, in that "they 'stick' to those that are involved with them." See Timothy Morton, *Hyperobjects: Philosophy and Ecology after the End of the World* (Minneapolis: University of Minnesota Press, 2013), 1.

14 Margaret Cohen, "Literary Studies on the Terraqueous Globe," *PMLA* 125, no. 3 (2010): 658.

15 See Philip E. Steinberg, *The Social Construction of the Ocean* (Cambridge: Cambridge University Press, 2001).

16 Allan Sekula, *Fish Story* (London: MACK, 1995), 49, 54.

17 See Ralph Shanks, Wick York, and Lisa Woo Shanks, *The U.S. Life-Saving Service: Heroes, Rescues, and Architecture of the Early Coast Guard* (Novato, CA: Costaño Books, 1996), 129.

18 For local examples, see Nancy L. Hobbs and Donella J. Lucero, *The Long Beach Peninsula* (Charleston, SC: Arcadia, 2005), and David Pinyerd, *Lighthouses and Life-Saving on the Oregon Coast* (Charleston, SC: Arcadia, 2007).

19 John Kopp, *CG 41332: Surfmen, the Cape Disappointment Motor Lifeboat School, and the Forgotten Tragedy that Transformed U.S. Coast Guard Operations* (n.p.: Remis Velisque, 2023). For more on lifesaving at the mouth of the Columbia, see Chris D'Amelio with Reid Maruyama, *Life and Death at Cape Disappointment: Becoming a Surfman on the Columbia River Bar* (Guilford, CT: Lyons, 2021).

20 Keith Keller, *Dangerous Waters: Wrecks and Rescues off the BC Coast* (Madeira Park, BC: Harbour, 1997), 148.

21 Two pages from Harvester's field notes appear in David C. Webster, *Nestucca: An Oil Spill Turns Creative* (Olympia: R. W. Morse, 1999), 110–111.

22 "Three Craft to Haul Stranded Ship Off Reef," *Seattle Times*, September 9, 1956, 1, 16, and "Rival Tug Puts Salvage Crew Aboard Stranded Ship," *Seattle Times*, September 11, 1956, 1.

23 Eric de Place and Ahren Stroming, "Fifty Years of Oil Spills in Washington's Waters: What Can the Past Tell Us about the Future?" Sightline Institute, January 12, 2015.

24 Eric de Place and Ahren Stroming, "Navy Sends Team to Scene of Ship Breakup," *Seattle Times*, January 10, 1972, B5, and "Nature Has Final Say on Wreck," *Seattle Times*, January 14, 1972, B7.

25 Webster, *Nestucca*, 12–13.

26 "Island Lucky This Time," *Victoria Daily Colonist*, March 19, 1972, 25.

27 "Pacific Rim Mop-Up Starting Today," *Victoria Daily Colonist*, March 17, 1972, 21; "Island Lucky This Time," *Victoria Daily Colonist*, March 19, 1972, 25; "Winds, Rain, High Tides Sweep Oil Threat Away," *Victoria Daily Colonist*, March 21, 1972, 1, 2; "Vanlene Wreck Picked Clean," *Victoria Daily Colonist*, April 4, 1972, 23, 35; "Scavengers Warned: Tires Deadly," *Victoria Daily Colonist*, April 8, 1972, 17.

28 Quoted in Webster, *Nestucca*, 55, 56.

29 Quoted in Webster, *Nestucca*, 153, 165.

30 Webster, *Nestucca*, 182, 226–227.

31 Webster, *Nestucca*, 270. In the end, Sause Brothers, the company that owned *Nestucca*, settled for $3.35 million in compensation to state, federal, and tribal governments.

32 Lynn Steinberg, "Spill Blackens Scenic Beaches—Thousands of Birds Threatened by Oil," *Seattle Post-Intelligencer*, July 29, 1991, A1.

33 Dylan Darling, "New Carissa 20 Years Later: Remembering the Beached Ship that Just Wouldn't Leave Oregon," *Register-Guard* (Eugene, OR), February 9, 2019.

34 "Ship Breaks Up," *Statesman Journal*, February 12, 1999, A1.

35 Roger Hull, *Henk Pander: Memory and Modern Life* (Seattle: University of Washington Press, 2011), 100.

36 "The Last Chapter of the New Carissa," *Marine Log*, November 2008, 71.

37 Richard G. Hildreth, Christina Otto Terenzi, and Lisa N. Thomas, "Evaluation of the New Carissa Incident for Improvements to State, Federal, and International Law," *Journal of Environmental Law and Litigation* 16, no. 1 (2001): 81–138.

38 "The Last Chapter of the New Carissa," 72.

39 Miranda L. Freeman, "The New Carissa Shipwreck: Aesthetic Impact on Coastal Recreation" (paper presented at American Agricultural Economics Association conference, Montreal, July 2003).

40 Kari Wergeland, *The Ballad of the New Carissa and Other Poems* (self-published, 2012), 68–69.

41 "Tribe Gets Murrelet Habitat in New Carissa Deal," *Oil Spill Intelligence Report* 30, no. 33 (August 9, 2007): 1.

42 See Zoltán Grossman and Alan Parker, eds., *Asserting Native Resilience: Pacific Rim Indigenous Nations Face the Climate Crisis* (Corvallis: Oregon State University Press, 2012).

43 "Hit Submerged Ledge," *Victoria Daily Colonist*, January 5, 1968, 1.

44 Eric Plummer, "Oil Removed from Nootka Sound Shipwreck," *Ha-Shilth-Sa*, July 14, 2021.

45 Plummer, "Oil Removed."

46 Rob Nixon, *Slow Violence and the Environmentalism of the Poor* (Cambridge, MA: Harvard University Press, 2011).

47 Anna Tsing, Nils Bubandt, Elaine Gan, and Heather Anne Swanson, eds., *Arts of Living on a Damaged Planet: Ghosts and Monsters of the Anthropocene* (Minneapolis: University of Minnesota Press, 2017), G1, G2.

48 Bruno Latour, *Down to Earth: Politics in the New Climatic Regime* (Cambridge: Polity, 2018), 19.

49 Latour, *Down to Earth*, 20. Latour also dips into nineteenth-century literature to further explicate his theory of shipwreck as a metaphor for the apprehension of ecological catastrophe: "To agree to look unblinkingly at such a situation is to position oneself like the hero of Edgar Allen Poe's 'Descent into the Maelstrom.' What distinguishes the sole survivor from the drowned victims is the cold-blooded attention with which the old sailor from the Lofoten Islands observes the movement of all the debris swirling around the vortex. When the ship is pulled into the abyss, the narrator manages to survive by attaching himself to an empty barrel. One has to be as astute as that old sailor to believe that escape is possible, to keep paying close attention to all the wreckage as it drifts:

such attention may make it possible to understand suddenly why some of the debris is sucked toward the bottom while other objects, because of their form, can serve as life preservers. 'My kingdom for a barrel!'" Latour, *Down to Earth*, 44–45.

50 Literary theorist Steve Mentz takes things a step further. Wading into the debate over what we should call our historical and geological epoch, Mentz takes issue with the term *Anthropocene*. Instead of a single framing—often too male, too technocratic, and too Western—Mentz argues that "multiple possible conceptions of this epoch must overlap, connect, and entangle in ways that may seem only partially legible." Surveying the many terms that have been coined to describe the era in which human activity has irreversibly shifted the planet's makeup—not just *Anthropocene*, but *Petrocene*, *Capitalocene*, *Chthulucene*, *Necrocene*, and more—Mentz goes so far as to offer *Neologismcene* as an apt descriptor for the welter of new words created in the attempt to define our era. And most relevant to our purposes, Mentz has added his own neologism to this mix: the *Naufragocene*, from *naufrage*, the French word for shipwreck, arguing that the rise of global maritime trade attendant to the last five hundred or so years overlaps with the ecological, economic, and social changes that many observers associate with the Anthropocene. Shipwreck, Mentz argues, is the perfect metaphor for our time. See Steve Mentz, *Shipwreck Modernity: Ecologies of Globalization, 1550–1719* (Minneapolis: University of Minnesota Press, 2015) and *Break Up the Anthropocene* (Minneapolis: University of Minnesota Press, 2019), 4.

51 *Ghost Adventures*, "Graveyard of the Pacific" (My Entertainment, 2018), season 20, episodes 6–9, aired October 6, 2018, on the Travel Channel.

SIX Neahkahnie's Archive

1 "Legendary Spanish Galleon Discovered on Oregon's Coast," *National Geographic*, June 16, 2022, http://www.nationalgeographic.com.

2 For several articles on this particular wreck, see the *Oregon Historical Quarterly* special issue, 119, no. 2 (2018). For a more theoretically driven analysis of the wreck and its possible meanings, see Aaron M. Hyman and Dana Leibsohn, "Lost and Found at Sea, or a Shipwreck's Art History," *West 86th* 28, no. 1 (2021).

3 Manu Karuka, *Tracks of Empire: Indigenous Nations, Chinese Workers, and the Transcontinental Railroad* (Berkeley: University of California Press, 2019), 12.

4   *The Goonies*, dir. Richard Donner (Burbank, CA: Warner Brothers, 1985).

5   Leah Sottile, "The Ghost Hunter," *Atavist Magazine*, no. 99 (2020), http://www.atavist.com.

6   For discussion of the statute and its eventual repeal, see Cameron La Follette, Dennis Griffin, and Douglas Deur, "The Mountain of a Thousand Holes: Shipwreck Traditions and Treasure Hunting on Oregon's North Coast," *Oregon Historical Quarterly* 119, no. 2 (2018): 287–293.

7   See La Follette, Griffin, and Deur, "The Mountain of a Thousand Holes," 292–293.

8   La Follette, Griffin, and Deur, "The Mountain of a Thousand Holes," 295–298.

9   La Follette, Griffin, and Deur, "The Mountain of a Thousand Holes," 294–295.

10 Herbert K. Beals and Harvey Steele, *Chinese Porcelains from Site 35-TI-1, Netarts Sand Spit, Tillamook County, Oregon* (Eugene: University of Oregon, 1981). See also Jessica Lally, *Analysis of Chinese Porcelain Associated with the Beeswax Wreck, Nehalem, Oregon* (master's thesis, Central Washington University, 2008).

11 La Follette, Griffin, and Deur, "The Mountain of a Thousand Holes," 301.

12 Radio script #4, "Neahkahnie Mountain," Kenneth Tilson, "Oregon Album," March 31, 1946, KGW, MSS 2492, folder 1, Oregon Historical Society.

13 La Follette, Griffin, and Deur, "The Mountain of a Thousand Holes," 293–294, 300–301.

14 John Erlandson, Robert J. Losey, and Neil Peterson, "Early Maritime Contact on the Northern Oregon Coast: Some Notes on the 17th Century Nehalem Beeswax Ship," in *Changing Landscapes: "Telling Our Stories" Proceedings of the Fourth Annual Coquille Cultural Preservation Conference*, ed. Jason Younker, Mark A. Tveskov, and David G. Lewis (North Bend, OR: Coquille Indian Tribe, 2001), 49–50.

15 J. Neilson Barry, "Astorians Who Became Permanent Settlers (Continued)," *Washington Historical Quarterly* 24, no. 4 (1933), 297.

16 Elizabeth D. Jacobs, *Ethnographic Notes on Three Months' Fieldwork among the Tillamook Salish, Garibaldi, Oregon* (Seattle: Melville Jacobs Collection, University of Washington Libraries, 1933), 7–8.

17 D. F. Howard, *Oregon's First White Men* (Rainier, OR: Rainier Review Press, 1927), 58, 60.

18 La Follette, Griffin, and Deur, "The Mountain of a Thousand Holes," 286.

19   Silas B. Smith, "Tales of Early Wrecks on the Oregon Coast, and How the Bees-Wax Got There: Address to the Oregon Historical Society, December 16, 1899," *Oregon Native Son*, no. 1 (1899–1900), 443–444.

20   Clipping from *Yamhill County Record*, September 22, 1899, in E. W. Giesecke, *Beeswax, Teak, and Castaways: Searching for Oregon's Lost Protohistoric Asian Ship* (Manzanita, OR: Nehalem Valley Historical Society, 2007).

21   Thomas H. Rogers, *Nehalem: A Story of the Pacific A.D. 1700* (McMinnville, OR: H. L. Heath, 1898).

22   E. W. Wright, ed., *Lewis & Dryden's Marine History of the Pacific Northwest* (Portland: Lewis & Dryden Printing, 1895), 2.

23   Frances Fuller Victor, *Atlantis Arisen; or, Talks of a Tourist around Oregon and Washington* (Philadelphia: J. B. Lippincott, 1891), 38–39.

24   See Giesecke, *Beeswax, Teak, and Castaways.*

25   George Gibbs, "Tribes of Western Washington and Northwestern Oregon," in *Tribes of the Extreme Northwest*, edited by W. H. Dall (Washington, DC: Government Printing Office, 1877), 236–238.

26   James G. Swan, *The Northwest Coast; or Three Years' Residence in Washington Territory* (New York: Harper & Brothers, 1857), 206.

27   Ruby Hult, *Lost Mines and Treasures of the Pacific Northwest* (Portland: Binford & Mort, 1964), 19, 37–38. Cited in La Follette, Griffin, and Deur, "The Mountain of a Thousand Holes," 285.

28   *Oregonian*, June 20, 1894, 6.

29   Elliott Coues, ed., *New Light on the Early History of the Greater Northwest: The Manuscript Journals of Alexander Henry, Fur Trader of the Northwest Company, and of David Thompson, Official of That Same Company, 1799–1814* (New York: Francis P. Harper, 1897), 2:878.

30   Gary Moulton, ed., *Journals of the Lewis & Clark Expedition*, accessed March 5, 2021, http://www.lewisandclarkjournals.unl.edu.

31   Coues, *New Light*, 2:768.

32   Ross Cox, *Adventures on the Columbia River, Including the Narrative of a Residence of Six Years on the Western Side of the Rocky Mountains among Various Tribes of Indians Hitherto Unknown: Together with a Journey across the American Continent* (London: J. & J. Harper, 1832), 1:151.

33   Gabriel Franchère, *Narrative of a Voyage to the Northwest Coast of America in the Years 1811, 1812, 1813, and 1814, or the First American Settlement on the Pacific* (New York: Redfield, 1854), 112–113.

34 Warren N. Vaughan, *Till Broad Daylight: A History of Early Settlement in Oregon's Tillamook County* (Wallowa, OR: Bear Creek Press, 2004), 83.

35 Samuel A. Clarke, *Pioneer Days of Oregon History* (Portland: Oregon Historical Society, 1905), 153, 173.

36 See Curt D. Peterson, Scott S. Williams, Kenneth M. Cruikshank, and John R. Dubè, "Geoarchaeology of the Nehalem Spit: Redistribution of Beeswax Galleon Wreck Debris by Cascadia Earthquake and Tsunami (~1700), Oregon, USA," *Geoarchaeology* 26, no. 2 (2021): 77–85.

37 For the context of the galleons, see Shirley Fish, *The Manila-Acapulco Galleons: The Treasure Ships of the Pacific* (Milton Keynes: Authorhouse, 2011); Arturo Giraldez, *The Age of Trade: The Manila Galleons and the Dawn of the Global Economy* (London: Rowman & Littlefield, 2015); and Peter Gordon and Juan José Morales, *The Silver Way: China, Spanish America, and the Birth of Globalization, 1615–1815* (New York: Penguin, 2017).

38 Sottile, "The Ghost Hunter", and January 16, 2024, interview with Robert Kentta.

39 Sottile, "The Ghost Hunter."

40 Fernand Braudel, *The Mediterranean and the Mediterranean World in the Age of Philip II*, trans. Siân Reynolds (New York, Harper & Row, 1972–1973), 2:543.

Epilogue

1 "Bark Peter Iredale Ashore on Clatsop Spit," *Morning Astorian*, October 26, 1906, 1.

2 "About the City," *Morning Astorian*, October 13, 1893, 3.

3 *Morning Astorian*, October 14, 1893, 3.

4 *Morning Astorian*, September 7, 1893, 3; *Morning Astorian*, September 9, 1893, 3; and *Capital Journal*, October 12, 1893, 1.

5 "Stranded Iredale News Items," *Morning Astorian*, October 27, 1906, 5; *Morning Astorian*, October 28, 1906, 4; *San Francisco Call*, October 29, 1906, 11; "Spar, Dock and Buoy," *Morning Astorian*, October 31, 1906, 4; "Wrecked Near Point Adams," *Oregon Mist*, November 2, 1906, 1; "Bar, Bay and River," *Morning Astorian*, November 9, 1906, 4; *Morning Astorian*, November 15, 1906, 4; *Morning Astorian*, January 1, 1907, 4.

6 Original Transcript of the Naval Court Findings, Issued in London by the Board of Trade on the 24th December 1906. "No. 7011, Peter Iredale," 1–2.

7   "To the Wrecks," *Morning Astorian*, November 17, 1906, 5; "Immense Interest," *Morning Astorian*, November 20, 1906, 5; "Sunday at the Wreck," *Morning Astorian*, October 30, 1906, 5; and *Morning Astorian*, December 4, 1906, 4. For a general history of the ship's demise, see Rowena L. Alcorn and Gordon D. Alcorn, "The Wreck of the 'Peter Iredale,'" *Oregon Historical Quarterly* 64, no. 1 (1963): 68–72.

8   "Personal Mention," *Morning Astorian*, November 11, 1906, 4; "Judd Arrested," *Morning Astorian*, December 5, 1906, 5; "Not Guilty," *Morning Astorian*, December 8, 1906, 5; "Marine Memoranda," *Morning Astorian*, December 11, 1906, 4; and "Soft, Easy and Safe," *Morning Astorian*, January 17, 1909, 2.

9   *Morning Astorian*, January 17, 1909, 2.

10 Gordon R. Newell, *SOS North Pacific: Tales of Shipwrecks off the Washington, British Columbia, and Alaska Coasts* (Portland: Binfords & Mort, 1955), xi.

11 Don Marshall, *Oregon Shipwrecks* (Portland: Binford & Mort, 1984), 101.

12 "Plan to Scrap Iredale Arouses Local Ire," *Marine Digest* 38, no. 41 (June 11, 1960): 21.

13 For a general biography of Peter Iredale, collated by one of his descendants, see Thomas P. Iredale, "Peter Iredale Biography," accessed November 29, 2023, http://www.iredale.de/maritime/biograph.htm. For Iredale's obituaries and the account of his funeral, see "Death of Mr. Peter Iredale," *Liverpool Daily Post*, October 27, 1899; "Death of a Liverpool Ship Owner," *Liverpool Mercury*, October 27, 1899; "Death of a Liverpool Ship Owner," *Liverpool Courier*, October 27, 1899; and "The Late Mr. Peter Iredale—Impressive Ceremony," *Liverpool Daily Post*, October 30, 1899.

14 Frank H. Shaw, *Seas of Memory* (London: Oldbourne, 1958), 36.

15 Christina Sharpe, *In the Wake: On Blackness and Being* (Durham, NC: Duke University Press, 2016), 29.

16 For discussion of Liverpool and slavery, see Katie Donington, Ryan Hanley, and Jessica Moody, eds., *Britain's History and Memory of Transatlantic Slavery: Local Nuances of a "National" Sin* (Liverpool: Liverpool University Press, 2016); David Richardson, Suzanne Schwarz, and Anthony Tibbles, eds., *Liverpool and Transatlantic Slavery* (Chicago: University of Chicago Press, 2010); and Jessica Moody, *The Persistence of Memory: Remembering Slavery in Liverpool* (Liverpool: Liverpool University Press, 2020).

17 For racist policies in early Oregon history, see Jacki Hedlund Tyler, *Leveraging*

an Empire: Settler Colonialism and the Legalities of Citizenship in the Pacific Northwest (Lincoln: University of Nebraska Press, 2021).

18 See Coll Thrush with Ruth S. Ludwin, "Finding Fault: Indigenous Seismology, Colonial Science, and the Rediscovery of Earthquakes and Tsunamis in Cascadia," *American Indian Culture & Research Journal* 31, no. 4 (2007), 1–24. Drawing on sources ranging from Indigenous histories, geology, archaeology, dendrochronology, and Japanese archival records, an interdisciplinary investigation of the last great Cascadia subduction zone—in which I played a small part as a graduate student—determined that the coast had last experienced such a traumatic geological event around nine p.m. on January 26, 1700. Over the past two decades, knowledge of the 1700 event has become an increasingly well-known aspect of the region's history, informing present-day awareness and mitigation of seismic risk, even as it highlights the temporal shallowness of settler society. For further discussions of the event, see Brian F. Atwater, Kenji Sataki, and Satoko Musumi-Rokkaku, *The Orphan Tsunami of 1700: Japanese Clues to a Parent Earthquake in North America* (Seattle: University of Washington Press, 2005), and Jerry Thompson, *Cascadia's Fault: The Coming Earthquake and Tsunami That Could Devastate North America* (New York: Counterpoint, 2012).

19 Lisa Lowe, *The Intimacies of Four Continents* (Durham, NC: Duke University Press, 2015).

INDEX

Page numbers in **bold** refer to illustrations.

RECENT BOOKS FROM THE
*Emil and Kathleen Sick Series
in Western History and Biography*

For a complete list of books in the series, visit uwapress.uw.edu

PHOTO BY MATT HAGEN

Coll Thrush (born 1970) is a settler historian who was raised in Auburn, Washington, in the treaty territory of the Muckleshoot Indian Tribe. A graduate of Fairhaven College at Western Washington University in Bellingham and the University of Washington in Seattle, Coll is professor of history and associate faculty in critical Indigenous studies at the University of British Columbia in Vancouver, on unceded Musqueam territory. He is author of *Native Seattle: Histories from the Crossing-Over Place* (2007/2017), coeditor of *Phantom Past, Indigenous Presence: Native Ghosts in North American Culture and History* (2011), and author of *Indigenous London: Native Travelers at the Heart of Empire* (2016). He lives in Vancouver's Kitsilano neighborhood with his husband and a little black dog.